Is It Nation Time?

Is It Nation Time?

Contemporary Essays on Black Power and Black Nationalism

EDITED BY
Eddie S. Glaude Jr.

The University of Chicago Press
Chicago and London

The University of Chicago Press, Chicago 60637
The University of Chicago Press, Ltd., London
© 2002 by The University of Chicago
All rights reserved. Published 2002
Printed in the United States of America
11 10 09 08 07 06 05 04 03 02   1 2 3 4 5

The publishers and authors have generously given permission to reprint the follow-
ing essays: Cornel West, "The Paradox of the African American Rebellion," in *The
Sixties: Without Apology,* ed. Sohnya Sayres et al. (Minneapolis: University of Minnesota Press, 1984), 44–58, reprinted by permission of the author and University
of Minnesota Press; Adolph L. Reed Jr., "Black Particularity Reconsidered," *Telos* 39
(Spring 1979): 71–93, reprinted by permission of Telos Press Ltd.; E. Frances
White, "Africa on My Mind: Gender, Counter Discourse, and African American
Nationalism," *Journal of Women's History* 2, no. 1 (Spring 1990): 73–97, reprinted
by permission of Indiana University Press; Wahneema Lubiano, "Standing in for
the State: Black Nationalism and 'Writing' the Black Subject," *Alphabet City* 3
(October 1993), reprinted by permission of the author; Phillip Brian Harper,
"Nationalism and Social Division in Black Arts Poetry of the 1960s," *Critical
Inquiry* 19, no. 2 (Winter 1993): 234–55, reprinted by permission of The
University of Chicago Press.

ISBN: 0-226-29821-3 (cloth)
ISBN: 0-226-29822-1 (paper)

Library of Congress Cataloging-in-Publication Data

Is it nation time? : contemporary essays on black power and black nationalism /
edited by Eddie S. Glaude Jr.
    p. cm.
    ISBN 0-226-29821-3 (cloth : alk. paper)—ISBN 0-226-29822-1 (paper : alk.
paper)
    1. Black power—United States—History—20th century. 2. Black national-
ism—United States—History—20th century. 3. African Americans—Politics and
government—20th century. 4. African Americans—Intellectual life—20th century. I. Glaude, Eddie S., 1968–
E185.615 .I78 2002
305.896'073—dc21

                                  2001043392

♾ The paper used in this publication meets the minimum requirements of the
American National Standard for Information Sciences—Permanence of Paper for
Printed Library Materials, ANSI Z39.48-1992.

For Marie and Langston

CONTENTS

ACKNOWLEDGMENTS

My understanding of black radicalism during my days at More-house College and Temple University was bound up in the languages and images of the Black Power era. In order to be militant I *had* to be Malcolm X. I bought my horn-rim glasses. I grew my goatee (I still have it!). And in an odd reversal I joined, for a brief period, the Nation of Islam. For three months, I lived Malcolm's life. This was for me, and I want to contend a large number of young black people in America, the only way radicalism could be imagined. The essays in this collection have helped me understand more fully that impulse.

I owe a great deal to the contributors to *Is It Nation Time?* In particu-lar, Robin D. G. Kelley, Gerald Horne, Farah Jasmine Griffin, S. Craig Watkins, Will Walker, and Jeffrey Stout have been more than generous. Each, without hesitation, agreed to write a new essay for the volume when it was in its formative stages. They have stuck with me throughout this process. I am forever in their debt. I am also grateful to my editor at Chi-cago, Alan Thomas, for his extraordinary patience and confidence in my work. Thanks to Leslie Keros and the other folks who assisted the produc-tion, and to the publishers of several journals for allowing me to reproduce essays first appearing in their pages.

Special thanks go to the readers of the earlier manuscript who helped me achieve what I was trying to do with the collection. Their brilliant in-sights and suggestions for revisions have made this a much better book. Also thanks to Elizabeth Pritchard who read portions of the collection. Her comments were invaluable.

Of course, most of my work finds its beginnings in conversations and disagreements with my friend and mentor, Cornel West. Words can not express how deeply blessed I am to have him as a friend.

I would also like to thank Wahneema Lubiano, Adolph Reed, E. Frances White, Phillip Brian Harper, Lucius Outlaw, Kimberly Benston, Howard Winant, Fasaha Traylor, Paul Jefferson, Paul Gilroy, William Hart, Albert Raboteau, Arnold Rampersad, Penny Von Eschen, Kevin Gaines, Jeffrey Tucker, Judith Jackson-Fossett, Marcellus Barksdale, Gloria Wade-Gayles, Daniel Black, Rodney Patterson, Nathaniel Norment, and Orlando Brown. I am especially indebted to my boys from Morehouse who journeyed with me through the black nationalist brook of fire: Paul Taylor, Charles McKinney, Samuel T. Lee, Ronald S. Sullivan Jr., William T. Crawley, and Mark Jefferson.

Ultimately, though, this work was made possible—as are all of my writings—by my family: my parents, Eddie and Juanita Glaude; my brother, Alvin Jones; my sisters, Bonita Glaude and Angela Glaude-Hosch; my grandparents, Delores Cox and Bernice Glaude; and my partner for life, Winnifred Brown-Glaude and our "little man," Langston Ellis Glaude.

Introduction: Black Power Revisited

Eddie S. Glaude Jr.

One of the first things I think young people, especially nowadays, should learn is how to see for yourself and listen for yourself and think for yourself. . . . This generation, especially of our people, has a burden, more so than any other time in history. The most important thing that we can learn to do today is think for ourselves.

Malcolm X

1

The essays in this collection examine closely the ambiguous legacy of the Black Power movement. By highlighting the complexities and nuances of specific historical formations and events during the period, they help us see the various ways the Black Power era has influenced the way we now live our lives as well as talk about racial matters. In some ways, then, these essays initiate, by way of historical reconstruction, a sustained critical examination of how the political choices and failures of the Black Power movement inform our nation's racial landscape. They take seriously the fact that from early 1968 to as late as 1975[1] the various politics of this moment provided the dominant ideological framework through which many young, poor, and middle-class blacks made sense of their lives and articulated a political vision for their futures. This proximity to our contemporary moment alone warrants more careful examination of the period. In fact, *Is It Nation Time?*

implies that failure to examine seriously the period's accomplishments and deficiencies, its internal fissures, and its effect on the form and content of our contemporary political languages dooms us to continuously misunderstand the complex political and cultural desires of black America. For example, what do we make of marches on Washington under the banner of what can be called black nationalism? How do we interpret the complex relation between nationalist desire and contemporary hip hop culture? the market value of Afrocentrism? How do we make sense of the political cash-value of these formations in relation to present-day problems like disproportionate sentencing, bad schools, and rising illiteracy rates? All of these questions require, I believe, closer scrutiny of the ambiguities and ambivalences of a period that continues to capture the political and cultural imaginations of many African Americans.

This volume aims then to distance itself from nationalist historiography, a form of historical work driven by the ideological presuppositions of black nationalism (in whatever guise), which supposedly tells the story of 1960s radicalism and its relevance for contemporary problems. In these accounts, the ambiguity of the Black Power movement remains offstage while the melodramatic battle for black self-determination implicates itself in the story of our contemporary moment. The works of Molefi Asante and Maulana Karenga stand as examples of this kind of historiography which celebrates uncritically the rise of black consciousness and its particular construction of a race-based politics.[2] Taken collectively, the essays in this volume offer neither a romantic embrace of Black Power nor an ideologically charged critical stance toward it. Each of these temperaments loads the evidence in one way or another, making for a more sentimental or hard-hearted view of the period. *Is It Nation Time?* also then critically intervenes in the rather narrow contemporary conversations about black nationalism as simply a political expression of racial essentialism. The work of Henry Louis Gates Jr. and K. Anthony Appiah opens up a range of considerations about the limitations of a certain kind of race-based politics.[3] But neither Gates nor Appiah provides a nuanced account of Black Power and black nationalism as a complicated historical formation with a number of different strands and political outcomes. The ambiguity is lost; both are simply expressions of racial essentialism. And this is a bad thing.

Thus, the essays in this volume occupy the middle ground between celebratory and hypercritical accounts of Black Power and black nationalism.[4] The volume commends an approach to the period which regards it as (1) a historically specific formation (2) with various conceptions of the good animating the political choices of a number of groups under its description, which (3) when examined closely can produce intellectual instrumentalities that can better equip us to understand and respond to the contemporary issues of race and racism in the United States. Descriptive and proscriptive concerns then organize the volume. In fact, the essays alternate between those that engage in thick descriptions of specific historical formations and those that critique the consequences of narrow political articulations with an eye fixed intensely on the task of reconstructing the way many of us think about racial matters. The ambiguity remains. Our task is to tell better stories about the Black Power era and its complicated legacies.

2

Blackness is our ultimate reality.

Maulana Karenga

In the spring and summer months of 1964–68, as black rebellions engulfed almost every major city outside of the South, a tremendous outpouring of dissatisfaction served notice to the country and to black America's traditional leadership. The Watts rebellion in 1965, in particular, signaled a shift in the basic orientation of the movement for black freedom as individuals and organizations were forced to reassess their allegiances and methods in the face of thirty-four deaths and over 40 million dollars in property damage. In this same year, Malcolm X was assassinated and quickly became the symbol of the new Black Power radicalism. His religion made his allegiance to this country suspect. He advocated self-defense instead of nonviolence—refusing to assume the role of the suffering servant—and his rhetoric dripped with what can be called radical rage, an intelligent articulation of the physical and psychical wounds caused by white supremacy. To be sure, Malcolm X represented the "mood" that loosely connected the disparate political projects of what would become the Black Power era.

African Americans also saw in 1965 the escalation of protests against the Vietnam War, the passage of the Voting Rights Act, and the failure of Selma. A conflict arose between the Student Nonviolent Coordinating Committee (SNCC) and traditional civil rights leaders and organizations over the efficacy of nonviolence. On June 16, 1966, in Greenwood, Mississippi, Stokely Carmichael announced: "This is the twenty-seventh time I have been arrested. I ain't going to jail no more. What we gonna start saying now is 'Black Power.'"[5] An immediate debate ensued about the efficacy of the phrase. Many rejected the implications of Carmichael's outburst; they saw it as a call for violence or as an unnecessary distraction. For some, the phrase became a shorthand to articulate a critique of the middle-class focus of civil rights reform. For others, "Black Power" was a catchphrase pushing black America to get its fair share of American capitalism. And still others saw in the phrase a call for African Americans to celebrate themselves as beautiful and their culture as significant. As Debbie Louis contended, in the Black Power era "the black community stood as a conglomeration of often contradictory interests and directions, dubiously tied together by a common mood which combined centuries of anger with new hope, increasing desperation with new confidence."[6]

This mood served notice to white America that a new black man and woman had been born and that their subordination would be, if necessary, violently resisted. Many African Americans mobilized throughout the country to "close ranks" and articulate forms of racial solidarity as the grounds for various political interventions. New organizations claiming Malcolm X as their patron saint emerged: the Black Panther Party for Self-Defense (BPP), the US Organization, and the Dodge Revolutionary Union Movement (DRUM) joined the ranks of the Nation of Islam and Malcolm X's Organization of African American Unity (OAAU) as "militant" organizations.

The political import of these various organizations was ambiguous. Their politics ranged from calls for complete separation from the United States and the formation of an independent nation-state to demands that African Americans should own and operate the businesses in their communities to efforts for the cultural retrieval of an African identity.[7] At the heart of the disparate political projects of each of these organizations, however, was what can be called a politics of transvaluation.[8] They not only believed that African Americans had to challenge directly the state and its white citizens, they also maintained that a fundamental psychological and cultural conversion from their socialization as a subordinate people to a self-determining nation needed to take place. In other words, and this is central to the mood and tone of the period, a revolution of the mind was a prerequisite for the success of the black revolution—a necessary condition for any embrace of power among African Americans. As William Van Deburg writes of the period:

> To become self-directed, to be assertive, to take pride in skin color
> and heritage was to remove the negative connotations of race that
> had long served as a constraining psychological and social force.

Whites, of course, might still factor supposed racial limitations into their own plans for continued societal domination, but black people endowed with a "national" consciousness no longer would agree to play by the old rules. Instead of meekly responding to white stimuli or linking arms with paternalistic white liberals, they would dare to be pro-black—to look, feel, be, and *do* black.[9]

This politics of transvaluation is best understood as a reassessment of "blackness"[10] in terms of its value for black lives and struggle. That is to say, it is a reconsideration of the extent to which a celebration of "blackness" is conducive to the preservation and enhancement of black individuals and communities throughout the United States.

The politics of transvaluation went beyond a reversal of value determinations. It was not simply a move to deify that which was previously demonized (as in the case of the Nation of Islam). Rather, the politics aimed to recast and revise "blackness" in a manner necessary for black individual and communal flourishing in a racist culture. This was not a reconstruction of blackness couched only in a rhetoric of *ressentiment*. This transvaluation was part of what Kimberly Benston sees as a black modernist sensibility within which certain cultural and political practices were "perceived to be evasions of a liberation praxis responsive to perceived conditions of blackness."[11] On one level, as Phillip Brian Harper argues, the politics aimed to convert those "negroes" and "niggers" who failed to see that the prerequisite for revolution was an acceptance of the "gospel of blackness." This missionary work required, as best as possible, an inventory of answers to questions of who do we take ourselves to be and how do we orient ourselves to "others," how do we conceive of our obligations to those whom we consider to be "one of us," and what constitutes the good for us. In other words, this politics affected how notions of virtue, right, and the good were understood in the context of this community of experience. As the SNCC position paper on Black Power maintained: "A thorough re-examination must be made by black people concerning the contributions that we have made in shaping this country. . . . Any re-evaluation that we must make will, for the most part, deal with identification. Who are black people, what are black people; what is their relationship to America and the world?"[12] At its best, the politics of transvaluation was merely instrumental, orienting a subject people in such a way that they struggled for themselves. At its worst, as Adolph Reed suggests in his essay in this volume, it led to a hypostatization of "blackness." Blackness would become the principal object of concern. Nevertheless, in both instances, the politics of transvaluation reordered allegiances and helped redefine the way many African Americans publicly deliberated about racial issues.

In some ways, then, the Black Power era was differentiated from other forms of black political expression primarily on the basis of what can be called its conceptions of piety, the rhetorical means by which the various political projects under its rubric articulated their desired aims, and the politics of transvaluation, which provided the form and content of both. That is to say, "blackness" became a determining category in how African Americans understood themselves as agents, *and* the articulation of "blackness" as a positive value became a means to defiantly challenge the state. Martin Luther King Jr., for example, stated the difference between the ambitions of the Black Power movement and civil rights reform quite succinctly in his last Southern Christian Leadership Conference (SCLC) presidential address:

> Now a lot of us are preachers, and all of us have moral convictions and concerns, and so often have problems with power. There is nothing wrong with power if power is used correctly. You see, what happened is that some of our philosophers got off base. And one of the great problems of history is that the concepts of love and power have usually been contrasted as opposites—polar opposites—so that love is identified with a resignation of power, and power with a denial of love. . . . What is needed is a realization that power without love is reckless and abusive, and love without power is sentimental and anemic. Power at its best is love implementing the demands of justice, and justice at its best is power correcting everything that stands against love. . . . [A] few extremists today . . . advocate for Negroes the same destructive and conscienceless power that they have justly abhorred in whites. It is precisely this collision of immoral power with powerless morality which constitutes the major crisis of our times.[13]

For King and others, the Christian language of love informed their actions and guided their demands for broad-based inclusion in America. Their piety found its power in their Christian conviction and in an allegiance to the ideals of the nation, not in notions of *the* race or the *black* nation.[14]

For many of the proponents of Black Power, however, Christian piety was not a ready resource for revolution. They looked instead to the revolutions and nation-building efforts in Africa, Asia, and Latin America for models. Robin D. G. Kelley illustrates this with his essay on the Revolutionary Action Movement. The political languages of the organization were based in international efforts to break loose from the colonial grip of the West. The conditions of black Americans then were understood within a broader set of considerations about capital and the general exploitation of darker peoples around the world. As Julius Lester, a SNCC staff member, noted, Black Power was "only another manifestation of what is transpiring in Latin America, Asia and Africa. People are reclaiming their lives on those continents and blacks in America are reclaiming theirs."[15] Nationalism formed and shaped in the context of anticolonial struggles was the principal form of the politics and the root of a cultural logic, and certain forms of black nationalism in the United States translated the distinctive discourse of race in America into that idiom. It projected, as Jeffrey Stout suggests in his essay, "an imagined national community—a people—for whom blackness serve[d] as an emblem."[16] The concept of blackness became a shorthand for talking about the complexities of black conditions of living in the United States and the world.

This way of thinking about race bound African Americans to one another, grounded the work of cultural recovery, and steadied their lives by way of a reverent attachment to the putative sources of their being. Following George Santayana, I call this a kind of piety. Santayana characterizes piety as "loyalty to the sources of one's being."[17] These sources are open-ended in that they could range from "parents to country to culture to the planet and, ultimately, to whatever powers in the cosmos there are that support human life."[18] Understanding piety in this way leaves open what the sources of our being may be and how we may conceive of them. For many proponents of Black Power, blackness came to be recognized as the source of black individual existence, and efforts to be cognizant of this source and to act appropriately toward it (whatever that might entail) became a critical feature of the politics of the Black Power era.

This kind of piety—and the politics of transvaluation that drives it—presupposed two basic ideas that directly affect the political languages of contemporary black America (one of which is certainly not the Christian idea of love!). First, many Black Power proponents assumed what Adolph Reed notes as a homogeneity of black political interests. As the concluding section of the Gary Declaration in 1972 noted: "When we turn to a Black Agenda for the seventies, we move in the truth of history, in the reality of the moment. We move recognizing that no one else is going to represent *our* interest but ourselves."[19] This view presupposes that because the sources of our individual identities are the wellsprings for the flourishing of the nation, our political interests ought to reflect, on pain of accusations of impious action, the interests of the nation—that is, its continued flourishing as a specific manifestation of our inheritance (blackness) which requires appropriate expressions of gratitude and loyalty. To act otherwise is to risk being labeled an Uncle Tom or race traitor. Second, this view of piety assumes a pristine cultural history, a form of life in which our cultural identities reflect the common historical experiences and shared cultural vocabularies that provide us with stable and unchanging frames of reference—historical experiences and cultural vocabularies that make us, in short, essentially *one* people.[20] It assumes that black people preferred this, their own form of life, to others, and that this specific inheritance strengthens them in a world of white supremacists with state power.

This piety was joined with a rhetorical stance that found its power in the expression of rage. The Black Power moment was distinctive, I believe, precisely because of its proponents' willingness to express, without any reservation, how they felt about white folk and the conditions of black America. The movement, in one sense, was attractive because of what Jeffrey Stout calls its rhetoric of excess and the fantasy of vengeance. Malcolm X said it best:

> If he [the white man] was made to realize how black people really feel and how fed up we are. Without that old compromising sweet talk. Why you're the one that makes it hard for yourself. The white man believes you when you go to him with that old sweet talk. 'Cause you been sweet talking him ever since he brought you here. Stop sweet talking him. Tell him how you feel. Tell him . . . what kind of hell you've been catching. And let him know that if he is not ready to clean his house up (dramatic pause). If he is not ready to clean his house up. He shouldn't have a house. It should catch on fire and burn down.[21]

The rhetoric of Black Power invoked the danger of violence and aimed to provoke African Americans to think the unthinkable: to imagine freedom apart from white people (and to define themselves not by white standards but by the piety of the black nation).

The politics of transvaluation sharpened the rhetoric's edges by celebrating "blackness" and using it, to some degree, to challenge the privilege of whiteness. Note, for example, the edge to Amiri Baraka's voice in his poem "It's Nation Time" (1970), and the way the politics of transvaluation grounds his intended aim:

> . . . when the brothers strike niggers come out
> Come out niggers
> When the brothers take over the school
> Help niggers
> Come out niggers
> All niggers negroes must change up
> Come together in unity unify
> For nation time
> It's nation time
> Boom
> Booom
> BOOM
> Boom
> Dadadadadadadadadadad
> Boom . . . .
> . . . when the brothers wanna stop animals
> come out niggers come out
> come out niggers niggers niggers come out
> help us stop the devil
> help us build a new world
> niggers come out, brothers are we
> with you and your sons your daughters are ours
> and we are the same, all the blackness from one black allah
> when the world is clear you'll be with us
> come out niggers come out
> come out niggers come out
> It's nation time eye ime
> It's nation ti eye ime
> Chant with bells and drum
> It's nation time . . .[22]

The cadence of Baraka's poem not only challenged the state, it also aimed to secure social cohesion among black individuals as a basis for that challenge. The poem presupposes, in one sense, an undifferentiated "blackness" as the basis of its aesthetic and political articulation and simultaneously seeks to create that black mass through the disciplining language of inside/outside.

with you and your sons your daughters are ours
and we are the same, all the blackness from one black allah
when the world is clear you'll be with us

These words betray a reality that runs counter to the presuppositions of the poem. One can assume that brothers and niggers are not unified. So, social cohesion is the intended consequence of the artifice "blackness." In short, Baraka's words direct us to the proselytizing dimension of the politics of transvaluation: as a conversion experience of sorts, those who had not experienced the grace of "blackness" had to be placed on the mourner's bench and urged to the thrashing floor! "Come out niggers come out!"

The language of nation, of course, was a crucial tool of expression for this experience. It captured the distinctiveness of African American experiences in relation to America. It also anchored the idea of unity (homogeneity of black interests) in a deeper awareness of particularity. Indeed, the redemptive promise of the language served as a source for personal identity construction and the maintenance of social cohesion. When black nationalists of the sixties and seventies spoke of a black revolution, when they donned the garb of Africa, when they indicted and convicted white America, somehow black America's suffering was to be alleviated, the evil of white supremacy was to be no more, and African Americans were to be made whole again—saved, in effect. The rhetorical excesses of Black Power sought to offer many African Americans a glimpse of paradise, a way of seeing beyond the immediacy of evil (white folk).[23]

However, this language simultaneously suppressed the very real tensions within the sixties revolution in that the language of nation and the idea of blackness it often presupposed collapsed the differences among African Americans into an ambivalent similarity. Black bourgeois interests often hid behind the totalizing trope of blackness. As Cornel West notes in his essay, "beneath the rhetoric of Black Power, black control, and black self-determination was a budding, 'new,' black, middle class hungry for power and starving for status." And for many black men of the period, the politics of Black Power meant that *their* well-being was the primary aim and end of political struggle. Many believed that white supremacy fundamentally emasculated black men, and since nationalisms are relational phenomena—they are always shaped, to a certain extent, by what they oppose—many black nationalists of the period equated freedom with patriarchal authority and manhood.[24] I point this out not to deny that black nationalists' imaginings of the nation stood in opposition to the evil effects of racial domination; rather, as E. Frances White and Wahneema Lubiano argue, to note that nationalist constructions of political memory set up standards of social relations that were both liberating *and* confining.

At least two specific consequences follow from these dueling tendencies. First, and this is one of Adolph Reed's central insights in his essay, the politics of Black Power helped politicize black culture in such a way that a certain form of identity politics surfaced as the predominant arena of struggle. It was assumed that black people could only reach freedom by cultivating their peculiar national identity. This national identity found its beginnings in Africa. Archaeological efforts to reconstruct a collective African culture aimed then to build and solidify social cohesion.[25] These projects offered images of African American life in which repressive social relations were justified with appeals to an "Africa" before European colonialism. Such efforts abstracted blackness from lived experience and, in many cases, a politics of blackness—a form of identity politics that determines the relative value of any kind of cultural work by its functional role in the revolution and its expression of black piety—became the predominant form of struggle, instantiating, in its more crude and extreme moments, a litmus test of "blackness." Signs of one's commitment had to be demonstrated: the dashiki, a certain language proficiency—in essence, a particular style had to be embraced for one to enter "the community of black saints."

This leads to the second consequence. The nationalist politics of Black Power often detached black cultural forms from their historical contexts. In their search for a pristine cultural history, black nationalists of the period ironically often stepped outside of history to account for black America's and, by extension, their own conditions of possibility. "Blackness" then became all-pervasive, to the extent that all aspects of black life—the social and political spheres and the private domain—were reducible to it. As such, black cultural practices in the context of a politics of blackness took on a commodity form.[26] African Americans could literally buy their salvation.

3

Reconstruction can be nothing less than the work of developing, of forming, of producing the intellectual instrumentalities which will progressively direct inquiry into the deeply and inclusively human—that is to say, moral—facts of the present scene and situation.

John Dewey

Historical reconstruction then is absolutely essential if we are to understand this complex moment and its effects. We must map the different ways the issues that concerned many proponents of Black Power came to be issues that mattered, and track how those concerns either fell to the side or were transformed in the face of the historical, social, economic, and ideological shifts that shape our lives today. All of the essays in *Is It Nation Time?* are important pieces in this regard. Cornel West's "The Paradox of the African American Rebellion" offers some historical background for the volume as he highlights the rise in the sixties and seventies of a new, relatively privileged black middle class, the role of the Black Power movement in its emergence, and its complex relationship to the black working poor. In some ways, West's essay lays out the general themes that are explored in the volume. He sees the politics of blackness as the political expression of a black petite bourgeoisie, congratulating and justifying itself on its newfound status as a middle class in America. Certain consequences followed from this view: (1) we were left with a truncated black leadership class whose political languages and orientation blocked the way for more progressive voices and alliances to speak to the conditions of black America; (2) these languages were often predicated on hypermasculinist assumptions, thereby alienating many black women and severing the ties with an emerging black feminist movement; and (3) the politics of this class lacked an organic relation with the black communities they supposedly represented. These three consequences, West maintains, continue to haunt us. If we are to get beyond them, he argues, we must revitalize progressive forms of black leadership that reject the politics of machismo and seek broad-based alliances with other progressive groups. We have to understand that the repoliticizing of the black working poor and underclass demands that more attention be given to black popular cultural forms. And, finally, we must recognize that the development of organic black leadership requires the revitalization of black civil society.

Adolph Reed, in his 1979 essay "Black Particularity Reconsidered," took on the monumental task of critically examining the politics of culture unleashed by the Black Power movement. West echoes some of Reed's earlier formulations but with an interesting difference. Reed argues that the black nationalisms of the sixties and seventies helped politicize black culture in such a way that identity politics became black America's principal preoccupation. Such a politics, he maintains, led to an oversimplification of the lives of African Americans and the reduction of regulative ideals to objects of immediate consumption. In the midst of this shift, Reed describes in detail the emergence of a particular stratum within the black community

(West's black petite bourgeoisie) which vigorously argued for "community control" of the political and economic institutions of what they understood to be "monolithic" black communities. Interestingly enough, they also situated themselves as the principal administrators or managers of these institutions. For Reed, black opposition during this period ultimately foundered on the fact that the language of opposition employed by this stratum was in fact the language of the dominant ideology. As he writes: "The movement 'failed' because it 'succeeded,' and its success can be measured by its impact on the administration of the social system." Unlike West, Reed does not commend attention to contemporary black popular culture as a site to reinvigorate the politics of the black working class. Instead, he views it as the evidence that black oppositional politics has been reduced to spectacle.

In "Stormy Weather: Reconstructing Black (Inter)Nationalism in the Cold War Era," Robin D. G. Kelley explodes the neat accounts of black nationalism(s) as an Americocentric affair. He gives voice to a black radical movement and discourse rooted in the late 1950s and early to mid-1960s by telling the history of an often forgotten organization: the Revolutionary Action Movement, a precursor to the black radical organizations of the late sixties and seventies. Kelley's essay serves as a qualification of West's and Reed's account. He points to a tradition of black political insurgency during the Black Power era that rejects the politics of a particular class of black elites for a more internationalist focus on Western imperialism and its relation to the darker people of the world. This "left-leaning" nationalism, in many ways, escapes the criticisms of Reed and West, and demonstrates that the politics of the period spanned the ideological spectrum. Kelley's historical narrative aims then to reactivate this hidden dimension of the period and show that the particular concerns associated with narrow forms of black nationalism have been and continue to be articulated within a more expansive political understanding of the nature of black oppression and its relation to capitalism. Kelley recognizes, however, that even these formulations suffered from the politics of machismo and from romantic visions of revolution.

Gerald Horne, in his essay "Reflecting Black: Zimbabwe and U.S. Black Nationalism," demonstrates the influence of the Black Power movement beyond U.S. national borders. In particular, he examines the effects of U.S. black nationalism—for better or worse—on the political environment of Zimbabwe (and how this played itself out against the backdrop of the Cold War). So, like Kelley, Horne turns to the international scene to expand our understanding of the politics of the Black Power era. Horne shows, however, how the political expressions of a particular form of U.S. black nationalism constrained the political and cultural imaginations of certain segments of the Zimbabwean revolution. More progressive voices and broad-based alliances were effectively blocked there just as they were in the United States by a narrow nationalist vision. Horne suggests that certain lessons can be learned by examining the congruities between black nationalism in Zimbabwe and the United States. With the fall of the Soviet Union and the devastating critiques of the more troubling aspects of black nationalism, Horne hopes that a new language might emerge (drawing on the best of the socialist and nationalist tradition) to speak to the newfangled problems that confront the African diaspora.

Although West, Reed, Kelley, and Horne end with somewhat trenchant critiques of the shortcomings of black nationalism, each begins his analysis with a serious engagement with the political formation. Neither draws on the rather easy and somewhat drawn-out critiques of racial essentialism as a shorthand for and quick dismissal of a very complex politics. Farah Jasmine Griffin recommends this kind of engagement to black feminists who have been rather quick (and, in some cases, rightly so) to dismiss black nationalism and, by extension, the black women who embrace that politics. Griffin's exhortations serve as general advice for those of us who desire to speak to black pain and suffering: we must take seriously (though not necessarily agree with) the languages that many black people use to express and respond to their experiences.

In "Conflict and Chorus: Reconsidering Toni Cade's *The Black Woman: An Anthology*," Griffin explores the complex relationship of contemporary black feminist thought to black women's lives and related struggles of black liberation. She cautions black feminists against easy dismissals of black nationalist women and passionately urges for an ongoing dialogue and debate—in the vein of Toni Cade Bambara's life and work—between black women across ideological differences. Through illustrations from autobiographical accounts and the example of Toni Cade Bambara's work within black nationalist circles, Griffin demonstrates the kinds of engagement that enable both serious criticism of the politics and continued constructive engagement with these sites where a number of black women are located (for a variety of interesting reasons).

E. Frances White's now classic essay, "Africa on My Mind: Gender, Counter Discourse, and African American Nationalism," serves as the best example of the kind of dialogue Griffin calls for. White examines the double-edged character of black nationalist constructions of memory and desire in the United States. She shows how specific ways of imagining social and political relations based on a supposedly pure and authentic African past serve both to resist racist structures and simultaneously construct repressive gender relations. White's close readings of Afrocentric theories and black feminist attempts to combine these theories with their own insights disclose her commitment to talking across these ideological divides. On one level, her essay is paradigmatic of the kind of engagement *Is It Nation Time?* calls for. She builds her critique out of a serious encounter with the insights and limitations of the politics. As she describes her kind of black feminism: It "recognizes the dangers of criticizing internal relations in the face of racist attacks but also argues that we will fail to transform ourselves into a liberated community if we do not engage in dialogue on the difficult issues that confront us."

Wahneema Lubiano, in her essay "Standing In for the State: Black Nationalism and 'Writing' the Black Subject," suggests that by understanding black nationalism(s) as the "common sense" of black America, we can gain some insight into the complicated ways this politics, particularly that of the Black Arts movement, does the work of the state by reproducing forms of subjectivity that are patriarchal, masculinist, and heterosexist. She urges that we take another critical glance at the kind of work this subjectivity is doing. On the one hand, its oppositional relation to white supremacy legitimizes it while, on the other, this same oppositional relation forecloses any sort of critical assessment "precisely because [this black subjectivity] presents itself as a need to fill the vacuum resulting from our abandonment by and resistance to the state." Lubiano recognizes, then, like White, the double-edged character of black nationalist(s) imaginings and situates the work of black feminist resistance to those imaginings as part of the fight against "the U.S. state's attempt to create its own version of a black subject."

We can trace the effects of this black nationalist understanding (and its contestation), Lubiano suggests, by looking more closely at the cultural work of black writers, filmmakers, and hip hop artists. Rap artist Common, for example, opens his track "The 6ᵗʰ Sense" with the old-school clarity of vinyl and these words:

> The Revolution will not be televised
> The Revolution is here . . . yeah
> This is Common Sense and D. J. Premier
> We gon' help ya'll see clear
> This is real hip hop music from the soul, ya'll

Common characterizes the lyrics that follow this introduction as, in some way, instantiating the revolution. And, of course, if this is the case, the revolution *is* televised. We all see it on BET. Ironically, Common brings together Gil Scott-Heron's critique of the commodification of black oppositional politics and the commodity form: after all, like Scott-Heron's, this is a song for sale (raising, of course, the hackles on Adolph Reed's neck!). But what is interesting is the way the "common sense" of black nationalism, as Lubiano describes it, does a certain kind of work amid this ambiguity. Common raps:

> Reality is friskin' me
> This industry'll make you lose intensity
> The common sense in me remembers the basement
> I'm Morphius in this hip hop matrix
> Exposing fake shit

The idea of a more authentic space for the expression of a black subjectivity (the common sense of the basement) not only serves as a basis for critiquing the music industry but also as a marker for distinguishing "the real" and "the fake." The refrain of the track hypnotically reinforces this distinction: "And you know . . . yes you know . . . This is rap for real . . . This is rap for the black people."

Obviously, some black people do not know this or Common's particular positioning of himself would lose its critical edge. So, on one level, his lyrics establish the divisions within the hip hop community in order to further reinforce the legitimacy of a particular understanding of black subjectivity (Common's "common sense"). Phillip Brian Harper's essay, "Nationalism and Social Division in Black Arts Poetry of the 1960s," implicitly traces this impulse back to the poetry of the Black Arts movement. Harper considers conventional assessments of Black Arts poetry as primarily defined by a call to violence against whites. He argues that such a reading fails to recognize the complex ways that rhetoric establishes divisions within black America. To some extent, "niggers" and "negroes" are as central to the construction of a certain kind of black nationalist subject as "crackers" and "ofays." Both oppositions solidify and insulate a particular imagining of "blackness." Harper maintains that a thicker account of this axis of black nationalism(s) will move us a bit further to understanding more fully the import of what he calls "the nationalist imperative" for black cultural production.

Craig Watkins's essay, "Black Is Back, and It's Bound to Sell!" takes us to the heart of the issue. Watkins examines the complex interaction of the ideology of black nationalism(s) and black popular culture. He examines three episodes: (1) the transformation of black popular music in the late 1960s and early 1970s; (2) the rise of political rap in the late 1980s and early 1990s; and (3) its profound influence on the black youth popular culture and, more generally, its impact on the bourgeois nationalism of filmmaker Spike Lee. Watkins explores each of these episodes in light of an effort to think about the "new repertoires of black youth agency, cultural production, and nation discourse" that have been and are made possible by technological innovation and consumer culture. With Cornel West and Adolph Reed, he sees the important role of an anxious black student middle class in the articulation of hip hop nationalism. He also recognizes, like Lubiano and Harper, the disciplinary character of the black subject and its style that is produced within hip hop culture. But Watkins urges that we nuance our understanding of the production of this black subject and its relation to commodification by linking it to a black nationalist desire for economic control. In other words, for Watkins, the discourse of "keeping it real" is much more than the spectacle that Adolph Reed denounces. As he puts it, "when critics charge that commodity culture has become a substitute for black political intervention . . . they often fail to see how it has become, in effect, a site of intervention"—extending the ambiguous legacies of the Black Power era to our contemporary moment in ways that are both enjoyable and problematic.

The final two essays bear a family resemblance in that they both draw on the work of black writers and their critiques/embrace of certain impulses behind the politics of the Black Power era. Will Walker's "After *The Fire Next Time:* James Baldwin's Postconsensus Double Bind" explores the impact of James Baldwin's southern tour and the rise of the Black Power movement on his aesthetic vision. He gives special attention to Baldwin's long essay *No Name in the Street* and concludes that Baldwin assumes the validity of the black nationalist(s') story about black oppression in the United States but discards what he takes to be the troublesome politics of blackness which denies the cultural and racial hybridity of America.

Jeffrey Stout extends an account of black nationalism inspired by the works of James Baldwin and Ralph Ellison. His "Theses on Black Nationalism" broadens the concerns of the preceding essays to a set of provocative considerations about the nature of our associations, the forms of our communities, and the roles each play in our lives. As he puts it, "Both Baldwin and Ellison cared . . . about the peoplehood of their people. They suspected that black nationalists were preoccupied with it. To be preoccupied with something is to care about it in such a way that other things tend, over time and not merely for a moment or two, to be excluded from one's concern." For Stout, the writings of Baldwin and Ellison provide us with a possible language to take seriously the realities of white supremacy while simultaneously resisting the temptation of the idolatry of blackness.

The central theme connecting all of these essays is that the Black Power movement was a complicated affair and its cultural legacies have a powerful hold on a number of African Americans today. For those of us who struggle to imagine a race-based politics—one in which the politics of blackness is continuously critiqued—we must begin to unravel the subtle and not so subtle ways the ideologies of the Black Power movement and their consequences inform our contemporary thinking about race and racial politics. Specifically, we must begin to assess the languages, style, and aims of contemporary forms of black nationalism and give particular attention to its expression in black popular culture. Toni Cade Bambara, James Baldwin, and Ralph Ellison emerge as exemplars for the kind of engagement needed. Each of these figures takes us beyond narrow considerations about racial essentialism and naive humanism. Instead, we are challenged by these thinkers to consider more broadly our politics and the problems African Americans (read: America) face. This collection represents then a first step. It aims to convince other scholars of the historical significance of the Black Power era and its importance to comprehending the complexities of our contemporary racial landscape.

NOTES

1. This time frame was chosen because, by 1968, the call for Black Power in Greenwood, Mississippi, had sedimented into black national consciousness, particularly with the assassination of Martin Luther King Jr. The year 1975 is a somewhat arbitrary cut-off date, but it marks the beginning of the end of the Great Debate between left-leaning and narrow cultural nationalists. As Manning Marable notes, "the struggle between the competing tendencies became increasingly fratricidal. Organizations collapsed beneath the weight of polemics." And, in effect, black militants turned on themselves. This is also the year Elijah Muhammed died and the Nation of Islam was thrown into turmoil. See Manning Marable, *Race, Reform, and Rebellion: The Second Reconstruction in Black America, 1945–1982* (Jackson, Miss., 1984), p. 152; see chap. 6 in particular.

2. See Molefi Asante, *The Afrocentric Idea* (Philadelphia, 1987), *"Malcolm X as Cultural Hero" and Other Afrocentric Essays* (Trenton, N.J., 1993), and an edited volume, *In Their Faces: Situating Alternatives to Afrocentrism* (Philadelphia, 1995); and Maulana Karenga, *Introduction to Black Studies* (Los Angeles, 1993), *Kawaida Theory: An Introduc-*

tory Outline (Los Angeles, 1980), and *Essays on Struggle: Position and Analysis* (Los Angeles, 1978).

3. See Henry Louis Gates Jr., ed., *"Race," Writing, and Difference* (Chicago, 1986). Also see Anthony Appiah's essay in that volume, "The Uncompleted Argument: Du Bois and the Illusion of Race" (pp. 38–58); Henry Louis Gates Jr., *Loose Canons: The Culture Wars* (New York, 1992); and Anthony Appiah, *In My Father's House: Africa in the Philosophy of Culture* (New York, 1992). For a much more nuanced version of the claims in "Uncompleted Argument," see Anthony Appiah and Amy Gutman, *Color Conscious: The Political Morality of Race* (Princeton, N.J., 1996). A somewhat similar treatment of black nationalism and race language also can be found in Paul Gilroy, *The Black Atlantic: Modernity and Double Consciousness* (Cambridge, Mass., 1993), and in his latest book, *Against Race: Imagining Political Culture beyond the Color Line* (Cambridge, Mass., 2000).

4. The approach of the volume can be found in the general works of Robin D. G. Kelley; the brilliant book of Timothy Tyson, *Radio Free Dixie: Robert Williams and the Roots of Black Power* (Chapel Hill, N.C., 1999); and Komozoi Woodard's *A Nation within a Nation: Amiri Baraka and Black Power Politics in Newark* (Chapel Hill, N.C., 1999).

5. Quoted in Clayborne Carson, *In Struggle: SNCC and the Black Awakening of the 1960s* (Cambridge, Mass., 1995), p. 210. Also see Gene Roberts, "Mississippi Reduces Police Protection for Marchers," *New York Times,* June 17, 1966.

6. Debbie Louis, *And We Are Not Saved: A History of the Movement as People* (Garden City, N.Y., 1970), p. 296. Also quoted in Marable, *Race, Reform, and Rebellion,* p. 110.

7. Three categories can help us map the general political tendencies of the Black Power movement: revolutionary, pluralist, and culturalist. Revolutionists "view the overthrow of existing political and economic institutions as a prerequisite for black liberation" (see John Bracey Jr., August Meier, and Elliot Rudwick, eds., *Black Nationalism in America* [Indianapolis, 1970]). They often call for a complete separation of black and white Americans based on different ways of life and different experiences of political and economic structures in the West (e.g., demanding control of a number of the southern states or simply a mass exodus back to Africa). Pluralists hold the view "that African-Americans had to mobilize, close ranks, and move toward a position of community and of group strength. This difficult process involved all aspects of black life—political, economic, psychological, and cultural. Once unity had been achieved in these areas, blacks would form a significant power bloc" (see William Van Deburg, *New Day in Babylon: The Black Power Movement and American Culture, 1965–1975* (Chicago, 1992). Culturalists contend "that black people have a culture, style of life, cosmology, approach to the problems of existence, and aesthetic values distinct from that of white Americans in particular and white Europeans or Westerners in general" (see *Black Nationalism in America*). For them, this distinct form of life constitutes a nation and a national identity: something to be retrieved in light of the desires and effects of white supremacy, and something to be preserved for posterity.

8. I have adapted the idea of the politics of transvaluation from Friedrich Nietzsche's notion of the transvaluation of values. See Nietzsche, *Beyond Good and Evil: Prelude to a Philosophy of the Future,* sec. 4 (New York, 1966) and the preface to his *Genealogy of Morals* (New York, 1956). I am not suggesting here that all political projects during the Black Power era thought about this revolution of the mind in the same way. Not at all. Huey P. Newton on May 15, 1968, made it abundantly clear that the political outcomes of a certain politics of transvaluation were to be rejected: "Cultural nationalism, or pork-chop

nationalism as I sometimes call it, is basically a problem of having the wrong political perspective. It seems to be a reaction to, instead of an action against, political oppression. The cultural nationalists are concerned with returning to the old African culture and thereby regaining their identity and freedom. In other words, they feel assuming the African culture is *enough* to buy political freedom. Many cultural nationalists fall into line as reactionary nationalists" (Philip Foner, *The Black Panther Speaks* [Philadelphia, 1970], p. 92; emphasis added). What is striking is not the well-known rejection of cultural nationalism but Newton's implicit acknowledgment of the value of the politics of transvaluation. He understood it, however, instrumentally: as a dimension of a broader strategy of struggle.

9. William Van Deburg, "Introduction," *Modern Black Nationalism: From Marcus Garvey to Louis Farrakhan,* ed. William Van Deburg (New York, 1997), p. 15.

10. I place "blackness" in quotation marks throughout the introduction to signal its particular meaning in the context of a politics of transvaluation. I believe it an egregious error to conflate the idea of blackness with all uses of race language. Race language is not only a tool in problem solving that goes beyond a celebration of "black" identity, it also invokes narratives, stories of a community's sojourn. I would personally find it difficult to tell the story of the horrors of lynching or the triumphs of the civil rights movement without the language of race. Indeed, the language singles out some events, places, and personalities that are constitutive of what can be called "black" communities. I am well aware of the potential negative consequences of narratives about community. Romantic reconstructions of an African past that are gynophobic and heterosexist are just one example among many of the pernicious ways communal narratives can police our individual identities. But I remain convinced that the quality of individuality depends on the types of communities in which we live, which in turn depends on the kinds of stories we tell. Race language invokes the specific pain and suffering and the joy and triumph that are definitive of a particular community of experience in the United States, and to discard that language because of a sloppy conflation with what can be a problematic notion of "blackness" is tantamount to removing our capacity to tell that story. See my essay, "Pragmatism and Black Identity: An Alternative Approach," *Nepantia* 2, no. 2 (July 2001).

11. Kimberly Benston, *Performing Blackness: Enactments of African-American Modernism* (London and New York, 2000), p. 353 n. 21.

12. SNCC, "Position Paper on Black Power, 1966," in *Modern Black Nationalism,* pp. 125–26.

13. Martin Luther King Jr., "Where Do We Go from Here?" in *A Testament of Hope: The Essential Writings and Speeches of Martin Luther King, Jr.,* ed. James Melvin Washington (New York, 1986), pp. 246–47.

14. Of course, the black theological project of James Cone and others attempts to bring these discourses together. See his texts, *Black Theology and Black Power* (New York, 1989) and *A Black Theology of Liberation* (New York, 1990). Also see *Black Theology: A Documentary History,* vol. 1, *1966–1979,* ed. James Cone and Gayraud Wilmore (New York, 1993). For an analysis of some of the problems this attempt at translation yielded, see my "Pragmatic Historicism and the Problem of History in Black Theology," *American Journal of Theology and Philosophy* 19, no. 2 (May 1998).

15. Quoted in Marable, *Race, Reform, and Rebellion,* p. 107.

16. See Jeffrey Stout, "Theses on Black Nationalism," in this volume.

17. George Santayana, *The Life of Reason,* 5 vols. (New York, 1905–6), 3:183.

18. Henry Samuel Levinson, *Santayana, Pragmatism, and the Spiritual Life* (Chapel Hill, N.C., 1992), p. 158. My use of piety is greatly influenced by Jeffrey Stout's essay in this volume and his Efroymson Lectures.

19. "The Gary Declaration, 1972," in *Modern Black Nationalism*, p. 142.

20. Stuart Hall, "Cultural Identity and Diaspora," in *Colonial Discourse and Post-Colonial Theory: A Reader* (New York, 1994), p. 393.

21. *Malcolm X: Make It Plain* (Boston: WGHB; distributed by PBS video, 1994).

22. William J. Harris, ed., *The Leroi Jones/Amiri Baraka Reader* (New York, 1995), pp. 240–42.

23. Vincent Harding recognized this effect of the movement early on. See his essay, "The Religion of Black Power," in *Black Theology: A Documentary History*, vol. 1. The essay originally appeared in Donald R. Cutler, ed., *The Religious Situation: 1968* (Boston, 1968).

24. Here Baraka, echoing the words of Maulana Karenga, makes this point explicitly: "We say that a black woman must first be able to inspire her man, then she must be able to teach her children and contribute to the social development of the nation. . . . How do you inspire black men; [*sic*] by being the conscious rising essence of Blackness. Blackness conscious of itself, which is what we mean by cultural. Blackness, Maulana has said, is Color, Culture, and Consciousness. By race, by identity, and by action you inspire Black Man by being Black Woman. By being the nation, as the house, the smallest example of how the nation should be. So you are my 'house', I live in you, and together we have a house, and that must be the microcosm, by example, of the entire black nation." See Amiri Baraka, *Raise Race Ray Raze: Essays since 1965* (New York, 1971), pp. 148–49.

25. I am referring here to culturalist expressions of black nationalism. Robin D. G. Kelley goes to great length in his essay in this volume to show that such a characterization alone does not help us understand the more radical strains of black nationalism. See also Komozoi Woodward, *A Nation within a Nation* (Chapel Hill, N.C., 1999).

26. I am not suggesting through my usage of commodification that "blackness" is being cheapened and degraded in its apparent transformation into consumer goods. This would suggest that I believe that there is a more authentic basis for black identity. Far from it. My intention here is to show how the commodification of blackness obscures further the fact that "blackness," like all race language, has pragmatic value—that blackness is one tool among many in a certain kind of problem-solving activity (whose efficacy is determined by its consequences). For me, and I don't have the space to argue for this view here, black identity is not about discovery, an archaeological project in which black folk uncover their true "black" selves. Rather, taken together, our problem-solving activity turns out to be our lives.

The Paradox of the African American Rebellion

Cornel West

The distinctive feature of African American life in the sixties was the rise on the historical stage of a small yet determined petite bourgeoisie promoting liberal reforms, and the revolt of the masses, whose aspirations exceeded those of liberalism but whose containment was secured by political appeasement, cultural control, and state repression. African America encountered the modern American capitalist order (in its expansionist phase)—as urban dwellers, industrial workers, and franchised citizens—on a broad scale for the first time. This essay will highlight the emergence of the black parvenu petite bourgeoisie—the new, relatively privileged, middle class—and its complex relations to the black working poor and underclass. I will try to show how the political strategies, ideological struggles, and cultural anxieties of this predominantly white-collar stratum both propelled the freedom movement in an unprecedented manner and circumscribed its vision, analysis, and praxis within liberal capitalist perimeters.

For interpretive purposes, the sixties is not a chronological category which encompasses a decade, but rather a historical construct or heuristic rubric that renders noteworthy historical processes and events intelligible. The major historical processes that set the context for the first stage of the black freedom movement in the sixties were the modernization of southern agriculture, the judicial repudiation of certain forms of southern racism, and the violent white backlash against perceived black progress. The modernization of southern agriculture made obsolete much of the traditional tenant labor force, thereby forcing large numbers of black rural folk into southern and northern urban centers in search of employment. The judicial repudiation of certain forms of southern racism, prompted by the gallant struggles of the National Association for the Advancement of Colored People (NAACP) and exemplified in the *Brown v. Board of Education* decision of 1954, was not only a legal blow against tax-supported school segregation; it also added historical momentum and political legitimacy to black struggles against racism. Yet there quickly surfaced an often violent white reaction to this momentum and legitimacy. For example, Rev. George W. Lee was fatally shot in May 1955 for refusing to take his name off the voter registration list. Sixty-three-year-old Lamar Smith was killed in broad daylight in August 1955 for trying to get out the black vote in an upcoming primary election. And most notably, Emmett L. Till, a fourteen-year-old lad from Chicago visiting his relatives, was murdered in late August 1955. These wanton acts of violence against black people in Mississippi, though part of the American southern way of life, reflected the conservative white reaction to perceived black progress. In 1955, this white reaction was met with widespread black resistance.

The greatness of Rev. Dr. Martin Luther King Jr.—the major American prophet of this century and black leader in the sixties—was his ability to mobilize and organize this southern resistance, such that the delicate balance between the emerging "new" black petite bourgeoisie, black working poor, and black underclass was maintained for a few years. The arrest of Rosa Parks on December 1, 1955, in Montgomery, Alabama—as a result of one of a series of black acts of civil disobedience against Montgomery's bus line that year—led to the creation of the Montgomery Improvement Association (MIA), the adoption of a citywide black boycott, and the placement of King at the head of the movement. After nearly a year of the boycott, the U.S. Supreme Court declared Alabama's state and local bus segregation laws unconstitutional. Judicial repudiation of southern racism again gave the black struggle for freedom momentum and legitimacy.

King is the exemplary figure of the first stage of the black freedom movement in the sixties not only because he was its gifted and courageous leader, or simply because of his organizational achievements, but, more important, because he consolidated the most progressive potential available in the black southern community at that time: the cultural potency of prophetic black churches, the skills of engaged black preachers, trade unionists, and professionals, and the spirit of rebellion and resistance of the black working poor and underclass. In this sense, King was an organic intellectual of the first order—a highly educated and informed thinker with organic links to ordinary folk. Despite his petit bourgeois origins, his deep roots in the black church gave him direct access to the life-worlds of the majority of black Southerners. In addition, his education at Morehouse College, Crozier Theological Seminary, and Boston University provided him with opportunities to reflect upon various anticolonial struggles around the world, especially those in India and Ghana, and also entitled him to respect and admiration in the eyes of black people, including the "old," black, middle class (composed primarily of teachers and preachers). Last, his Christian outlook and personal temperament facilitated relations with progressive nonblack people, thereby insuring openness to potential allies.

King institutionalized his sense of the social engagement of black churches, his Christian-informed techniques of nonviolence, and his early liberal vision of America with the founding in February, 1957, in New Orleans of the Southern Christian Leadership Conference (SCLC). This courageous group of prophetic black preachers from ten southern states served as the models for young black southern activists. I stress the adjective "southern" not simply because most black people in the United States at this time lived in the South, but also because the core of the first stage of the black freedom movement was a church-led movement in the belly of the violence-prone, underindustrialized, colonylike southern United States. Of course, the North was quite active—especially Harlem's Rev. Adam Clayton Powell Jr. in Congress and the Nation of Islam's Malcolm X in the streets—but activity in the North was not the major thrust of this first stage.

Like David against Goliath, black activists openly challenged the entrenched, racist, white status quo in the South. Widespread white economic sanctions and physical attacks on black people, fueled by the so-called Southern Manifesto promoted in 1956 by Senator J. Strom Thurmond of South Carolina along with over a hundred congressmen, rendered both the Democratic and Republican parties relatively silent regarding the civil rights issues affecting black people. Two diluted civil rights bills (in 1957 and 1960) limped through Congress, and the Supreme Court, owing to congressional pressure, took much of the bite out of its earlier *Brown* decision. Black resistance intensified.

Inspired by the praxis of King, MIA, and SCLC—as well as the sit-in techniques employed by the Congress of Racial Equality (CORE) in the North—four black freshmen students at North Carolina Agricultural and Technical College in Greensboro staged a sit-in at the local Woolworth's on February 1, 1960. Within a week, their day-to-day sit-in had been joined by black and white students from the Women's College of the University of North Carolina, North Carolina College, and Duke University. Within two weeks, the sit-in movement had spread to fifteen other cities in Virginia, Tennessee, and South Carolina. Within two months, there were sit-ins in seventy-eight cities. By the end of 1960, over fifty thousand people throughout the South had participated in sit-in demonstrations, with over 25 percent of the black students in predominantly black colleges participating. In short, young black people (and some progressive white people) had taken seriously King's techniques of nonviolence and the spirit of resistance.

This spontaneous rebellion of young black people against the southern taboo of black and white people eating together in public places exemplified a major component in the first stage of the black freedom movement: the emergence of politicized, black, parvenu, petit bourgeois students. These students, especially young preachers and Christian activists, prefigured the disposition and orientation of the vastly increasing number of black college students in the sixties: they would give first priority to social activism and justify their newly acquired privileges by personal risk and sacrifice. So the young black student movement was not simply a rejection of segregation in restaurants. It was also a revolt against the perceived complacency of the "old" black petite bourgeoisie. It is no accident that at the first general conference on student sit-in activity, which began Good Friday (April 15) 1960, the two keynote speakers—Rev. James Lawson and Rev. Martin Luther King Jr.—launched devastating critiques of the NAACP and other "old" black middle-class groups. King articulated this viewpoint when he characterized the sit-in movement as "a revolt against those Negroes in the middle class who have indulged themselves in big cars and ranch-style homes rather than in joining a movement for freedom." The organization which emerged later in the year from this gathering—the Student Nonviolent Coordinating Committee (SNCC)—epitomized this revolt against the political reticence of the "old" black middle class.

The major achievement of SNCC was, in many ways, its very existence. SNCC initiated a new style and outlook among black students in particular and the "new" black petite bourgeoisie in general. Its activist, countercultural orientation even influenced disenchanted white students on elite university campuses. Yet SNCC's central shortcoming was discernible at its inception: if pushed far enough, the revolt against middle-class status and outlook would not only include their models but also themselves, given their privileged student status and probable upward social mobility.

The influence of SNCC's new style was seen when James Farmer departed from the program directorship of the NAACP to become National Director of CORE. Within six weeks, he announced that CORE would conduct "Freedom Rides"—modeled on the 1947 Journey of Reconciliation led by CORE—to challenge segregation in interstate bus depots and terminals. On May 4, 1961, seven black people and six white people left Washington, D.C. Within ten days, one of the buses had been burned to the ground and many riders had been viciously attacked in Birmingham and Montgomery. This Freedom Ride was disbanded in Montgomery on May 17. A second Freedom Ride was initiated by SNCC, led by Diane Nash, composed of white and black people from CORE and SNCC. Violence ensued again, with twenty-seven people arrested and given suspended two-month sentences and fines of two hundred dollars. They refused to pay and were taken to Parchman Prison.

These two Freedom Rides—though responsible for the desegregation of bus and train stations on September 22, 1961, by the Interstate Commerce Commission—served as a portent of the two basic realities that would help bring the initial stage of the black freedom movement to a close: first, the slow but sure rift between SNCC and King, and, second, the ambiguous attitude of Democratic Party liberals to the movement. Both aspects came to the fore at the crucial August 1961 staff meeting at SNCC at the Highlander Folk School in Tennessee. It was well known that the Kennedy administration had called for a "cooling off" period, motivated primarily by its fear of alienating powerful southern Democratic comrades in Congress. At the meeting, Tim Jenkins, a fellow traveler of the Democratic Party, proposed that SNCC drop its emphasis on direct action and focus on voter education and registration. The majority of the SNCC staff opposed Jenkins's project, owing to its connections with the Kennedy administration and the open approval of it by King's SCLC. In the eyes of many SNCC members, the "establishment" against which they were struggling began to encompass both the Democratic Party's liberals and the SCLC's black activist liberals. This slow rupture would result in some glaring defeats in the civil rights movement, most notably the Albany (Georgia) movement in December 1961, and also led to the gradual breakaway of SNCC from the techniques of nonviolence.

Yet in 1963, the first stage of the black freedom movement would culminate in its most successful endeavors: Birmingham and the March on Washington. The televised confrontation between the civil rights marchers and the Commissioner of Public Safety, Eugene "Bull" Connor, as well as the dramatic arrest of King, gave the movement much sympathy and support throughout the country. And the use of hundreds of black children in the struggle reinforced this effective histrionic strategy. Despite the bombing of the black Gaston Hotel, of King's brother's home, and black spontaneous rebellions in Birmingham, the massive nonviolent direct action—including over three thousand people imprisoned—proved successful. The city of Birmingham, often referred to as the "American Johannesburg," accepted the black demands for desegregation and black employment opportunities. Furthermore, President Kennedy responded to the Birmingham campaign with a televised address to the nation in which he pledged his support for a comprehensive civil rights bill. However, the assassination of Medgar Evers, state executive secretary of the Mississippi NAACP, only hours after Kennedy's speech cast an ominous shadow over the Birmingham victory.

The famous March on Washington in August 1963—the occasion for King's powerful and poignant "I have a dream" speech—was not the zenith of the civil rights movement. The movement had peaked in Birmingham. Rather the March on Washington was the historic gathering of that coalition of liberal forces—white trade unionists, Christians, Jews, and civil rights activists—whose potency was declining, whose fragile cohesion was falling apart. The central dilemma of the first stage of the black freedom movement emerged: the existence and sustenance of the civil rights movement neither needed nor required white aid or allies, yet its *success* required white liberal support in the Democratic Party, Congress, and the White House.

The March on Washington exemplified this debilitating limitation of the civil rights movement. With white liberal support, the movement would achieve limited success but slowly lose its legitimacy in the eyes of the now more politicized black petit bourgeois students, working poor, and underclass. Without white liberal support, the movement could raise more fundamental issues of concern to the black working poor and underclass, yet thereby render the movement marginal to mainstream American politics and hence risk severe repression. It comes as no surprise that the March on Washington witnessed both the most powerful rhetoric and the most salient reality of the civil rights movement: King's great speech and the Kennedy administration's supervision of the March.

In summary, the first stage of the black freedom movement in the sixties—the civil rights struggle—began as a black response to white violent attacks and took the form of a critique of everyday life in the American South. This critique primarily consisted of attacking everyday cultural folkways that insulted black dignity. It was generated, in part, from the multifarious effects of the economic transformation of dispossessed southern rural peasants into downtrodden industrial workers, maids, and unemployed city dwellers within the racist American South. In this regard, the civil rights movement prefigured the fundamental concerns of the American New Left: linking private troubles to public issues, accenting the relation of cultural hegemony to political control and economic exploitation.

The major achievements of the civil rights movement were noteworthy: the transformation of everyday life (especially the elimination of terror as a primary mode of social control) of central regions in the American South; the federal commitment to the civil and voting rights of African Americans; and the sense of confidence among black people that effective mobilization and organization were not only possible but imperative if the struggle for freedom was to continue. The pressing challenges were immense: transforming the power relations in the American South and North, obtaining federal support for employment and economic rights of the underprivileged, sustaining black organizational potency in the face of increasing class differentiation within the black community, and taking seriously the long-overlooked specific needs and interests of black women. The first stage came to a close principally because the civil rights struggle achieved its liberal aims, namely, absorption into mainstream American politics, reputable interest-group status in the (soon to falter) liberal coalition of the Democratic Party.

The second stage centered primarily on the issue of the legitimacy and accountability of the black political leadership. Like the first stage, this historical movement was engendered by a sense of black resistance and rebellion, and led by black petit bourgeois figures. Yet these "new," black, middle-class figures had been highly politicized and radicalized by the strengths and weaknesses of King's movement, by the rise of the New Left movement among white privileged students, and by the revolutionary anticolonial struggles in the Caribbean (Cuba), Africa (Ghana and Guinea), Latin America (Chile and Bolivia), and Southeast Asia (Vietnam). The transitional events were the Mississippi Freedom Summer in 1964, the Democratic National Convention in Atlantic City, late August 1964, and the Selma campaign of 1965. The Freedom Summer brought to the surface the deep cultural and personal problems of interracial political struggle in America: white attitudes of paternalism, guilt and sexual jealousy, and black sensibilities of one-upsmanship, manipulation, and sexual adventure. The Atlantic City convention illustrated the self-serving machinery of the Democratic Party, whose support even King at this point solicited at the risk of white-controlled compromise. Finally, King's Selma campaign, initiated by SNCC years earlier, was sustained primarily by federal support, escort, and legitimacy. In short, the bubble was about to burst: the vision, analysis, and praxis of significant elements of the black freedom movement were to move beyond the perimeters of prevailing American bourgeois politics.

The Watts explosion in August 1965 revealed the depths of the problem of legitimacy and accountability of black political leadership. The rebellion and resistance (especially in northern urban centers) could no longer find an organizational form of expression. In the cities, it had become sheer anarchic energy and existential assertion without political direction and social vision. The Watts rebellion was a watershed event in the black freedom movement, in that it drew the line of demarcation between those who would cling to liberal rhetoric, ties to the Democratic Party, and middle-class concerns, and those who would attempt to go beyond liberalism, expose the absorptive role and function of the Democratic Party, and focus more on black proletarian and lumpenproletarian interests.

The pressing challenges of the second stage were taken up by Martin Luther King Jr. His Chicago campaign in 1966—though rejected by most of his liberal black and white comrades in SCLC—pushed for the radical unionization of slum-dwellers against exploitative landlords. His aborted poor people's campaign of 1967–68, initiated after his break with President Johnson and the Democratic Party, which had been precipitated by his fierce opposition to the Vietnam War, was even more attuned to black, Latino, and white working poor and underclass concerns. Yet, despite his immense talent, energy, and courage, it became clear that King lacked the organization and support to address these concerns. Notwithstanding his 1968 murder—preceded by intense FBI harassments and threats—the widespread ideological fragmentation and increased class and strata differentiation in African America precluded King from effectively meeting the pressing challenges. His new focus on the urban poor led to black middle-class abandonment of his movement; his nonviolent approach perturbed black committed leftists who otherwise welcomed his new focus; his Christianity disturbed black secularists and Muslims already working in urban ghettos; and his integrationist perspective met with staunch opposition from black nationalists who were quickly seizing hegemony over the black freedom movement. In other words, King was near death politically and organizationally before he was murdered, though he will never die in the hearts and minds of progressive people in the United States and abroad.

Ironically, King's later path was blazed by his early vociferous critic, Malcolm X. Even as a narrow black nationalist under the late Honorable Elijah Muhammad, Malcolm X rejected outright white liberal support and ties to the Democratic Party, and he highlighted the plight of urban black working poor and unemployed people. More than any other black figure during the first stage, Malcolm X articulated the underlying, almost visceral, feelings and sensibilities of black urban America—North and South, Christian and non-Christian, young and old. His early rhetoric was simply prescient: too honest, too candid, precisely the things black folk often felt but never said publicly due to fear of white retaliation, even in the early sixties. In fact, his piercing rhetoric had primarily a cathartic function for black people; it purged them of their deferential and defensive attitudes toward white people.

Although Malcolm X moved toward a more Marxist-informed humanist position just prior to his assassination by rival Black Muslims in February 1965, he became the major symbol for (and of) the second stage of the black freedom movement in the sixties. What were accented were neither his political successes nor his organizational achievements but rather his rhetorical eloquence and homespun honesty. Malcolm X did not hesitate to tell black and white America "like it is," even if it resulted in little political and practical payoff. This eloquence and honesty were admired at a distance by the black working poor and underclass: it expressed their gut feelings and addressed their situation but provided little means or hope as to how to change their predicament. The "old," black, middle class was horrified; they publicly and secretly tried to discredit him. The "new" black petite bourgeoisie, especially black students, welcomed Malcolm X's rhetoric and honesty with open arms. It resonated with their own newly acquired sense of political engagement and black pride; it also spoke to a more fundamental problem they faced—the problem of becoming black leaders and elites with organic, existential, and rhetorical ties to the black community.

In a complex way, Malcolm X's candid talk both fueled more protracted black rebellion and provided a means to contain it. In short, his rhetoric was double-edged and functioned in contradictory ways. On the one hand, it served as an ideological pillar for revolutionary black nationalism. On the other hand, his rhetoric was employed by manipulative black petit bourgeois politicians, professionals, administrators, and students to promote their own upward social mobility. The adulation of Malcolm X in the black community is profound. Yet an often overlooked component of this adulation among the "new" black middle class was (and is) their subtle use of his truth-telling for their narrow, self-serving aims. The relative silence regarding his black sexist values and attitudes also reveals the deep patriarchal sensibilities in the black community.

The revolt of the black masses, with hundreds of rebellions throughout the country, set the framework for the second stage. The repressive state apparatus in American capitalist society jumped at this opportunity to express its contempt for black people. And the basic mechanism of pacifying the erupting black ghettos—the drug industry—fundamentally changed the content and character of the black community. The drug industry, aided and abetted by underground capitalists, invaded black communities with intense force, police indifference, and political silence. It accelerated black white-collar and solid blue-collar working-class suburban flight, and transformed black poor neighborhoods into terrains of human bondage to the commodity form, enslavement to the buying and selling of drugs. For the first time in African American history, fear and trepidation among black folk toward one another became pervasive. As crime moved toward civil terrorism, black distrust of and distance from the black poor and underclass deepened. And, of course, black presence in jails and prisons rapidly increased.

The revolt of the black masses precipitated a deep crisis—with political, intellectual, and existential forms—among the "new" black petite bourgeoisie. What should the appropriate black middle-class response be to such black working poor and underclass rebellions? This complex response is best seen in the internal dynamics of the Black Power movement. This movement, more than any other at the time, projected the aspirations and anxieties of the recently politicized and radicalized black petite bourgeoisie. From Adam Clayton Powell Jr.'s Howard University baccalaurcate address of 1966, through the Meredith March, to the Newark Black Power Conference, the message was clear: beneath the rhetoric of Black Power, black control, and black self-determination was a budding, "new," black, middle class hungry for power and starving for status. Needless to say, most young black intellectuals were duped by this petit bourgeois rhetoric, primarily owing to their own identity crisis and self-interest. In contrast, the "new" black business, professional, and political elites heard the bourgeois melody behind the radical rhetoric and manipulated the movement for their own benefit. The rebellious black working poor and underclass often either became dependent on growing welfare support or seduced by the drug culture.

The second stage was primarily a black nationalist affair. The veneration of "black" symbols, rituals, styles, hairdos, values, sensibilities, and flag escalated. The "Black Is Beautiful" slogan was heard throughout the black community, and James Brown's "Say It Loud, I'm Black and I'm Proud" became an exemplary—and healthy—expression of the cultural reversal of alienating Anglo-American ideals of beauty and behavior. Yet this cantankerous reversal (like the black rediscovery of jazz) was principally a "new" black middle-class phenomenon.

The working poor and underclass watched as the "new" black middle class visibly grappled with its new identity, social position, and radical political rhetoric. For the most part, the black underclass continued to hustle, rebel when appropriate, get high, and listen to romantic proletarian love songs produced by Detroit's Motown; they remained perplexed at their idolization by the "new" black middle class, which they sometimes envied. The black working poor persisted in their weekly church attendance, struggled to make ends meet, and waited to see what the beneficial results would be after all the bourgeois hoopla was over. In short, the black nationalist moment, despite its powerful and progressive critique of American cultural imperialism, was principally the activity of black petit bourgeois self-congratulation and self-justification upon reaching an anxiety-ridden, middle-class status in racist American society.

To no surprise, the leading black, petit bourgeois, nationalist groups such as SNCC (after 1966), CORE, Ron Karenga's US, and Imamu Amiri Baraka's Congress of African People were viewed by black proletarian and lumpenproletarian organizations as "pork-chop nationalists" who confused superficial nation-talk with authentic cultural distinctiveness, middle-class guilt with working-class aspirations, and identity crises with revolutionary situations. The late Honorable Elijah Muhammad's Nation of Islam, though petit bourgeois in intent, was staunchly working poor and underclass (and especially strong in American prisons) in composition. Devoid of leading black intellectuals yet full of eloquent spokesmen, the Nation of Islam put to shame the pork-chop nationalists, not only by being "blacker than thou" in both mythology and ideology, but also by producing discernible results in the personal, organizational, and financial life of its members and the black community.

The Black Panther Party (founded in Oakland, California, 1966) was the leading black lumpenproletarian revolutionary party in the sixties. It thoroughly rejected and consistently struggled against petit bourgeois nationalism from a viewpoint of strong black leftist internationalism. Yet it was overwhelmed by the undisciplined character of black underclass life, seduced by the histrionic enticements of mass media, and crushed by state repression. The only other major national response of black progressives against black petit bourgeois nationalism was George Wiley's and Fannie Lou Hamer's National Welfare Rights Organization (founded in August 1967). But it was unable to sustain broad membership and thereby control encroaching bureaucratic leadership. The League of Revolutionary Black Workers (founded in Detroit, Michigan, 1969), though regional in scope, was the most important revolutionary group among black industrial workers in the country. It eventually split over the issue of the role of black nationalism in a Marxist organization.

The rift between black petit bourgeois nationalists and black revolutionary leftists was best illustrated in the American response to James Forman's historic Black Manifesto. Forman, a former executive director of SNCC, ex-minister of Foreign Affairs of the Black Panther Party, and leader of the short-lived Black Workers' Congress, proposed at the National Black Economic Development Conference in Detroit and later, more dramatically, at New York City's Riverside Church's 11:00 P.M. service, reparation funds of 500 million dollars from white Christian churches and Jewish synagogues in order to finance the black revolutionary overthrow of the U.S. government. This "revolution" would turn into an "armed, well-disciplined, black-controlled government."

This symbolic gesture represented the peak of the black nationalist moment in the sixties, though it was enacted by a black Marxist. It also signified liberal white America's absorption and domestication of black nationalism. Despite the manifesto's Marxist critique and demands of American capitalist society—such as the call for a black revolutionary vanguard party and even the call for white progressive people to accept this black leadership—the most salient issue became that of reparations to existing black middle-class groups.

The white American response to these demands on the ecclesiastical, educational, and corporate levels was widespread. Of course, the major funds were not given to Forman's group (though it received about three hundred thousand dollars), but rather to church agencies, denominational caucuses, minority-oriented programs and, above all, black businesses and banks. Regardless of Forman's naive revolutionary intent, the black petit bourgeois nationalists triumphed. Soon the federal government and even the Nixon administration would openly support such moves in the name of "black self-determination" and "black capitalism."

The hegemonic role of black petit bourgeois nationalism had four deleterious consequences for African America. First, it isolated progressive black leftists such that orthodox Marxism became the primary refuge for those concerned with class struggle and internationalism. And even in these new Marxist formations, the Black Nation thesis—the claim that black people constitute a nation within the United States—once again became the widely accepted understanding of African American oppression. Second, the machismo lifestyles of black nationalists (of the petit bourgeois and revolutionary varieties) so marginalized black women that the black feminist movement of the seventies and eighties was often forced to sever ties with black male-dominated groups, thereby encouraging an understandable but innocuous black feminist separatism. Third, black nationalism disarmed and delimited a large number of young black intellectuals by confining them to parochial black rhetoric, pockets of "internal dialogues," which resulted in posing almost insurmountable walls of separation between progressive white, brown, red, yellow, and black intellectuals. Last, black nationalist rhetoric contributed greatly to the black freedom movement's loss of meaningful anchorage and organic ties to the black community, especially the churches. In short, besides the severe state repression and the pervasive drug invasion, the black petit bourgeois nationalist perspectives and practices were primarily responsible for the radically decentered state of the black freedom movement in the seventies and eighties. This was so principally because they undergirded the needs and interests of the "new" black middle class.

The sixties in African American history witnessed an unforgettable appearance of the black masses on the historical stage, but they were quickly dragged off—killed, maimed, strung out, imprisoned, or paid off. Yet history continues and the growing black petite bourgeoisie still gropes for identity, direction, and vision. This black middle class is "new" not simply because significant numbers of black people recently arrived in the world of higher education, comfortable living, and professional occupations, but also because they achieved such status against the backdrop of undeniable political struggle, a struggle in which many of them participated. And the relation of their unprecedented opportunities and privileges to the revolt of the black masses is quite obvious to them. This is why the "new" black middle class will more than likely refuse to opt for political complacency. Its own position hangs on some form of political participation, on resisting subtle racist practices, housing policies, and educational opportunities. Only persistent pressure can ensure a managerial job at IBM, partnership in a Wall Street firm, a home in Westchester, or a slot at Harvard College, whereas in the past little resistance by the "old" black middle class was required to service the black community, live in the Gold Coast of Washington, D.C., or send the kid to Howard, Fisk, or Morehouse. The roots of the "new" black middle class are in political struggle, in SCLC, SNCC, CORE, in the values and sensibilities these groups generated.

The major challenge of the "new," black, petite bourgeoisie is no longer whether it will take politics seriously (as posed in E. Franklin Frazier's classic *Black Bourgeoisie* in 1957). Rather it is what kind of politics the "new" black middle class will promote in the present national context of austere economic policies, declining state support of black rights, escalating racist violence, and the prevailing international context of the crisis of capitalism, the nuclear arms race, and anti-imperialist struggles. Like any other petite bourgeoisie, the "new" black middle class will most likely pursue power-seeking lifestyles, promote black entrepreneurial growth, and perpetuate professional advancement. Yet the rampant racism in American society truncates such lifestyles, growth, and advancement. The "new" black middle class can become only a "truncated" petite bourgeoisie in American society, far removed from real ownership and control over the crucial sectors of the economy and with intractable ceilings imposed upon its upward social mobility.

Presently, there are three major political options for this "truncated" black middle class: electoral politics in the bosom of the centrist Democratic Party or conservative Republican Party; social democratic and democratic socialist politics on the margin of the liberal wing of the Democratic Party (for instance, the Democratic Socialists of America) and inside grassroots, black leftist, nationalist, preparty formations (for instance, the National Black United Front); or orthodox revolutionary politics far removed from both bourgeois American politics and black grassroots groupings. The effects of the second stage of the black freedom movement in the sixties—beneath and between the endless ideological debates about violence versus nonviolence, the viability of black-white coalitions, reform versus revolution—primarily consisted of an oscillation between the first and third options, between vulgar realpolitik and antiquated orthodoxy, bourgeois politics and utopian rhetoric, with no mediating moment, hence little acknowledgment of the historical complexity of the prevailing African American predicament.

The prospects of galvanizing and organizing renewed black resistance are open-ended. The major tasks are repoliticizing the black working poor and underclass, revitalizing progressive black proletarian and petit bourgeois organizations, retooling black organic and traditional intellectuals, and forging meaningful alliances and beneficial fusions with progressive Latino, Asian, Native American, and white groups.

Despite the historical limitations of the "new" black petite bourgeoisie, the African American predicament dictates that this group play a crucial role in carrying out these tasks. This is principally because the black middle class—preachers, teachers, lawyers, doctors, and politicians—possesses the requisite skills and legitimacy in the eyes of the majority of

African Americans for the articulation of the needs and interests of African America. This unfortunate but inescapable situation requires that the politicized progressive wing of the black petite bourgeoisie and stable working class incessantly push beyond the self-serving liberalism of major black leaders and raise issues of fundamental concern to the black working poor and underclass. In short, the "new" black middle class must not be prematurely abandoned or denigrated. Rather, black progressives must keep persistent pressure on, and radical fire under, their liberal reformism until more effective political mobilization and organization emerge among the black working poor and underclass.

The repoliticizing of the black working poor and underclass should focus primarily on the black cultural apparatus, especially the ideological form and content of black popular music. African American life is permeated by black popular music. Since black musicians play such an important role in African American life, they have a special mission and responsibility: to present beautiful music which both sustains and motivates black people and provides visions of what black people should aspire to. Despite the richness of the black musical tradition and the vitality of black contemporary music, most black musicians fall far short of this crucial mission and responsibility. There are exceptions—Gil Scott-Heron, Brian Jackson, Stevie Wonder, Kenneth Gamble, and Leon Huff—but more political black popular music is needed. Jamaican reggae music and Nigeria's Fela Anikulapo Kuti can serve as inspiring models in this regard. The radical politicization of black popular music, as best seen in Grandmaster Flash and the Furious Five's "The Message" and "New York, New York" (despite their virulent sexism) in the early years of rap is a necessary, though not sufficient, condition for the repoliticization of the black working poor and underclass. Black activists must make black musicians accountable in some way to the urgent needs and interests of the black community.

The major prerequisite for renewed organizational black resistance is the political revitalization of existing black groups—fraternities, sororities, lodges, trade unions, and, especially, black churches. Without black religious participation, there can be no widespread black resistance. The prophetic wing of the black church has always been at the center of the black freedom movement. Without a strong organizational base with deep organic connections in the black community, there can be no effective renewed black resistance. Only the political revitalization of black prophetic churches can provide this broad organizational base—as Rev. Herbert Daughtry's African Peoples' Christian Organization and other such groups are attempting to do.

The role of black intellectuals—organic ones closely affiliated with the everyday operations of black organizations or traditional ones nesting in comfortable places geared toward theoretical and historical analyses, social visions, and practical conclusions—is crucial for renewed black resistance. Without vision, the black freedom movement is devoid of hope. Without analysis, it lacks direction. Without protracted struggle, it ossifies. Yet the vision must be guided by profound, not provincial, conceptions of what it is to be a human being, an African human being in predominantly white, postindustrial, capitalist America, and of how human potential can be best realized in an overcoming of existing economic exploitation, racial and sexual oppression. Likewise, the analysis must be informed by the most sophisticated and cultivated, not self-serving and cathartic, tools available in order to grasp the complexity and specificity of the prevailing African American predicament on the local, regional, national, and international levels. Last, the political praxis, though motivated by social vision and guided by keen analysis, must be grounded in moral convictions. Personal integrity is as important as correct analysis or desirable vision. It should be noted that while black intellectuals deserve no special privilege and treatment in the black freedom movement, the services they provide should be respected and encouraged.

It should be obvious that African Americans cannot fundamentally transform capitalist, patriarchal, racist America by themselves. If renewed black resistance is to achieve its aim, alliances and coalitions with other progressive peoples are inescapable. Without such alliances and coalitions, African Americans are doomed to unfreedom. Yet, the more consolidated the black resistance, the better the chance for meaningful and effective alliances and coalitions with others. Of course, each alliance and coalition must be made in light of the specific circumstances and the particular contexts. The important point here is that any serious form of black resistance must be open to such alliances and coalitions with progressive Latino, Asian, Native American, and white peoples.

In conclusion, the legacy of the black freedom movement in the sixties still haunts us. In its positive form, it flows through our veins as blood to be spilt if necessary for the cause of human freedom, and in the visions, analyses, and practices that build on, yet go beyond, those in the sixties. In its negative form, it reminds us of the tenuous status of the "new" black petite bourgeoisie—its progressive potential and its self-serving interests, its capacity to transcend its parochial past and its present white subordination. The challenge of the black freedom movement in the late twentieth century is neither a discovery of another Rev. Martin Luther King Jr.—though it would not hurt—nor a leap of faith in a messianic black working class or underclass—though the role of both is crucial. Rather the challenge is a fusing and transforming of indigenous forms of American radicalism—of which black resistance is a central expression—into a major movement that promotes workers' self-management, cultural heterogeneity (including nonracist and nonsexist ways of life), and individual liberties.

2

Black Particularity Reconsidered

Adolph L. Reed Jr.

Over forty years ago Walter Benjamin pointed out that "mass reproduction is aided especially by the reproduction of masses."[1] This statement captures the central cultural dynamic of a "late" capitalism. The triumph of the commodity form over every sphere of social existence has been made possible by a profound homogenization of work, play, aspirations, and self-definition among subject populations—a condition Herbert Marcuse has characterized as one-dimensionality.[2] Ironically, while U.S. radicals in the late 1960s fantasized about a "new man" in the abstract, capital was in the process of concretely putting the finishing touches on *its new individual.* Beneath the current black-female-student-chicano-homosexual-old-young-handicapped, etc., etc., ad nauseam, "struggles" lies a simple truth: there is no coherent opposition to the present administrative apparatus.

Certainly, repression contributed significantly to the extermination of opposition, and there is a long record of systematic corporate and state terror, from the Palmer Raids to the FBI campaign against the Black Panthers. Likewise, co-optation of individuals and programs has blunted opposition to bourgeois hegemony throughout this century, and co-optative mechanisms have become inextricable parts of strategies of containment. However, repression and co-optation can never fully explain the failure of opposition, and an exclusive focus on such external factors diverts attention from possible sources of failure within the opposition, thus paving the way for the reproduction of the pattern of failure. The opposition must investigate its own complicity.

During the 1960s theoretical reflexiveness was difficult because of the intensity of activism. When sharply drawn political issues demanded unambiguous responses, reflection on unintended consequences seemed treasonous. A decade later, coming to terms with what happened during that period is blocked by nostalgic glorification of fallen heroes and by a surrender that David Gross describes as the "ironic frame-of-mind."[3] Irony and nostalgia are two sides of the coin of resignation, the product of a cynical inwardness that makes retrospective critique seem tiresome or uncomfortable.[4]

At any rate, things have not moved in an emancipatory direction despite all claims that the protest of the 1960s has extended equalitarian democracy. In general, opportunities to determine one's destiny are no greater now than before and, more important, the critique of life-as-it-is disappeared as a practical activity; that is, an ethical and political commitment to emancipation seems no longer legitimate, reasonable, or valid. The amnestic principle, which imprisons the social past, also subverts any hope, which ends up seeking refuge in the predominant forms of alienation.

This is also true in the black community. Black opposition has dissolved into celebration and wish fulfillment. Today's political criticism within the black community—both Marxist-Leninist and nationalist—lacks a base and is unlikely to attract substantial constituencies. This complete collapse of political opposition among blacks, however, is anomalous. From the 1956 Montgomery bus boycott to the 1972 African Liberation Day demonstration, there was almost constant political motion among blacks. Since the early 1970s there has been a thorough pacification; or these antagonisms have been so depoliticized that they can surface only in alienated forms. Moreover, few attempts have been made to explain the atrophy of opposition within the black community.[5] Theoretical reflexiveness is as rare behind Du Bois's veil as on the other side!

This critical failing is especially regrettable because black radical protests and the system's adjustments to them have served as catalysts in universalizing one-dimensionality *and* in moving into a new era of monopoly capitalism. In this new era, which Paul Piccone has called the age of "artificial negativity," traditional forms of opposition have been made obsolete by a new pattern of social management.[6] Now, the social order legitimates itself by integrating potentially antagonistic forces into a logic of centralized administration. Once integrated, these forces regulate domination and prevent disruptive excess. Furthermore, when these internal regulatory mechanisms do not exist, the system must create them. To the extent that the black community has been pivotal in this new mode of administered domination, reconstruction of the trajectory of the 1960s' black activism can throw light on the current situation and the paradoxes it generates.

A common interpretation of the demise of black militance suggests that the waning of radical political activity is a result of the satisfaction of black aspirations. This satisfaction allegedly consists in: (1) extension of the social welfare apparatus; (2) elimination of legally sanctioned racial barriers to social mobility, which in turn has allowed for (3) expansion of possibilities open to blacks *within* the existing social system; all of which have precipitated (4) a redefinition of "appropriate" black political strategy in line with these achievements.[7] This new strategy is grounded in a pluralist orientation that construes political issues solely in terms of competition for the redistribution of goods and services within the bounds of fixed system priorities. These four items constitute the "gains of the 1960s."[8] Intrinsic to this interpretation is the thesis that black political activity during the 1960s became radical because blacks had been excluded from society and politics and were therefore unable effectively to solve group problems through the "normal" political process. Extraordinary actions were thus required to pave the way for regular participation.

This interpretation is not entirely untenable. With passage of the 1964 and 1965 legislation the program of the civil rights movement appeared to have been fulfilled. Soon, however, it became clear that the ideals of freedom and dignity had not been realized, and, within a year, those ideals reasserted themselves in the demand for black power. A social program was elaborated, but again its underpinning ideals were not realized. The dilemma lay in translating abstract ideals into concrete political goals, and it is here also that the "gains of the sixties" interpretation founders. It collapses ideals and appropriateness of the programs in question.

To be sure, racial segregation has been eliminated in the South, thus removing a tremendous oppression from black life. Yet, the dismantlement of the system of racial segregation only removed a fetter blocking the *possibility* of emancipation. In this context, computation of the "gains of the sixties" can begin only at the point where that extraordinary subjugation was eliminated. What, then, are those "gains" which followed the passage of civil rights legislation, and how have they affected black life?

In 1967 black unemployment was over 7 percent; for the first five months of 1978, it averaged over 12 percent.[9] Between 1969 and 1974 the proportion of the black population classified as "low income" has remained virtually the same.[10] Black median income did not improve significantly in relation to white family income in the decade after passage of civil rights legislation,[11] and between 1970 and 1974 black purchasing power actually declined.[12] Moreover, blacks are still far more likely to live in inadequate housing than whites, and black male life expectancy has declined, both absolutely and relative to whites, since 1959–61.[13]

Thus, the material conditions of the black population as a whole have not improved appreciably. Therefore, if the disappearance of black opposition is linked directly with the satisfaction of aspirations, the criteria of fulfillment cannot be drawn from the general level of material existence in the black community. The same can be said for categories such as "access to political decision-making." Although the number of blacks elected or appointed to public office has risen by leaps and bounds since the middle 1960s, that increase has not demonstrably improved life in the black community.

The problem is one of focus. The "gains of the sixties" thesis seems to hold only as long as the "black community" is seen as a monolithic social aggregation. Although black life *as a whole* has not improved considerably beyond the elimination of racial segregation, in the 1970s certain strata within the black community have actually benefited. This development is a direct outcome of the 1960s activism: of the interplay of the "movement" and the integrative logic of administrative capitalism. And this "gains of the sixties" interpretation cannot spell out what "satisfaction" is because it is itself the ideology of precisely those strata which have benefited from the events of the 1960s within the black community. These "leadership" strata tend to generalize their own interests since they see their legitimacy and integrity tied to a monolithic conceptualization of black life. Indeed, this conceptualization appeared in the unitarian mythology of late 1960s black nationalism. The representation of the black community as a collective subject neatly concealed the system of hierarchy which mediated the relation of the "leaders" and the "led."[14]

To analyze the genesis of this new elite is to analyze simultaneously the development of domination in American society in general. Consequently, the following will focus on sources of the pacification of the 1970s and will expose the limitations of any oppositionist activity which proceeds uncritically from models of mass-organization politics. This approach tends to capitulate to the predominant logic of domination.

Black resistance to oppression hardly began in Montgomery, Alabama, in 1955. Yet, it was only then that opposition to racial subjugation assumed the form of a mass movement. Why was this so? Despite many allusions to the impact of "decolonization" in Africa, international experiences of blacks in World War II, and so on, the reasons why black activism exploded in the late 1950s have seldom been addressed systematically.[15]

Although resistance before 1955 was undoubtedly reinforced by the anti-colonial movements abroad, what was significant for post-1955 growth of civil rights activity were those forces reshaping the entire American social order. A historically thorough perspective on the development of black opposition requires an understanding of the Cold War era in which it took shape.

Although popularly symbolized by "brinksmanship," "domino theory," fallout shelters, and the atmosphere of terror characterized by McCarthy, HUAC, and legions of meticulously anticommunist liberals, the Cold War was a much broader cultural phenomenon. Ultimately, it was a period of consolidation of the new mode of domination which had been developing for over two decades. Piccone has noted that the Cold War era was the culmination of a dynamic of political and cultural adjustment over the American economy by the 1920s.[16] On the political front, the New Deal redefined the role of the state apparatus in terms of an aggressive, countercyclical intervention in the economy and everyday reality. At the same time, mass production required intensification of consumption. This requirement was met by the development and expansion of a consciously manipulative culture industry and by the proliferation of an ideology of consumerism through mass communications and entertainment media.[17] Consumerism and the New Deal led to an intensification of Taylorization of labor, which homogenized American life according to the dictates of bureaucratic-instrumental rationality. By the 1950s, Americanization had been institutionalized. Rigid political, intellectual, and cultural conformism (David Riesman's "other directedness") evidenced a social integration achieved through introjection and reproduction of the imperatives of the system of domination at the level of everyday life.[18]

Pressures toward homogenization exerted for decades at work, in schools, and through the culture industry had eliminated any authentic cultural particularity among ethnic groups. What remained were residues of the lost cultures—empty mannerisms and ambivalent ethnic identities mobilizable for Democratic electoral politics.[19] Moreover, the pluralist model was already available for integrating the already depoliticized labor movement. In this context, the ruthless elimination of whatever opposition remained through the witch-hunts was only the coup de grâce in a battle already won.

For various reasons, throughout this period, one region was bypassed in the monopolistic reorganization of American life and remained unintegrated into the new social order. At the end of World War II, the South remained the only internal frontier available for large-scale capital penetration. However, even though the South could entice industry with a docile workforce accustomed to low wages, full domestication of this region required certain basic adjustments.

For one thing, the castelike organization of southern society seriously inhibited development of a rational labor supply. While much has been made of the utility of the segregated workforce as a depressant of general wage levels, the maintenance of dual labor markets creates a barrier to labor recruitment.[20] As a pariah caste, blacks could not adequately become an industrial reserve army since they were kept out of certain jobs. Consequently, in periods of rapid expansion the suppressed black labor pool could not be fully used. Nor could blacks be mobilized as a potential strike-breaking force as readily as in other regions since employment of blacks in traditionally "white" jobs could trigger widespread disruptions.

The dual labor system was irreconcilable with the principle of reducing *all* labor to "abstract labor."[21] Scientific management has sought to reduce work processes to homogeneous and interchangeable hand and eye motions, eventually hoping to eliminate specialized labor.[22] A workforce stratified on the basis of an economically irrational criterion such as race constitutes a serious impediment to realization of the ideal of a labor pool comprised of equivalent units. (Consider further the wastefulness of having to provide two sets of toilets in the plants!) In addition, the existing system of black subjugation, grounded in brutality, was intrinsically unstable. The racial order which demanded for its maintenance constant terror raised at every instant the possibility of rebellion and to that extent endangered "rational" administration. Given this state of affairs, the corporate elite's support for an antisegregationist initiative makes sense.

The relation of the corporate liberal social agenda to civil rights protest is not a causal one. True, the Supreme Court had been chipping away at legal segregation for nearly twenty years, and the 1954 *Brown* decision finally provided the spark for intensified black protest. Yet, the eruption of resistance from southern blacks had its own roots. Hence, to claim that the civil rights movement was bourgeois conspiracy would be to succumb to the order's myth of its own omnipotence. Thus, the important question is not whether sectors of the corporate elite orchestrated the civil rights movement but instead what deficiencies within the civil rights movement were sufficiently compatible with the social agenda of corporate elites to prompt the latter to acquiesce to and encourage them. In order to answer this, it is necessary to identify both the social forces operative *within* the black community during segregation and those forces' engagement in civil rights activism. An analysis of the internal dynamic of the 1960s activism shows overlaps between the goals of the "New Deal offensive" and the objectives of the "movement" (and, by extension, the black community).[23]

For the purposes of this analysis, the most salient aspects of the black community in the segregated South lie within a management dimension. Externally, the black population was managed by means of codified subordination, reinforced by customary dehumanization and the omnipresent specter of terror. The abominable details of this system are well known.[24] Furthermore, blacks were systematically excluded from formal participation in public life. By extracting tax revenues without returning public services or allowing blacks to participate in public policy formation, the local political system intensified the normal exploitation in the workplace. Public administration of the black community was carried out by whites. The daily indignity of the apartheid-like social organization was both a product of this political-administrative disenfranchisement as well as a motor of its reproduction. Thus, the abstract ideal of freedom spawned within the civil rights movement addressed primarily this issue.

Despite the black population's alienation from public policy making, an internal stratum existed which performed notable, but limited, social management functions. This elite stratum was comprised mainly of low-level state functionaries, merchants, and "professionals" servicing black markets, and the clergy. While it failed to escape the general subordination, this indigenous elite usually succeeded by virtue of its comparatively secure living standard and informal relations with significant whites, in avoiding the extremes of racial oppression. The importance of this stratum was that it stabilized and coordinated the adjustment of the black population to social policy imperatives formulated outside the black community.

Insofar as black public functionaries had assimilated bureaucratic rationality, the domination of fellow blacks was carried out in "doing one's job." For parts of the black elite such as the clergy, the ministerial practice of "easing community tensions" has always meant accommodation of black life to the existing forms of domination. Similarly, the independent merchants and professionals owed their relatively comfortable position within the black community to the special, captive markets created by segregation. Moreover, in the role of "responsible Negro spokesmen," this sector was able to elicit considerable *politesse,* if not solicitousness, from "enlightened" members of the white elite. Interracial "cooperation" on policy matters was thus smoothly accomplished, and the "public interest" seemed to be met simply because opposition to white ruling group initiatives had been effectively neutralized. The activating factor in this management relation was a notion of "Negro leadership" (later "black" or even "Black") that was generated outside the black community. A bitter observation made from time to time by the radical fringe of the movement was that the social category "leaders" seemed only to apply to the black community. No "white leaders" were assumed to represent a singular white population. But certain blacks were declared opinion makers and carriers of the interests of an anonymous black population. These "leaders" legitimated their role through their ability to win occasional favors from powerful whites and through the status positions they already occupied in the black community.[25]

This mode of domination could not thoroughly pacify black life: only the transformation of the segregated order could begin to do that. Furthermore, the internal management strategy generated centrifugal pressures of its own. In addition to segregation, three other disruptive elements stand out within the black community in the 1950s. First, the United States's emergence from World War II as the major world power projected American culture onto an international scene. Thus, the anticolonial movements that grew in Africa and Asia amid the crumbling of French and British colonial empires had a significant impact on black resistance in this country.[26] Second, the logic of one-dimensionality itself became a disruptive element. The homogenizing egalitarianism of the New Deal generated a sense of righteousness able to sustain a lengthy battle with southern segregation. The challenge to racial domination was justified in terms of the American Dream and an ideal of freedom expressed in a demand for full citizenship.[27] Thus, the same forces that since the 1920s had sought to integrate the various immigrant populations also generated an American national consciousness among blacks. By the 1950s a sense of participation in a national society had taken root even in the South, fertilized by the mass culture industry (including black publications), schools, and a defensive Cold War ideology. In the face of this growing national consciousness, "separate but equal" existence was utterly intolerable to blacks. This is not to say that a perception rooted in the nation-state was universal among southern blacks in the 1950s, especially since the chief mechanisms of cultural adjustment such as television, popular films, compulsory schooling, and so on, had not fully invaded the black community. Yet, mass culture and its corollary ideologies had extensively penetrated the private sphere of the black elite: the stratum from which systematic opposition arose.[28]

Third, given the racial barrier, social mobility for the black elite was limited, relative to its white counterpart. Because of de facto proscription of black tenure in most professions, few possibilities existed for advancement. At the same time, the number of people seeking to become members of the elite had increased beyond what a segregated society could accommodate as a result of population growth and rising college attendance. In addition, upward mobility was being defined by the larger national culture in a way that further weakened the capability of the black elite to integrate its youth. Where ideology demanded nuclear physics and corporate management, black upward mobility rested with mortuary service and the Elks Lodge! The disjunction between ideals and possibilities delegitimized the elite's claim to brokerage and spokesmanship. With its role in question, the entrenched black elite was no longer able to effectively perform its internal management function and lost any authority with its "recruits" and the black community in general. As a result, a social space was cleared within which dissatisfaction with segregation could thrive as systematic opposition.

From this social management perspective, the sources of the "Freedom Movement" are identifiable within and on the periphery of its indigenous elite stratum. As soon as black opposition spilled beyond the boundaries of the black community, however, the internal management perspective became inadequate to understand further developments in the civil rights movement. When opposition to segregation became political rebellion, black protest required a response from white ruling elites. That response reflected the congruence of the interests of blacks and of corporate elites in reconstructing southern society and helped define the logic of all subsequent black political activity. Both sets of interests shared an interest in rationalizing race relations in the South. The civil rights movement brought the two sets together.[29]

The alliance of corporate liberalism and black protest was evident in the aggressive endorsement of civil rights activity that was mobilized by the New Deal coalition. Major labor organizations and "enlightened" corporate sectors immediately climbed aboard the freedom train through the "progressive" wing of the Democratic party and private foundations. Moreover, it was through its coverage of black resistance in the South that television developed and refined its remarkable capabilities for creating public opinion by means of "objective" news reportage (a talent that reached its acme years later with the expulsion of Richard Nixon from the presidency). But television was not alone on the cultural front of the ideological struggle. *Life, Look, Saturday Evening Post,* major nonsouthern newspapers, and other national publications featured an abundance of photo-essays that emphasized the degradation and brutalization of black life under Jim Crow.

Even popular cinema sought to thematize black life in line with civil rights consciousness in films such as *The Defiant Ones* (1958), *All the Young Men* (1960), *Raisin in the Sun* (1961), *Band of Angels* (1957), and the instructively titled *Nothing but a Man* (1964). Those and other films were marked by an effort to portray blacks with a measure of human depth and complexity previously absent from Hollywood productions. By 1957 even the great taboo of miscegenation could be portrayed on the screen in *Island in the Sun,* and a decade later the cultural campaign had been so successful that this theme could be explored in the parlor rather than in back streets and resolved with a happy ending in *Guess Who's Coming to Dinner.* It is interesting that Dorothy Dandridge became the first black in a leading role to be nominated for an academy award for her role in *Carmen* in 1954—the year of the *Brown* decision—and that the most productive periods of civil rights activism and Sidney Poitier's film career coincided. Poitier's lead performance in the maudlin *Lilies of the Field* won an Oscar for him in 1963, on the eve of the passage of the Public Accommodations Act! Thus endorsed by the culture industry (which affronted white supremacy in the late 1950s by broadcasting a Perry Como show in which comedienne Molly Goldberg kissed black ballplayer Ernie Banks), the civil rights movement was virtually assured success.

While the civil rights coalition was made possible by the compatibility of the allies' interests in reorganizing the South, its success was facilitated by the ideals and ideologies generated in the protest. Even though there had been ties between black southern elites and corporate-liberal elements for a long time, if the civil rights program had raised fundamental questions regarding social structure, the corporate-elite response may have been suppression rather than support—especially given the Cold War context. Instead, from the very beginning the American establishment outside of Dixie supported the abolition of segregation.[30] At any rate, it is clear that the civil rights ideology fit very well with the goals of monopoly capitalism. The civil rights movement appealed to egalitarianism and social rationality. On both counts segregation was found wanting while leaving nonracial features of the social order unquestioned.

The egalitarian argument was moral as well as constitutional. The moral argument was in the bourgeois tradition from the Reformation to the French Revolution. It claimed equal rights for all human beings as well as entitlement to equal life chances. This abstract and ahistorical moral imperative did not grasp social relations beyond their phenomenal forms and therefore could only denounce racial exclusion as an evil anomaly. The predominant form of social organization was uncritically accepted and the moral imperative was predictably construed in terms of American constitutional law. Equality before the law and equality of opportunity to participate in all areas of citizenship were projected as the needed extension to blacks in the backward South to fulfill the promise of democracy.

Coexisting with this egalitarian ideology was the civil rights movement's appeal to a functionalist conception of social rationality. To the extent that it blocked individual aspirations, segregation was seen as restricting artificially social growth and progress. Similarly, by raising artificial barriers such as the construction of blacks' consumer power through Jim Crow legislation and, indirectly, through low black wages, segregation impeded, so the argument went, the free functioning of the market. Consequently, segregation was seen not only as detrimental to the blacks who suffered under it but also to economic progress as such. Needless to say, the two lines of argument were met with approval by corporate liberals.[31]

It is apparent now that the egalitarian ideology coincided with corporate liberalism's cultural program of homogenization. Civil rights egalitarianism demanded that any one unit of labor be equivalent to any other, that one citizen-consumer be considered equivalent to another, and that the Negro be thought of as "any other American." There is more than a little irony that the civil rights movement demanded for blacks the same "eradication of otherness" that had been forced upon immigrant populations. The demand hardly went unheard; through the blanket concept "integration" and the alliance with a corporate elite that was all too ready to help clarify issues and refine strategies and objectives, the abstract ideals of civil rights activism were concretized in the corporate elite's plan for pacification and reorganization.

The elimination of segregation in the South destroyed the specificity of both the South as a region and blacks as a group, and the rationality in whose name the movement had appealed paved the way for reconstruction of new modes of domination of black life. The movement had begun as a result of the frustrations of the black elite, and it ended with the achievement of autonomy and mobility among those elements. Public accommodations and voting rights legislation officially defined new terms for the management of blacks and an expanded managerial role for the elite.

Although the civil rights movement did have a radical faction, this wing failed to develop a systematic critique of civil rights ideology or the alliance with corporate liberalism. Moreover, the radicals—mainly within SNCC—never repudiated the leadership ideology which reinforced the movement's character as an elite brokerage relation with powerful whites outside the South. Thus, the radicals helped isolate their own position by acquiescing to a conception of the black community as a passive recipient of political symbols and directives. When the dust settled, the black "mainstream" elements and their corporate allies—who together monopolized the symbols of legitimacy—proclaimed that freedom had been achieved, and the handful of radicals could only feel uneasy that voting rights and "social equality" were somehow insufficient.[32]

Outside the South, rebellion arose from different conditions. Racial segregation was not rigidly codified and the management subsystems in the black community were correspondingly more fluidly integrated within the local administrative apparatus. Yet, structural, generational, and ideological pressures, broadly similar to those in the South, existed within the black elite in the northern, western, and midwestern cities that had gained large black populations in the first half of the twentieth century. In nonsegregated urban contexts, formal political participation and democratized consumption had long since been achieved: there the salient political issue was the extension of the administrative purview of the elite within the black community. The centrality of the administrative nexus in the "revolt of the cities" is evident from the ideological programs it generated.

Black Power came about as a call for indigenous control of economic and political institutions in the black community.[33] Because one of the early slogans of Black Power was a vague demand for "community control," the emancipatory character of the rebellion was open to considerable misinterpretation. Moreover, the diversity and "militance" of its rhetoric encouraged extravagance in assessing the movement's depth. It soon became clear, however, that "community control" called not for direction of pertinent institutions—schools, hospitals, police, retail businesses, and so on—by their black constituents, but for administration of those institutions by alleged representatives *in the name of* a black community. Given an existing elite structure whose legitimacy had already been certified by federal social welfare agencies, the selection of "appropriate" representatives was predictable. Indeed, as Robert Allen has shown,[34] the empowerment of this elite was actively assisted by corporate-state elements. Thus, "black liberation" quickly turned into black "equity," "community control" became simply "black control," and the Nixon "blackonomics" strategy was readily able to "co-opt" the most rebellious tendency of 1960s black activism. Ironically, Black Power's supersession of the civil rights program led to further consolidation of the management elite's hegemony within the black community. The black elite broadened its administrative control by uncritically assuming the legitimacy of the social context within which that elite operated. Black control was by no means equivalent to democratization.

This state of affairs remained unclear even to Black Power's radical fringe. Such a failure of political perception cannot be written off as crass opportunism or as underdeveloped consciousness. Though not altogether false, explanations of this kind only beg the question. Indeed, Black Power radicalism, which absorbed most of the floundering left wing of the civil rights movement and generated subsequent "nationalist" tendencies, actually blurred the roots of the new wave of rebellion. As civil rights activism exhausted itself and as spontaneous uprisings proliferated among urban blacks, the civil rights radicals sought to generate an ideology able to unify and politicize these uprisings. This effort, however, was based on two mystifications that implicitly rationalized the elite's control of the movement.

First, Black Power presupposed a mass-organizational model built on the assumption of a homogeneity of black political interests to be dealt with through community leadership. It is this notion of "black community" that has blocked development of a radical critique in the civil rights movement by contraposing an undifferentiated mass to a leadership stratum representing it. This understanding ruled out any analysis of cleavages or particularities within the black population: "community control" and "black control" became synonymous. The implications of this ideology have already been discussed: having internalized the predominant elite-pluralist model of organization of black life, the radical wing could not develop any critical perspective. Internal critique could not go beyond banal symbols of "blackness" and thus ended up by stimulating demand for a new array of "revolutionary" consumer goods. Notwithstanding all its bombast, Black Power construed racial politics within the ideological universe through which the containment of the black population was mediated.

Acceptance of this model not only prevented Black Power from transcending the social program of the indigenous administrative elite, but it also indicated the extent to which, as Harold Cruse was aware at the time,[35] Black Power radicalism was itself a frantic statement of the elite's agenda—hence the radicals' chronic ambivalence over "black bourgeoisie," capitalism, socialism, and "black unity." Their mystification of the social structure of the black community was largely the result of a failure to come to terms with their own privileged relation to the corporate elite's program of social reconstruction. This state of affairs precipitated a still more profound mystification that illuminates the other side of Black Power rebellion: the reaction against massification.

The civil rights movement's demand for integration was superfluous outside the South, and Black Power was as much a reaction against integrationist ideology as against racial domination. Thus, while militant black nationalism developed as a reaction to the assimilationist approach of the civil rights movement, it simultaneously envisioned an obsolete model of black life. This yearning was hypostatized to the level of a "black culture"—a romantic retrieval of a vanishing black particularity. This vision of black culture, of course, was grounded in residual features of black rural life prior to migrations to the North. They were primarily cultural patterns that had once been enmeshed in a lifeworld knitted together by kinship, voluntary association, and production within a historical context of rural racial domination. As that lifeworld disintegrated before urbanization and mass culture, black nationalism sought to reconstitute it.[36]

In that sense, the nationalist elaboration of Black Power was naive both in that it was not sufficiently self-conscious and in that it mistook artifacts and idiosyncrasies of culture for its totality and froze them into an ahistorical theory of authenticity. Two consequences followed. First, abstracted from its concrete historical context, black culture lost its dynamism and took on the commodity form (e.g., red, black, and green flags, dashikis, Afro-Sheen, "blaxploitation" films, collections of bad poetry). Second, while ostensibly politicizing culture by defining it as an arena for conflict, black nationalism actually depoliticized the movement inasmuch as the reified nationalist framework could relate to the present only through a simplistic politics of unity.[37] Hence, it forfeited hegemony over political programs to the best organized element in the black community: the administrative elite. In this fashion, black culture became a means of legitimation of the elite's political hegemony.

Black culture posited a functionalist, perfectly integrated black social order which was then projected backward through history as the *Truth* of black existence. The "natural" condition of harmony was said to have been disrupted only when divisiveness and conflict were introduced by alien forces. This myth delegitimated internal conflicts and hindered critical dialogue within the black community. Correspondingly, the intellectual climate that came to pervade the "movement" was best summarized in the nationalists' exhortation to "think black," a latter-day version of "thinking with one's blood." Thus was the circle completed: the original abstract rationalism that had ignored existing social relations of domination for a mythical, unitarian social ideal had turned into a militant and self-justifying irrationalism. Truth became a function of the speaker's "blackness," that is, validity claims were to be resolved not through discourse but by the claimant's manipulation of certain banal symbols of legitimacy. The resultant situation greatly favored the well-organized and highly visible elite.

The nationalist program functioned also as a mobilization myth. In defining a collective consciousness, the idealization of folkishness was simultaneously an exhortation to collectivized practice. The folk, in its Afro-American manifestation as well as elsewhere, was an ideological category of mass-organizational politics. The community was to be created and mobilized as a passively homogeneous mass, activated by a leadership elite.

While the politicized notion of black culture was a negative response to the estrangement and anomie experienced in the urban North, as a "solution" it only *affirmed the negation* of genuine black particularity.[38] The prescription of cohesion in the form of a mass leadership relation betrayed the movement's tacit acceptance of the agenda of the black management stratum. The negatively immanent in the cultural myth soon gave way to an opportunistic appeal to unity grounded on an unspecifiable "blackness" and a commodified idea of "soul." Black unity, elevated to an end in itself, became an ideology promoting consolidation of the management elite's expanded power over the black population. In practice, unity meant collective acceptance of a set of demands to be lobbied by a leadership elite before the corporate-state apparatus. To that extent, "radical" Black Power reproduced on a more elaborate ideological basis the old pluralist brokerage politics. Similarly, this phony unity restricted possibilities for development of a black public sphere.

To be sure, the movement stimulated widespread and lively political debate in the black community. Although it hardly approached an "ideal speech situation," various individuals and constituencies were drawn into political discourse on a considerably more democratized basis than had previously been the case. Yet, the rise of unitarian ideology, coupled with a mystified notion of "expertise," effectively reintroduced hierarchy within the newly expanded political arena.[39] At any rate, "grassroots" politics in the black community can be summarized as follows: the internal management elite claimed primacy in political discourse on the basis of its ability to project and realize a social program, and then mobilized the unitarian ideal to delegitimize any divergent positions. On the other hand, the "revolutionary" opposition offered no alternative; within its ranks the ideology of expertise was never repudiated. The radicals had merely replaced the elite's pragmatism with a mandarin version of expertise founded on mastery of the holy texts of Kawaida, Nkrumanism, or "scientific socialism." By the time of the 1971 National Black Political Convention in Gary, the mainstream elite strata were well on the way to becoming the sole effective voice in the black community. By the next convention in 1974 in Little Rock—after the election of a second wave of black officials—their hegemony was total.[40]

By now the reasons for the demise of black opposition in the U.S.

should be clear. The opposition's sources were formulated in terms of the predominant ideology and thereby readily integrated as an affirmation of the reality of the system as a whole. The movement "failed" because it "succeeded," and its success can be measured by its impact on the administration of the social system. The protest against racial discrimination in employment and education was answered by the middle 1970s by state-sponsored democratization of access to management and other "professional" occupations. Clear, quantifiable racial discrimination remained a pressing public issue only for those whose livelihood depended on finding continuous instances of racial discrimination.[41] Still, equalization of access should not be interpreted simply as a concession: it also rationalized recruitment of intermediate management personnel. In one sense the affirmative action effort can be viewed as a publicly subsidized state and corporate talent search.

Similarly, the protest against external administration of black life was met by an expansion in the scope of the black political-administrative apparatus. Through federal funding requirements of community representation, reapportionment of electoral jurisdictions, support for voter "education," and growth of the social welfare bureaucracy, the black elite was provided with broadened occupational opportunities and with official responsibility for administration of the black population. The rise of black officialdom in the latter 1970s signals the realization of the reconstructed elite's social program and the consolidation of its hegemony over black life. No longer do preachers, funeral directors, and occasional politicos vie for the right to rationalize an externally generated agenda to the black community. Now, black officials and professional political activists represent, interact among, and legitimate themselves before an attentive public of black functionaries in public and private sectors of the social management apparatus.[42] Even the ideological reproduction of the elite is assured: not only mass-market journalists, but black academicians as well (through black "scholarly" publications, research institutes, and professional organizations) almost invariably sing the praises of the newly empowered elite.[43]

It was in the ideological sphere as well that the third major protest, that against massification of the black community, was resolved. Although authentic Afro-American particularity had been undermined by the standardizing imperatives of mass capitalism, the black nationalist reaction paved the way for the constitution of an artificial particularity.[44] Residual idiomatic and physical traits, bereft of any distinctive content, were injected with racial stereotypes and the ordinary petit bourgeois *Weltanschauung* to create the pretext for an apparently unique black existence. A

thoroughly ideological construction of black uniqueness—which was projected universally in the mass market as black culture—fulfilled at least
three major functions. First, as a marketing device it facilitated the huck-
stering of innumerable commodities designed to enhance, embellish, or
glorify "blackness."[45] Second, artificial black particularity provided the basis for the myth of genuine black community and consequently legitimated
the organization of the black population into an administrative unit—and,
therefore, the black elite's claims to primacy. Finally, the otherness-without-
negativity provided by the ideologized blackness can be seen as a potential
antidote to the new contradictions generated by monopoly capitalism's
bureaucratic rationality. By constituting an independently given sector of
society responsive to administrative controls, the well-managed but recalcitrant black community justifies the existence of the administrative apparatus and legitimates existing forms of social integration.

In one sense, the decade and a half of black activism was a phenomenon vastly more significant than black activists appreciated, while in
another sense it was far less significant than has been claimed.[46] As an
emancipatory project for the Afro-American population, the "movement"—especially after the abolishment of segregation—had little impact
beyond strengthening the existing elite strata. Yet, as part of a program of
advanced capitalist reconstruction, black activism contributed to thawing
the Cold War and outlined a model to replace it.

By the latter 1960s the New Deal coalition had become obsolete and
was no longer able to fully integrate recalcitrant social strata such as the black
population.[47] The New Deal coalition initiated the process of social homogenization and depoliticization Marcuse described as one-dimensionality. As
Piccone observes, however, by the 1960s the transition to monopoly capitalism had been fully carried out and the whole strategy had become counter-
productive.[48] The drive toward homogenization and the total domination of
the commodity form had deprived the system of the "otherness" required
both to restrain the irrational tendencies of bureaucratic rationality and to locate lingering and potentially disruptive elements. Notwithstanding their
vast differences, the ethnic "liberation struggles" and counterculture activism, on the one side, and the "hard hat" reaction, on the other, were two
sides of the same rejection of homogenization. Not only did these various
positions challenge the one-dimensional order, but their very existence betrayed the inability of the totally administered society to pacify social existence while at the same time remaining sufficiently dynamic.

The development of black activism from spontaneous protest
through mass mobilization to system support indicated the arrival of a new

era of domination based on domesticating negativity by organizing spaces in which it could be legitimately expressed. Rather than suppressing opposition, the social system now creates its own. The proliferation of government-generated reference groups in addition to ethnic ones (the old, the young, battered wives, the handicapped, veterans, retarded and gifted children, etc.)[49] and the appearance of legions of "watchdog" agencies reveal the extent to which the system manufactures and markets its own illusory opposition.

What makes the "age of artificial negativity" possible is the overwhelming success of the process of massification undertaken since the Depression and in response to it. Universal fragmentation of consciousness, with the corollary decline in the ability to think critically and the regimentation of an alienated everyday life[50] set the stage for new forms of domination built in the very texture of organization. In mass society, organized activity on a large scale requires hierarchization. Along with hierarchy, however, the social management logic also comes into being to (1) protect existing privileges by delivering realizable, if inconsequential, payoffs and (2) to legitimate the administrative rationality as a valid and efficient model. To the extent that the organization strives to ground itself on the *mass* it is already integrated into the system of domination. The shibboleths which comprise its specific platform make little difference. What is important is that the organization reproduces the manipulative hierarchy and values typical of contemporary capitalism.

Equally important for the existence of this social-managerial form is that the traditional modes of opposition to capitalism have not been able to successfully negotiate the transition from entrepreneurial to administrative capitalism. Thus, the Left has not fully grasped the recent shifts in the structure of domination and continues to organize resistance along the very lines that reinforce the existing social order. As a consequence, the opposition finds itself perpetually outflanked. Unable to deliver the goods—political or otherwise—the Left collapses before the cretinization of its own constituency. Once the mass model is accepted, cretinization soon follows and from that point the opposition loses any genuine negativity. The civil rights and Black Power movements prefigured the coming of this new age; the feminist photocopy of the black road to nowhere was its farcical rerun.

The role of the mass culture industry in this context is to maintain and reproduce the new synthesis of domination. Here, again, the history of the "black revolution" is instructive. In its most radical stage Black Power lived and spread as a media event. Stokely Carmichael and Rap Brown entertained nightly on network news, and after ordinary black "militancy" had lost its dramatic appeal, the Black Panther Party added props and uniforms to make radical politics entirely a show business proposition. Although late 1960s black radicalism offered perhaps the most flamboyant examples of the peculiar relation of the mass media to the would-be opposition, that was only an extreme expression of a pattern at work since the early days of the civil rights movement. Since then, political opposition has sought to propagandize its efforts through the mass media. Given the prevailing cretinization and the role of the culture industry in reproducing the fragmented, commodified consciousness, such a strategy, if pursued uncritically, could only reinforce the current modes of domination.[51]

That all forms of political opposition accepted the manipulative mass-organization model gave the strategy a natural, uncomplicated appearance and prevented the development of a critical approach. The consequence was a propagation of a model of politics that reinforced oversimplification, the reduction of ideals to banalized objects of immediate consumption—that is, the commodity-form—and to an alienated dehumanized hero cultishness with the "revolutionary" replacing either hero or villain. In short, opposition increasingly becomes a spectacle in a society organized around reduction of all existence to a series of spectacles.[52]

So monopoly capitalism has entered a new stage typified by the extension of the administrative apparatus throughout everyday life. In this context genuine opposition is checkmated a priori by the legitimation and projection of a partial, fragmented criticism which can be readily made functional in further streamlining the predominant rationality. And in cases where existing bureaucratic structures need control mechanisms to prevent excesses, diffused uneasiness with predominant institutions ends up artificially channeled into forms of negativity able to fulfill the needed internal control function. Always a problem for opposition which seeks to sustain itself over time, under the new conditions of administered negativity, this one step backward, required by the organized opposition's need to broaden its constituency and conduct "positional warfare," becomes a one-way slide to affirmation of the social order. The logic of the transition to new forms of bourgeois hegemony requires adjustment of administrative rationality. The unrestrained drive to total integration now is mediated by peripheral, yet systematically controlled loci of criticism; one-dimensionality itself has been "humanized" by the cultivation of commodified facsimiles of diversity.[53]

An important question remains: what of the possibilities for genuine opposition? The picture that has been painted seems excessively pessimistic. Yet, this should not be understood to mean that opposition is futile. It *is* necessary, though, to closely examine the customary modes of opposition.

The theory of artificial negativity historicizes the critique of the post–Cold War Left and suggests at the same time some broad outlines for a reconceptualization of emancipatory strategy.

This examination of black radicalism in the wake of its integration offers a microcosmic view of the plight of the Left as a whole. Having accepted an organizational model based on massification, the radicals were forced to compete with the elite on the latter's terms—an impossible proposition since the elite had access to the cultural apparatus designed for mass mobilization. Moreover, even when opposition tried to reconstruct itself, it failed to generate a systematic critique of its own strategy and was therefore unable to come to terms with shifts in the structure of capitalist social relations. Instead, it remained caught within a theoretical structure adequate only for an earlier, preadministrative stage of capitalist development. Thus, the failure of mysticized black nationalism is reproduced in today's "ideological struggles," which reached their nadir in the 1978 dispute over whether Mao Tse-tung was really dead!

Still, what of possibilities? Certain implications follow from the previous analysis. It points in the direction of attempts to cultivate areas of unorganizable free space in the interstices of the social system and to reduce the scope of appropriate political intervention from mass organization to the reconstitution of individuality. Clearly, this sketch provides no blueprint. In fact, it does not point to any really "concrete" direction. Yet, charges of pessimism are unwarranted. Hope must seek its possibilities in the darkest moments of the present; it is despair which hides its head from history and refuses to see the undesirable.[54]

NOTES

1. Walter Benjamin, "The Work of Art in the Age of Mechanical Reproduction," in *Illuminations* (New York, 1968), p. 251.

2. Herbert Marcuse, *One-Dimensional Man: Studies in the Ideology of Advanced Industrial Society* (Boston, 1964).

3. David Gross, "Irony and the 'Disorders of the Soul,'" *Telos* (Winter 1977–78): 167.

4. Possible sources of the Left's failure to interpret its past meaningfully are discussed also by Christopher Lasch, "The Narcissist Society," *New York Review of Books*, September 30, 1976, 5 ff.; Russell Jacoby, "The Politics of Objectivity: Notes on the U.S. Left," *Telos* (Winter 1977–78): 74–88, and *Social Amnesia: A Critique of Conformist Psychology from Adler to Laing* (Boston, 1975), pp. 101–18; and by Andrew Feen-

berg, "Paths to Failure: The Dialectics of Organization and Ideology in the New Left," and David Gross, "Cultural Life-Style and Cultural Criticism," both [in *Race, Politics, and Culture: Critical Essays on the Radicalism of the 1960s,* ed. Adolph Reed Jr. (Westport, Conn., 1986)].

5. The work of Alex Willingham is the most consistent and noteworthy exception. See the following: "Ideology and Politics: Their Status in Afro-American Social Theory," *Endarch I* (Spring 1975): 4–25; "California Dreaming: Eldridge Cleaver's Epithet to the Activism of the Sixties," *Endarch I* (Winter 1976): 1–23.

6. Paul Piccone, "Beyond Critical Theory," mimeo, and "The Crisis of One-Dimensionality," *Telos* (Spring 1978): 43–54. See also Tim Luke, "Culture and Politics in the Age of Artificial Negativity," *Telos* (Spring 1978): 43–54.

7. See, e.g., Thomas R. Brooks, *Walls Come Tumbling Down: A History of the Civil Rights Movement, 1940–1970* (Englewood Cliffs, N.J., 1974), pp. 290 ff.; Eddie N. Williams, *From Protest to Politics: The Legacy of Martin Luther King, Jr.* (Washington, D.C.).

8. This slogan has risen to prominence on the back of the black elite's voluble reaction to the Bakke case, which is said to portend reversal of those alleged "gains." One interpretation of these gains is found in Richard Freeman, "Black Economic Progress since 1964," *Public Interest* (Summer 1978): 52–68.

9. U.S. Department of Labor, Bureau of Labor Statistics, *Employment and Earnings* 25 (1978); the National Commission for Manpower Policy, Special Report 9, *The Economic Position of Black Americans: 1976* (Washington, D.C., 1976), provides confirming trend data.

10. U.S. Department of Commerce, Bureau of the Census, *The Social and Economic Status of the Black Population in the United States: 1974* (Washington, D.C., 1975), p. 42.

11. Ibid., p. 25.

12. Barbara Jones, "Black Family Income: Patterns, Sources, and Trends," unpublished paper presented at the annual meetings of the National Economic Association, American Economic Association, Atlantic City, New Jersey, September 1976, p. 2.

13. Bureau of the Census, *Social and Economic Status,* pp. 123, 137.

14. That the leadership elite projects its interests over the entire black population is neither unique nor necessarily suggestive of insidious motives; however, it is just in the extent to which the elite's hegemony develops unconsciously that it is most important as a problem for emancipatory action. Compare Gouldner's critique of intellectuals and intelligentsia; Alvin W. Gouldner, "Prologue to a Theory of Revolutionary Intellectuals," *Telos* (Winter 1975–76): 3–36, and *The Dialectic of Ideology and Technology: The Origins, Grammar, and Future of Ideology* (New York, 1976), pp. 247–48 and passim.

15. John Hope Franklin does not raise the question in his standard volume, *From Slavery to Freedom: A History of Negro Americans,* 3d ed. (New York, 1969); nor surprisingly does Harold Cruse's *The Crisis of the Negro Intellectual: From Its Origins to the Present* (New York, 1967) which is a seminal contribution to a reflexive theory of black political activity. That Cruse and Franklin fail to raise the question is perhaps because both—reflecting an aspect of the conventional wisdom—see an unbroken, if not cumulating, legacy of black activism in the twentieth century. Franklin sees the civil rights movement simply as the culmination of a century or more of protest. Cruse, in establishing the continuities of the

poles of integrationism and nationalism, projects them back and forth from Douglass and Delaney to Black Power, glossing over significant historical differences in the process. In *The Making of Black Revolutionaries* (New York, 1972), James Forman is so consumed by the movement's manifest and organizational unfoldings that he is unable to subordinate it to history. His account of the 1950s focuses entirely on his personal awakening. Louis Lomax, *The Negro Revolt,* rev. ed. (New York, 1971); Lewis Killian, *The Impossible Revolution? Black Power and the American Dream* (New York, 1968); and the two period volumes by Lerone Bennett Jr., *The Negro Mood* (New York, 1964) and *Before the Mayflower: A History of the Negro in America, 1619–1964,* rev. ed. (Baltimore, 1969), all raise the question only to answer casually or to beg the question further. An all too common shortcoming, exemplified by each of the writers cited and extending throughout the study of black political activity, is a tendency to abstract black life from the currents of American history. The resulting scenarios of black existence suffer from superficiality.

16. Piccone, "Crisis of One-Dimensionality," pp. 45–46; "Beyond Critical Theory," p. 6.

17. John Alt observes that "The problem of legitimating industrial reorganization was solved through a new social practice and ideology structured around the pursuit of money, material comfort, and a higher standard of living through consumerism. Mass consumption, as the necessary otherness of Taylorized mass production, was itself offered as the ultimate justification for the rationalization of labor." "Beyond Class: The Decline of Industrial Labor and Leisure," *Telos* (Summer 1976): 71. Stuart Ewen identifies the Cold War period as the apotheosis of consumerism, whose enshrinement during those years was aided by the continued spread of popular journalism and the "mass marketing of television . . . (which) carried the consumer imagery into the back corners of home life." *Captains of Consciousness: Advertising and the Social Roots of the Consumer Culture* (New York, 1976), pp. 206–15.

18. Compare David Riesman (with Nathan Glazer and Reuel Denney), *The Lonely Crowd: A Study of the Changing American Character,* abr. ed. (New Haven, Conn., 1961), pp. 19–22, and Jules Henry's perceptive and telling study of the period, *Culture against Man* (New York, 1963). Marcuse went so far as to suggest that even the concept of introjection may not capture the extent to which the one-dimensional order is reproduced in the individual on the ground that "Introjection implies the existence of an inner dimension distinguished from and even antagonistic to the external exigencies—an individual consciousness and an individual unconscious *apart from* public opinion and behavior. . . . (However, mass) production and mass distribution claim the *entire* individual. . . . The manifold processes of introjection seem to be ossified in almost mechanical reactions. The result is not adjustment but mimesis: an immediate identification of the individual with *his* society and, through it, with the society as a whole." Marcuse, *One-Dimensional Man,* p. 10.

19. The point is not that ethnicity has lost its power as a basis for self-identification or associational activity. What has been obliterated, however, is the distinctiveness of the institutional forms which were the source of group consciousness in the first place. Warner and Srole pridefully acknowledge the centrality of the prevailing order in the determination of ethnic consciousness: "The forces which are most potent both in forming and changing the ethnic groups emanate from the institutions of the dominant American social system." W. Lloyd Warner and Leo Srole, *The Social Systems of American Ethnic Groups* (New Haven, Conn., 1945), pp. 283–84. Stuart and Elizabeth Ewen, "Americanization

and Consumption," *Telos* 37 (Fall 1978), observe that the dynamic of homogenization began with integration into the system of wage labor which "created great fissures and, ultimately, gaps in people's lives. Money . . . rendered much of the way in which non-industrial peoples understood themselves, and the reproduction of their daily lives, useless. The money system itself was a widely disseminated *mass medium* which ripped the structure of peoples' needs from their customary roots, and by necessity transplanted these needs in a soil nourished by the 'rationality' of corporate industry and the retail marketplace" (p. 47). Traditional ethnic ways of life hardly stood a chance under conditions in which the terms of survival were also those of massification! See also Maurice R. Stein, *The Eclipse of Community: An Interpretation of American Studies* (New York, 1960).

20. See, e.g., John V. Van Sickle, *Planning for the South: An Inquiry into the Economics of Regionalism* (Nashville, 1943), pp. 68–71; Gene Roberts Jr., "The Waste of Negro Talent in a Southern State," in Alan F. Westin, ed., *Freedom Now: The Civil Rights Struggle in America* (New York, 1954).

21. Harry Braverman, *Labor and Monopoly Capital: The Degradation of Work in the Twentieth Century* (New York, 1974), notes the ironic circumstance that capital has appropriated as a conscious ideal Marx's "abstraction from the concrete forms of labor" (pp. 181–82). In the logic of monopoly capitalism—characterized in part by constant reduction of labor's share of the overall costs of production and increasing sensitivity for optimizing profits over time in a stable production environment, cf. Andreas Papandreou, *Paternalistic Capitalism* (Minneapolis, 1972), esp. pp. 80–89—the short-term benefits likely to accrue from a dual labor market situation need not be expected to hold any great attractiveness.

22. Braverman, *Labor and Monopoly Capital,* p. 319 and passim. Also see David Noble, *America by Design: Science, Technology, and the Rise of Corporate Capitalism* (New York, 1977), pp. 82, 257–320.

23. A clarification is needed concerning use of the constructs "black community" and "black activism." Racial segregation and the movement against it were southern phenomena. Black Power "nationalism" was essentially a northern phenomenon for which legally sanctioned racial exclusion was not an immediate issue. Although the two historical currents of rebellion were closely related, they nevertheless were distinct. Consequently, they must be considered separately.

24. See, e.g., Charles S. Johnson, *Patterns of Negro Segregation* (New York, 1943), and *Growing Up in the Black Belt* (Washington, D.C., 1941); C. Vann Woodward, *The Strange Career of Jim Crow* (New York, 1966); Wilbur J. Cash, *The Mind of the South* (New York, 1941); Robert Penn Warren, *Segregation: The Inner Conflict in the South* (New York, 1956); John Dollard, *Caste and Class in a Southern Town* (New York, 1957); James W. Vander Zanden, *Race Relations in Transition* (New York, 1965); George B. Tindall, *The Emergence of the New South: 1913–1945* (Baton Rouge, 1967); Arthur Raper, *Preface to Peasantry: A Tale of Two Black Belt Countries* (Chapel Hill, 1936), and *The Tragedy of Lynching* (Chapel Hill, N.C., 1933); William L. Patterson, *We Charge Genocide* (New York, 1951); Martin Luther King Jr., *Why We Can't Wait* (New York, 1964). The following discussion draws freely from these sources.

25. Certainly, the bizarre notion of black leadership was not an invention of the postwar era. That strategy of pacification had been the primary nonterroristic means for subduing black opposition since Booker T. Washington's network of alliances with corpo-

rate progressives and New South Bourbon Democrats. Moreover, the notion of a leadership stratum which was supposed to speak for a monolithic black community became the ideological model and political ideal for 1960s radicalism—especially in its "nationalist" variants.

26. King's fascination with satyagraha suggests, although exaggeratedly, the influence which decolonization abroad had on the development of civil rights opposition. Compare David L. Lewis, *King: A Critical Biography* (Baltimore, 1970), pp. 100–103, and King, "Letter from Birmingham Jail," in *Why We Can't Wait*, pp. 76–95.

27. Lomax, *The Negro Revolt*, p. 21 and passim; Martin Luther King Jr., "I Have a Dream," in *Speeches by the Leaders: The March on Washington for Jobs and Freedom* (New York, n.d.); Whitney Young, *To Be Equal* (New York, 1964); and Samuel DuBois Cook, "The American Liberal Democratic Tradition, the Black Revolution and Martin Luther King, Jr.," in Hanes Walton, *The Political Philosophy of Martin Luther King, Jr.* (Westport, Conn., 1971), pp. xiii–xxxviii.

28. This does not mean that *Life* magazine and "Father Knows Best" taught blacks to "dream the dream of freedom." Rather, the integrative logic of massification exacerbated disruptive tendencies already present within the black elite.

29. Concepts such as duplicity and co-optation are inadequate to shed light on why corporate and liberal interests actively supported the civil rights movement. Interpretations so derived cannot fully explain programs and strategies which originated in the black community. They suggest that naive and trusting blacks, committed to an ideal of global emancipation, allowed themselves to be led away from this ideal by bourgeois wolves in sheep's clothing. This kind of "false consciousness" thesis is theoretically unacceptable. Consciousness is false not when it is a lie forced from outside but when it does not comprehend its historical one-sidedness.

30. Of course, suppression was the reaction of certain elements, most notably within the state apparatus whose bureaucratized priorities urged suppression of any disruptive presence in the society. Howard Zinn, *SNCC: The New Abolitionists* (Boston, 1965), as well as Forman and Sellers, shows that the federal apparatus, which later developed a reputation at the grass roots as the patron saint of equality, was at best lukewarm in response to black demands for enforcement of constitutional rights and often set out to suppress tendencies and distinct personalities in the movement. Nevertheless, the movement was not suppressed, and not because it "forced" its will upon history. That bit of romantic backslapping has as little credence as the one that contends that the antiwar movement ended the Vietnam War. The state hardly was mobilized against civil rights activism; the Supreme Court had authorized its legitimacy before it even began.

31. John F. Kennedy picked up the line and ran it as if it were his own; see his "Message to Congress," *Congressional Record* 88th Congress, 1st Session, February 28, 1963.

32. It was out of this milieu of muddled uneasiness that Rev. Willie Ricks gave the world the slogan "Black Power!" on the Meridith march in 1966. A flavor of the frustration of the radicals at the time can be gotten from Julius Lester, *Look Out, Whitey! Black Power's Gon' Get Your Mama* (New York, 1968). In some respects Lester's account, though more dated, has greater value for understanding this period than either Forman's or Sellers's because *Look Out, Whitey!* is written from within Black Power, rather than retrospectively from the vantage point of new ideologies and old involvements that need to be protected.

See also Stokely Carmichael, "Who Is Qualified?" in *Stokely Speaks: Black Power to Pan-Africanism* (New York, 1961).

33. See, e.g., Carmichael, "Power and Racism," in *Stokely Speaks.* This essay is perhaps the first attempt to articulate a systematic concept of the notion of Black Power.

34. Robert Allen, *Black Awakening in Capitalist America: An Analytic History* (Garden City, N.J., 1969), pp. 129–92. Allen's interpretation, however, cannot move beyond this descriptive point because he accepts a simplistic notion of co-optation to explain the black corporate elite nexus. Julius Lester charged by 1968 that the "principal beneficiaries of Black Power have been the black middle class." *Revolutionary Notes* (New York, 1969), p. 106.

35. Cruse, *Crisis,* pp. 544–65.

36. Jennifer Jordan notes this "nostalgic" character of 1960s culturalism and its grounding in the black elite in an essay, "Cultural Nationalism in the Sixties: Politics and Poetry" [in *Race, Politics, and Culture,* ed. Reed]. In the most systematic and thorough critical reconstruction of black cultural nationalism to date, Jordan identifies two core nationalist tendencies: one Afro-American preservationist, the other African retrievalist. Presumably, Ron Karenga is to be seen as a bridge between those tendencies with his commitment to "creation, recreation and circulation of Afro-American culture." "From the Quotable Karenga," in *The Black Power Revolt,* ed. Floyd Barbour (Boston, 1968), p. 162.

37. Compare Imamu Amiri Baraka (LeRoi Jones), "Toward the Creation of Political Institutions for All African Peoples," *Black World* 21 (October 1972): 54–78. "Unity will be the only method, it is part of the black value system because it is only with unity that we will get political power." Baraka, *Raise, Race, Rays, Raze* (New York, 1971), p. 109.

38. The fascination shared by most of the nationalists with the prospects of consciously creating a culture revealed both the loss of genuine cultural base *and* the extent of the nationalists' acceptance of manipulation as a strategy (cf. Karenga's "seven criteria for culture," *Black Power Revolt,* p. 166). The farther away the nationalists chose to go to find their cultural referent, the more clearly they demonstrated the passage of a self-driving, spontaneous black existence from the arena of American history. The ultimate extension of escapism came with the growth of Pan-Africanism as an ideology; that turn—at least in its most aggressive manifestations—conceded as a first step the inauthenticity of *all* black American life. See Carmichael, *Stokely Speaks,* pp. 175–227; Ideological Research Staff of Malcolm X Liberation University, *Understanding the African Struggle* (Greensboro, N.C., 1971); Owusu Sadaukai (Howard Fuller), *The Condition of Black People in the 1970s* (Chicago, 1972).

39. In this regard expertise translates into superficial articulateness and ability to negotiate with the social management apparatus.

40. Ronald Walters was able to gloat after Little Rock that the black elected officials had become the vanguard political force in the black community. "The Black Politician: Fulfilling the Legacy of Black Power," unpublished. Baraka, its former chairman and a central organizer, was very nearly expelled from the National Black Assembly in 1975 by a force of elected officials put off by his newfound "Marxism." Note, however, that even he had to admit the activists' marginality and weakness compared to the mainstream elite as early as 1970 at the Congress of African Peoples. Baraka, ed., *African Congress: A Documentary of the First Modern Pan-African Congress* (New York, 1972), p. 99.

41. This is not to say that blacks no longer are oppressed, nor that that oppression

no longer has racial characteristics. Nor still is it possible to agree with Wilson's simplistic claim that race is receding as a factor in the organization of American society; as Harold Barnette notes, the integration of affirmative action programs into the social management apparatus suggests race's continuing significance. See William Julius Wilson, *The Declining Significance of Race: Blacks and Changing American Institutions* (Chicago, 1978), and Barnette's review in *Southern Exposure* 7 (Spring 1979): 121–22. With legitimation and absorption of antiracism by the social management system, race has assumed a more substantial and pervasive function than ever before in American life. Moreover, this function is often life-sustaining; controlling discrimination has become a career specialty—complete with "professional," "paraprofessional," and "subprofessional" gradations—in public and private bureaucracies. However, "racial discrimination" fails as a basis from which to interpret or address black oppression.

"Racism" is bound to an "equality of opportunity" ideology which can express only the interests of the elite strata among the black population; equality of access to the meaningless, fragmented, and degrading jobs which comprise the bulk of work, for example, hardly is the stuff of "black liberation" and is ultimately a retrograde social demand. It is not an accident, therefore, that the only major battle produced by the struggle against racism in the 1970s has been the anti-Bakke movement, whose sole objective was protection of blacks' access to pursuit of professional employment status.

Racism makes its appearance as an opaque reification grafted onto otherwise acceptable institutions. Small wonder it is the only issue the black elite can find to contend! Not only does racism carry the elite's sole critique of U.S. society, but the claim that racism creates a bond of equivalent victimization among blacks is one of the sources of the elite's legitimation. It is interesting to recall in this context that "racism" became the orthodox explanation of black oppression when the Kerner Commission anointed it as the fundamental source of the 1964–67 urban uprisings. *Report of the National Advisory Commission on Civil Disorders* (New York, 1968), p. 203. This document goes far toward articulating the outlines of what became the new strategy for management of the black population.

42. The most significant shift in the occupational structure of the black population in the decade after the 1964 Civil Rights Act was relative expansion of its elite component. Between 1964 and 1974 the percentage of minority males classified as "professional and technical" workers increased by half; the percentage classified as nonfarm, salaried "managers and administrators" quadrupled over that period. Similar increases were realized by minority females. *Social and Economic Status of the Black Population*, pp. 73–74.

43. The celebration of the new elite is not, as once was the case, restricted to black media. Stephen Birmingham has testified to their presence and allowed them to expose their personal habits in his characteristically gossipy style of pop journalism in his *Certain People: America's Black Elite* (Boston, 1977). The *New York Times Sunday Magazine* twice at least has lionized the beautiful black stratum of the 1970s. See Peter Ross Range, "Making It in Atlanta: Capital of 'Black Is Bountiful,'" *New York Times Sunday Magazine,* April 7, 1974, and William Brashler, "The Black Middle Class: Making It," in the December 3, 1978, magazine. Each of these brassy accounts tends, despite occasional injections of "balance," to accept and project the elite's mystical view of itself and exaggerates its breadth and force in society. However, that the *Times* even would care to make the statement made by these two articles suggests minimally that the elite has been integrated into the corporate marketing strategy on an equal basis.

44. The distinction of "authentic" and "artificial" particularity is similar to Haber-

mas's distinction of "living" and "objectivistically prepared and strategically employed" cultural traditions. A cultural particularity is "authentic" insofar as it: (1) reproduces itself within the institutional environment that apparently delimits the groups, i.e., outside the social administrative system; and (2) is not mobilized by the mass culture industry. Compare Jürgen Habermas, *Legitimation Crisis* (Boston, 1975), pp. 70–72.

45. Jordan even contends that radical culturalism was most susceptible among all the 1960s oppositional forms to the logic of commodification because of its tendency to reduce identity to the artifact; cf. "Cultural Nationalism in the Sixties."

46. Compare, e.g., S. E. Anderson, "Black Students: Racial Consciousness and the Class Struggle, 1960–1976," *Black Scholar* 8 (January–February 1977): 35–43; Muhammad Ahmad, "On the Black Student Movement—1960–1970," *Black Scholar* 9 (May–June 1978): 2–11; James and Grace Lee Boggs, *Revolution and Evolution in the Twentieth Century* (New York, 1974), pp. 174 ff.

47. The coalition's bankruptcy was demonstrated by the defections from its electoral constituency to Nixon's "silent majority" in 1968 and wholesale collapse in the face of McGovernite and Republican challenges in 1972. Unable to end the Vietnam War and adjust to a new era of imperialism or to address the concerns of such post-scarcity era advocacy centers as the student and ecology movements, the productivist liberal-labor forces who had controlled the Democratic Party for a generation also found it impossible to establish a common discursive arena with the ethnic and feminist consciousness movements of the 1960s.

48. Piccone, "Crisis of One-Dimensionality," p. 46; "The Changing Function of Critical Theory," *New German Critique* (Fall 1977): 35–36.

49. Habermas calls these "quasi-groups" and maintains that they perform the additional function of absorbing the "secondary effects of the averted economic crisis," *Legitimation Crisis*, p. 39.

50. Russell Jacoby, "A Falling Rate of Intelligence?" *Telos* (Spring 1976): 141–46; Stanley Aronowitz, "Mass Culture and the Eclipse of Reason: The Implications for Pedagogy," *College English* 38 (April 1977): 768–74, and *False Promises: The Shaping of American Working Class Consciousness* (New York, 1973).

51. Julius Lester was one who saw the prominence of a media cult in the movement; *Revolutionary Notes*, pp. 176–80. On the peculiar style of the Panthers, see Earl Anthony, *Picking up the Gun* (New York, 1970).

52. "The spectacle presents itself as an enormous unalterable and inaccessible actuality. It says nothing more than 'that which appears is good, that which is good appears.' The attitude which it demands in principle is this passive acceptance, which in fact it has already obtained by its manner of appearing without reply, by its monopoly of appearance." Guy Debord, *Society of the Spectacle* (Detroit, 1970), par. 12.

53. A recent incident captures contemporary life: during the national telecast of the 1978 Miss Black America pageant, General Motors, a sponsor of the broadcast, featured a commercial in which a utility man at a plant listed the attractions of his job. Among them were pay, fringe benefits, security, opportunity to perform various tasks (a function solely of his particular position), congenial supervision, and a good union! In the metaphor of a colleague who is one of a vanishing breed of baseball fans, the bourgeoisie has a shut-out going with two away in the bottom of the ninth!

54. "The main thing is that utopian conscience and knowledge, through the pain it

suffers in facts, grows wise, yet does not grow to full wisdom. It is *rectified*—but never *refuted*—by the mere power of that which, at any particular time, *is*. On the contrary it confutes and judges the existent if it is failing, and failing inhumanly; indeed, first and foremost it provides the *standard* to measure such facticity precisely as departure from the Right." Ernst Bloch, *A Philosophy of the Future* (New York, 1970), p. 91.

3

Stormy Weather: Reconstructing Black (Inter)Nationalism in the Cold War Era

Robin D. G. Kelley

The spectre of a storm is haunting the Western world. . . . The Great Storm, the coming Black Revolution, is rolling like a tornado; roaring from the East; shaking the moorings of the earth as it passes through countries ruled by oppressive regimes; toppling the walls of mighty institutions; filling the well paved, colonial streets with crimson rivers of blood. Yes, all over this sullen planet, the multi-colored "hordes" of undernourished millions are on the move like never before in human history. They are moving to the rhythms of a New Song, a New Sound; dancing in the streets to a Universal Dream that haunts their wretched nights: they dream of Freedom! Their minds are fueled and refueled by the fires of that dream.

Rolland Snellings (Askia Muhammad Toure)

The story of the shift from civil rights to Black Power has been told so many times, in books, documentary films, in African American history courses all across the United States, that it has become a kind of common sense. It usually begins with the murder of Emmett Till, quickly followed by *Brown v. Board of Education* in 1954—both events spurring an already hopeful, if not angry, black community into action. Black anger and hopefulness are traced to black support for the Good War against fascism abroad a decade earlier; they were, after all, loyal to America, and now it was time for the state to grant black folk democracy and citizenship. Then

Montgomery showed the world what black protest could accomplish, thus giving birth to the modern civil rights movement. Local and national campaigns waged by the Southern Christian Leadership Conference (SCLC), the Congress on Racial Equality (CORE), the Student Nonviolent Coordinating Committee (SNCC), to name only the big three, fought for citizenship, the right to vote, and desegregation, and succeeded in getting the federal government to pass the Civil Rights Act (1964) and the Voting Rights Act (1965).

These were Pyrrhic victories, to say the least. Activists were snuffed out and the FBI did nothing about it; the Democratic Party rejected the only hope for real democracy in Mississippi, Fannie Lou Hamer's Mississippi Freedom Democratic Party; civil rights marchers in Selma were "turned back," striking a mighty blow to the morale of the movement. Meanwhile, the emergence of Malcolm X and his subsequent assassination, exacerbated by the wave of urban rebellions between 1964 and 1968, served as a catalyst for rising black nationalist sentiment. SNCC members started to carry guns to protect themselves, and their black leaders, particularly folks like Stokely Carmichael and Willie Ricks, began to question the movement's integrationist agenda. Then, during the summer of 1966, the slogan "Black Power" emerged full-blown among black SNCC and CORE militants. Tired and impatient with the slow pace of the civil rights establishment, a new attitude overtook the movement: no more compromise, no more "deals" with white liberals, no more subordinating the struggle to the needs of the Democratic Party. Out of bitter disappointment rose a new Black Revolution.

In other words, high expectations begat the civil rights movement; the movement's failure to achieve all of its goals or deal with urban poverty begat Black Power. The flowering of black nationalism in the mid- to late 1960s was an evolutionary process, a stage in the development of postwar black politics. It's a neat typology, to be sure, but one that obscures more than it reveals. First of all, it is a tale too often limited to the domestic sphere, to the U.S. nation-state. Even black nationalism tends to be cast in terms of riots and "buy black" campaigns rather than black activists' support for anticolonial movements and "Third World" solidarity.[1] Second, given our south to north trajectory, the northern urban political landscape of the late 1950s is overshadowed by the southern struggle, for after all, this is where the television cameras were before the riots. The third reason, of course, has to do with a general conspiracy of silence against the most radical elements of the black freedom movement, the movements and activists that spoke of revolution, socialism, self-determination, armed struggle—

those radicals who looked to the Third World for models of black liberation in the United States. These movements, while often small and sometimes isolated, confound our narrative of the black freedom movement, for they were independent of both the white Left and the mainstream civil rights movement.[2]

The following, therefore, is a brief and very incomplete effort to give voice to a black radical movement and discourse rooted in the late 1950s and early to mid-1960s. My own small contribution to recovering black radicalism in the so-called Cold War era and to reperiodizing the black freedom movement must be seen as part of a larger collective project involving a growing number of scholars and activists, including Ernest Allen, Muhammad Ahmad (Max Stanford), Rod Bush, Kevin Gaines, Van Gosse, Gerald Horne, Peniel Joseph, Brenda Gayle Plummer, Nikhil Singh, Clarence Taylor, Timothy Tyson, Akinyele Umoja, Penny von Eschen, and Fanon Wilkins, to name a few. To these writers I am deeply indebted. For the purposes of this essay, I will focus most of my remarks on one particular organization: the Revolutionary Action Movement (RAM). A semi-under ground organization that rarely gets more than a mention in histories of the modern black freedom movement, RAM was a precursor to the black radical organizations of the later sixties and seventies. Although RAM was homegrown in the sense that it drew many of its ideas from Malcolm X, Harold Cruse, and others, and developed in response to urban poverty and racism, police brutality, black student struggles, and the defense of Robert Williams, it was also a product of uprisings and revolutions in Africa, Asia, and Latin America. RAM's history and political ideology is incomprehensible without the Chinese and Cuban revolutions or the African independence movement; RAM leaders understood the African American condition through an analysis of global capitalism, imperialism, and Third World liberation. While Dr. Martin Luther King Jr., Ella Baker, and other major strategists of the civil rights movement also understood the black freedom struggle in international terms, RAM militants went a step further, attempting to develop a radical theory that would bring together black nationalism, Marxism, and Third World internationalism.

Roaring from the East

For many black radicals, the Cold War represented one of the "hottest" moments in world history. Despite the virtual suspension of democracy during the 1950s—from the wave of jailings and deportations of alleged

Communists to the outlawing of mainstream organizations such as the NAACP in the South—this was *the* revolutionary moment. It was the age of nationalist revolt, African independence, the first gathering of non-aligned nations in Bandung, Indonesia, the creation of the Organization of African Unity.[3] Ghana's independence in 1957 was cause to celebrate, and the CIA-sponsored assassination of Patrice Lumumba in the Congo inspired protest from all black activist circles. The Cuban Revolution and Fidel Castro's infamous residency at Harlem's Hotel Theresa during his visit to the United Nations brought black people face-to-face with an avowed socialist who extended a hand of solidarity to people of color the world over. Indeed, dozens of black radicals not only publicly defended the Cuban Revolution but visited the island through groups like the Fair Play for Cuba Committee.[4]

One of these visitors was Harold Cruse, himself an ex-Communist still committed to Marxism. He believed the Cuban, Chinese, and African revolutions could revitalize radical thought because they demonstrated the revolutionary potential of nationalism. In a provocative essay published in the *New Leader* in 1962, Cruse wrote that the new generation is looking to the former colonial world for its leaders and insights, and among its heroes is Mao:

> Already they have a pantheon of modern heroes—Lumumba,
> Kwame Nkrumah, Sekou Toure in Africa; Fidel Castro in Latin
> America; Malcolm X, the Muslim leader, in New York; Robert
> Williams in the South; and Mao Tse-tung in China. These men seem
> heroic to the Afro-Americans not because of their political philoso-
> phy, but because they were either former colonials who achieved
> complete independence, or because, like Malcolm X, they dared to
> look the white community in the face and say: "We don't think your
> civilization is worth the effort of any black man to try to integrate
> into." This to many Afro-Americans is an act of defiance that is truly
> revolutionary.[5]

The Chinese and Cuban ability to seize power by force of arms also made these revolutions attractive to black radicals in the age of nonviolent passive resistance. Of course, the era had its share of armed struggle in the South, with groups like the Deacons for Defense and Justice and Gloria Richardson's Cambridge movement defending nonviolent protesters when necessary. But the figure who best embodied black traditions of armed self-defense was Robert Williams, a hero to the new wave of black internationalists whose importance almost rivaled that of Malcolm X. A former U.S. Marine with extensive military training, Williams earned notoriety in 1957 for forming armed self-defense groups in Monroe, North Carolina, to fight the Ku Klux Klan. Two years later, Williams's statement that black people must "meet violence with violence" as the only way to end injustice in an uncivilized South led to his suspension as president of the Monroe Chapter of the NAACP.[6]

Williams's break with the NAACP and his open advocacy of armed self-defense pushed him further left, into the orbit of the Socialist Workers Party, the Workers World Party, and among some members of the old Communist Party (CPUSA). However, Williams had had contact with Communists since his days as a Detroit auto worker in the 1940s. He not only read the *Daily Worker* but published a story in its pages called "Some Day I Am Going Back South." Williams was also somewhat of an intellectual dabbler and autodidact, having studied at West Virginia State College, North Carolina College, and Johnson C. Smith College. Nevertheless, his more recent left associations had led him to Cuba and the Fair Play for Cuba Committee. Upon returning from his first trip in 1960, he hoisted the Cuban flag in his backyard and ran a series of articles in his mimeographed publication, the *Crusader,* about the transformation of working people's lives in Cuba as a result of the revolution. In one of his editorials published in August of 1960, Williams insisted that African Americans' fight for freedom "is related to the Africans', the Cubans', all of Latin Americans' and the Asians' struggles for self-determination." His support of the Chinese revolution was evident in the pages of the *Crusader* as well, emphasizing the importance of China as a beacon of strength for social justice movements the world over. Like Amiri Baraka, Williams took note of China's detonation of an atomic bomb in 1960 as a historic occasion for the oppressed. "With the bomb," he wrote "China will be respected and will add a powerful voice to those who already plead for justice for black as well as white."[7]

By 1961, as a result of trumped-up kidnapping charges and a federal warrant for his arrest, Williams and his family were forced to flee the country and seek political asylum in Cuba. During the next four years, Cuba became Williams's base for promoting black world revolution and elaborating an internationalist ideology that embraced black nationalism and Third World solidarity. With support from Fidel Castro, Williams hosted a radio show called "Radio Free Dixie" that was directed at African Americans, continued to edit the *Crusader* (which by now had progressed from a mimeo to a full-blown magazine), and completed his book *Negroes with Guns* (1962).

He did not, however, identify himself as a Marxist. At the same time, he rejected the "nationalist" label, calling himself an "internationalist" instead: "That is, I'm interested in the problems of Africa, of Asia, and of Latin America. I believe that we all have the same struggle; a struggle for liberation."[8]

Although Williams recalls having had good relations with Castro, political differences over race did lead to a rift between him and the Cuban Communists. "The Party," Williams remembered, "maintained that it was strictly a class issue and that once the class problem had been solved through a socialist administration, racism would be abolished."[9] Williams not only disagreed but had moved much closer to Che Guevara, who embodied much of what Williams had been advocating all along: Third World solidarity, the use of armed struggle, and a deep and unwavering interest in the African revolution. Indeed, Che's leanings toward China undoubtedly made an impact on Williams's decision to leave Cuba for Beijing. Given Che's break with Fidel and the solidification of Cuba's links to the Soviet Union, Williams saw no need to stay. He and his family packed up and moved to China in 1966.

As an exiled revolutionary in China during its most tumultuous era, Williams nevertheless predicted that urban rebellions in America's ghettos would transform the country. Although one might argue that by publishing the *Crusader* from Cuba and then China, Williams had very limited contact with the black freedom movement in the United States, his magazine reached a new generation of young black militants and promoted the vision of black world revolution articulated by critics such as Harold Cruse. The fact is, the *Crusader* and Williams's own example compelled a small group of black radical intellectuals and activists to form what might loosely be called the first black Maoist-influenced organization in history: the Revolutionary Action Movement (RAM).

The Coming Black Revolution

Williams's flight to Cuba turned out to be a major catalyst for the creation of RAM. In Ohio around 1961, black members of Students for a Democratic Society (SDS) as well as activists in SNCC and CORE met in a small group to discuss the significance of Williams's work in Monroe and his subsequent exile. Led by Donald Freeman, a black student at Case Western Reserve in Cleveland, the group's main core consisted of a newly formed

organization made up of Central State College students at Wilberforce calling themselves "Challenge." Members of Challenge were especially taken
with Harold Cruse's 1962 essay "Revolutionary Nationalism and the Afro-
American," which was circulated widely among young black militants. In it
he argued that black people in the United States were living under domestic
colonialism and that their struggles must be seen as part of the worldwide
anticolonial movement. "The failure of American Marxists," he wrote, "to
understand the bond between the Negro and the colonial peoples of the
world has led to their failure to develop theories that would be of value to
Negroes in the United States." He reversed the traditional argument that
the success of socialism in the developed West was key to the emancipation
of colonial subjects and the development of socialism in the Third World.
Instead, he saw the former colonies as the vanguard of the revolution, and
at the forefront of this new socialist revolution were Cuba and China. "The
revolutionary initiative has passed to the colonial world, and in the United
States is passing to the Negro, while Western Marxists theorize, temporize
and debate."[10]

Inspired by Cruse's interpretation of domestic colonialism and the
global importance of the black freedom struggle, Freeman hoped to turn
Challenge into a revolutionary nationalist movement akin to the Nation of
Islam but that would adopt the direct action tactics of SNCC. After a
lengthy debate, Challenge members decided to dissolve the organization
in the spring of 1962 and form the Revolutionary Action Movement
(RAM) (initially called a "Committee") with its primary leaders being Freeman, Max Stanford, and Wanda Marshall. Initially, the group called themselves the "Reform" Action Movement so as not to alarm the administration, but once they decided to maintain RAM as a semi-underground
organization, they changed the name and focused on developing a small, select vanguard of the black liberation movement.[11]

Freeman and RAM members in Cleveland continued to work publicly through the Afro-American Institute, an activist policy-oriented think
tank formed in the fall of 1962. Under Freeman's directorship, its board—
dubbed the Soul Circle—consisted of a small group of black men with ties
to community organizations, labor, civil rights, and student groups. Board
members such as Henry Glover, Arthur Evans, Nate Bryant, and Hanif
Wahab gave lectures on African history and politics, and organized forums
to discuss the future of the civil rights movement, black participation in
Cleveland politics, and the economic conditions of urban blacks. The institute even recruited the great drummer Max Roach to help organize a

panel entitled "The Role of the Black Artist in the Struggle for Freedom."
Institute members also used random leaflets and pamphlets to influence
black community thinking on a number of local and international issues.
Addressed "To Whom It May Concern," these short broadsides were intended to stimulate discussion and offer the black community a position
on pressing topics such as "elections, urban renewal, Black economic sub-
servience, the 'arms race,' and the struggle in the South." Within a year, the
institute graduated from random leafletting to a full-blown newsletter titled *Afropinion*. Through the Afro-American Institute, RAM members in
Cleveland worked with CORE activists and other community organizers to
demand improvements in hospital care for black patients and to protest the
exclusion of African and Afro-American history from the public school curriculum. Their most important campaign of 1963 was the defense of Mae
Mallory, a black woman who was being held in the county jail in Cleveland
for her association with Robert Williams in Monroe, North Carolina. Soon
after Williams's flight to Cuba, Mallory was arrested in Ohio and awaited
extradition charges. The institute and its allies, including the Nation of Islam in Cleveland, petitioned the governor of Ohio to revoke the warrant of
extradition and organized a mass demonstration in front of the county jail
demanding Mallory's immediate release.[12]

In northern California, RAM grew primarily out of the Afro-American
Association. Founded by Donald Warden in 1962, the Afro-American Association consisted of students from the University of California at Berkeley and Merritt College—many of whom, such as Leslie and Jim Lacy,
Cedric Robinson, Ernest Allen, and Huey Newton, would go on to play
important roles as radical activists and intellectuals. In Los Angeles, the
president of the Afro-American Association was a young man named Ron
Everett, who later changed his name to Ron Karenga and went on to found
US Organization. The Afro-American Association quickly developed a reputation as a group of militant intellectuals willing to debate anyone. By
challenging professors, debating groups such as the Young Socialist Alliance, and giving public lectures on black history and culture, these young
men left a deep impression on fellow students as well as the black community. In the East Bay, where the tradition of soapbox speakers died in the
1930s (save for individual campaigns by the Communist-led Civil Rights
Congress during the early 1950s), the Afro-American Association was
walking and talking proof that a vibrant, highly visible militant intellectual
culture could exist.[13]

Meanwhile, the Progressive Labor (PL) movement had begun sponsoring trips to Cuba and recruited several radical black students in the East Bay to go along. Among them was Ernest Allen, a transfer student from Merritt College to Berkeley who had been forced out of the Afro-American Association. A working-class kid from Oakland, Allen was part of a generation of black radicals whose dissatisfaction with the civil rights movement's strategy of nonviolent passive resistance drew them closer to Malcolm X and Third World liberation movements. Not surprisingly, through his trip to Cuba in 1964 he discovered the Revolutionary Action Movement. Allen's travel companions included a contingent of black militants from Detroit: Luke Tripp, Charles ("Mao") Johnson, Charles Simmons, and General Baker. All were members of the student group Uhuru, and all went on to play key roles in the formation of the Dodge Revolutionary Union Movement and the League of Revolutionary Black Workers. Incredibly, RAM leader Max Stanford was already on the island visiting Robert Williams. When it was time to go back to the states, Allen and the Detroit group were committed to building RAM. Allen stopped in Cleveland to meet with RAM members on his cross-country bus trip back to Oakland. Armed with copies of Williams's *Crusader* magazine and related RAM material, Allen returned to Oakland intent on establishing RAM's presence in the East Bay. Never more than a handful of people, folks such as Isaac Moore, Kenn Freeman (Mamadou Lumumba), Bobby Seale (future founder of the Black Panther Party), and Doug Allen (Ernie's brother) established a base at Merritt College through the Soul Students Advisory Council. The group's intellectual and cultural presence, however, was broadly felt. Allen, Freeman, and others founded a journal called *Soulbook: The Revolutionary Journal of the Black World* that published prose and poetry that is best described as left black nationalist in orientation. Freeman, in particular, was highly respected among RAM activists and widely read. He constantly pushed his members to think about black struggle in a global context. The editors of *Soulbook* also developed ties with "old" left black radicals, most notably former Communist Harry Haywood, whose work they published in an early issue.[14]

Although RAM had established itself in northern California and Cleveland, Ohio, by 1964 Philadelphia appeared to be RAM's home base. It was in Philadelphia, after all, that RAM maintained an open existence, operating under its own name rather than a variety of front organizations. The strength of the Philadelphia chapter had much to do with the fact that it was also the home of Max Stanford, RAM's national field chairman. It was out of Philadelphia that RAM published a bimonthly paper called

Black America and a one-page newsletter called *RAM Speaks,* made plans to build a national movement oriented toward revolutionary nationalism, youth organizing, and armed self-defense, and recruited several Philadelphia activists to the group, including Ethel Johnson (who had also worked with Williams in Monroe), Stan Daniels, and Playthell Benjamin.[15] Subsequently, RAM recruited a group of young Philadelphia militants who would go on to play key roles in radical organizations. These included Michael Simmons, one of the authors of SNCC's famous Black Consciousness Paper and whose resistance to the draft resulted in his serving a two-and-a-half-year prison sentence, and Tony Monteiro, who went on to become a leading national figure in the CPUSA during the 1970s and 1980s.[16]

At the outset, it seems as though RAM leaders were not all in agreement on the usefulness of Marxism for black liberation. Indeed, circumstantial evidence suggests that the Philadelphia leadership was to the left of people like Warden in California and Freeman in Ohio. Freeman did call for collectively owned black enterprises "in order to eliminate total subjugation to white capitalism," but he insisted that white "socialists and Marxists do not possess the solutions to the ills of Black America." Warden was even less ambivalent about black capitalism: "We must develop our own planned businesses where efficiency, thrift and sacrifice are stressed. . . . The capital for such industries also is available from our own community, if it could be diverted from the consumption of alcohol, bleaching creams and preachers' Cadillacs." On the other hand, we cannot assume that Warden's position was representative of the entire California Afro-American Association, for, as Ernie Allen reminds us and the pages of *Soulbook* indicate, Warden's ideas were constantly challenged from the Left.[17]

By the middle of 1964 and early 1965, the left wing of RAM had clearly won out. Under Max Stanford's leadership, RAM proclaimed its adherence to "Marxism-Leninism Mao Tse-tung thought" as it applied to the conditions of black people. They also claimed to be the first organization to advance "the theory that the Black liberation movement in the U.S. was part of the vanguard of the world socialist revolution."[18] RAM's greater leftward turn can be attributed in part to its ideological mentors, who in some respects bridged 1930s and 1940s radicalism with the black New Left. Young RAM militants sought political guidance not only from Williams but also from a number of former black Communists who either had been expelled for "ultra-leftism" or "bourgeois nationalism," or had bolted the party because of its "revisionism." Among this group of elders were Harold

Cruse, Harry Haywood, Abner Berry, and "Queen Mother" Audley Moore. Indeed, Moore would go on to become one of RAM's most important mentors on the East Coast, offering members training in black nationalist thought and Marxism. The Queen Mother's home, which she affectionately called Mount Addis Ababa, practically served as a school for a new generation of young black radicals. She founded the African American Party of National Liberation in 1963, which formed a provisional government and elected Robert Williams as premier in exile. They also turned to Detroit's legendary ex-Trotskyists James and Grace Lee Boggs, former comrades of C. L. R. James, whose Marxist and Pan-Africanist writings greatly influenced RAM members as well as other New Left activists. In fact, James Boggs briefly served as RAM's ideological chairman from mid-1964 to January 1965.[19]

Other sources of RAM's embrace of revolutionary Marxism and radical anti-imperialism were the urban uprisings that had just started during the summer of 1964. Even before the riot wave, RAM militants had read Williams's prophetic essay in the *Crusader* entitled "USA: The Potential of a Minority Revolution." His words were portentous: "This year, 1964 is going to be a violent one, the storm will reach hurricane proportions by 1965 and the eye of the hurricane will hover over America by 1966. America is a house on fire—FREEDOM NOW!—or let it burn, let it burn. Praise the Lord and pass the ammunition!!" He described in detail what weapons black urban guerrillas should use, how to make homemade bombs and flamethrowers, and how to knock out communications systems. In another installment of the same essay published almost three years later, Williams's directions for launching a ghetto rebellion were even more explicit. At times he sounded like the protagonist Freeman in Sam Greenlee's *The Spook Who Sat by the Door.* He informed his readers how to squeeze a trigger, called for selective fires "set over a wide area," and even suggested that brothers be sent to Africa for "specialized training in the manufacture and use of the poisonous dart." Most striking were his instructions on how to build the "Black Power Bomb." First, one must fill a gallon-size empty syrup container about three-fourths with gasoline and one-fourth with extra heavy motor oil. "The screw-on cap should be tightened after which a tampax, well soaked in gasoline, should be securely taped or wired to the jug. The soaked tampax or well soaked rag is lit when the individual is ready to heave the Black Power Bomb."[20]

RAM leaders echoed Williams's support for armed insurrection and drew inspiration and ideas directly from his theory of guerrilla warfare in the urban United States, even if they did not try to carry it out. In print, at least, RAM's official position was that such a war was not only possible but could be won in ninety days. The combination of mass chaos and revolutionary discipline was the key to victory. The Fall 1964 issue of *Black America* predicted Armageddon:

> Black men and women in the Armed Forces will defect and come over to join the Black Liberation forces. Whites who claim they want to help the revolution will be sent into the white communities to divide them, fight the fascists and frustrate the efforts of the counter-revolutionary forces. Chaos will be everywhere and with the break-down of mass communications, mutiny will occur in great numbers in all facets of the oppressors' government. The stock market will fall; Wall Street will stop functioning; Washington, D.C. will be torn apart by riots. Officials everywhere will run—run for their lives. The George Lincoln Rockwellers, Kennedys, Vanderbilts, Hunts, Johnsons, Wallaces, Barnetts, etc., will be the first to go. The revolution will "strike by night and spare none." . . . The Black Revolution will use sabotage in the cities, knocking out the electrical power first, then transportation and guerrilla warfare in the countryside in the South. With the cities powerless, the oppressor will be helpless.[21]

RAM not only prepared for war, it prepared for the coming society. Its twelve-point program called for the development of freedom schools, national black student organizations, rifle clubs, black farmer cooperatives (not just for economic development but to keep "community and guerrilla forces going for a while"), and a liberation guerrilla army made up of youth and unemployed. Its members also placed special emphasis on internationalism, pledging support for national liberation movements in Africa, Asia, and Latin America as well as the adoption of "Pan-African socialism." In line with Cruse's seminal essay, they saw themselves as colonial subjects fighting a "colonial war at home."[22] As colonial subjects with a right to self-determination, RAM saw Afro-America as a de facto member of the non-aligned nations. They even identified themselves as part of the "Bandung world," going so far as to hold a conference in November 1964 in Nashville on "The Black Revolution's Relationship to the Bandung World." In a 1965 article published in RAM's journal *Black America,* they started to develop a theory of Bandung Humanism or Revolutionary Black Internationalism, which argued that the battle between western imperialism and the Third World—more than the battle between labor and capital—repre-

sented the most fundamental contradiction in our time. They linked the
African American freedom struggle with what was happening in China,
Zanzibar, Cuba, Vietnam, Indonesia, and Algeria, and they characterized
their work as part of Mao's international strategy of encircling western capitalist countries and challenging imperialism. This position was echoed in a
particularly moving, eloquent essay by Rolland Snellings (better known as
Askia Muhammad Toure, the extraordinary poet and leader in the Black
Arts movement) titled "Afro American Youth and the Bandung World."
The urban rebellions in the United States were cast in terms of an international rebellion against imperialism, one where "Black America became one
with the students and people of Panama, Venezuela, Japan, South Vietnam,
the Congo, and all colonial peoples rioting in protest against injustice and
exploitation by puppet regimes stemming from or allied with White America, colossus of the West." These rebellions were not tragedies but celebra-
tions, temporarily freed spaces akin to liberated zones in which the
oppressed are "Dancing in the Streets!"[23]

After 1966, the term "Bandung Humanism" was dropped entirely
and replaced with "Black Internationalism." Precisely what "Black Internationalism" meant was laid out in an incredibly bold thirty-six-page
pamphlet published by RAM in 1966 titled *The World Black Revolution*.
Echoing *The Communist Manifesto* (its opening lines are "All over Africa,
Asia, South, Afro and Central America a revolution is haunting and sweep-
ing . . ."), the pamphlet identifies strongly with China against both the
capitalist West and the Soviet Empire. The "emergence of Revolutionary
China began to polarize caste and class contradictions within the world, in
both the bourgeoisie [*sic*] imperialist camp and also in the European bourgeois communist-socialist camp."[24] In other words, China was the wedge
that sharpened contradictions between colonial peoples and the West. Rejecting the idea that socialist revolution will arise in the developed countries
of the West, RAM insisted that the only true revolutionary solution was the
"dictatorship of the world by the Black Underclass through World Black
Revolution." Of course, they weren't working from today's definitions;
RAM used "underclass" to encompass all peoples of color in Asia, Latin
American, Africa, and elsewhere; the "Black Underclass" was merely a syn-
onym for the colonial world:

> The Black Underclass has only one alternative to free itself of colo-
> nialism, imperialism, capitalism and neo-colonialism; that is to com-
> pletely destroy Western (bourgeois) civilization (the cities of the
> world) through a World Black Revolution and establishing a Revolu-

tionary World Black Dictatorship can bring about the end of exploitation of man by mankind and the new revolutionary world be
created.[25]

To coordinate this revolution, RAM called for the creation of a Black International and the creation of a "People's Liberation Army on a world scale."

Although Mao's thought loomed large in *The World Black Revolution*,
much of the document reflects original thinking on the part of RAM members, who also drew from a wellspring of black radical thought. W. E. B. Du
Bois's pronouncement that the problem of the twentieth century is the
problem of the color line undergirds much of their argument. And just as
Du Bois argued in his magisterial book *Black Reconstruction in America*,
RAM maintained the position that the problem of the color line lay at the
heart of class struggle on a world scale. Furthermore, the pamphlet gives a
nod to Indian Communist leader M. N. Roy, who debated Lenin at the
Second Communist International Congress in 1920 over the "national-
colonial question." Roy, they argued, not only recognized nationalist and
anticolonial movements as revolutionary forces but insisted that class distinctions in the colonies placed the peasantry in a more pivotal position
than the colonial petite bourgeoisie for waging a revolutionary movement.
By resurrecting Roy, who had remained relatively obscure among the
panoply of Communist theoreticians, they revealed, once again, a stream of
radical thought from the Third World critical of western Marxism and capable of offering insights where European radicals had failed.[26]

For all of its strident nationalism, *The World Black Revolution* concludes that black nationalism "is really internationalism." Only by demol-
ishing white nationalism and white power can liberation be achieved for
everyone. Not only will national boundaries be eliminated with the "dictatorship of the Black Underclass," but "the need for nationalism in its aggressive form will be eliminated." This is a remarkable statement given
RAM's social and ideological roots. But rather than represent a unified position, the statement reflects various tensions that persisted throughout
RAM's history. On one side were nationalists who felt that revolutionaries
should fight for the black nation first and build socialism separate from the
rest of the United States. On the other side were socialists like James and
Grace Lee Boggs who wanted to know who would rule the "white" nation
and what such a presence would mean for black freedom. They also rejected
efforts to resurrect the Black Nation thesis—the old Communist line that
people in black majority counties of the South (the "black belt") have a
right to secede from the union. The Boggses contended that the real source

of power lay in the cities, not the rural black belt. In January of 1965, James Boggs resigned from his post as ideological chairman.

Moving to the Rhythms of a New Song

As an organization made up primarily of college-educated intellectuals (though many did not have degrees since they chose to drop out to participate in the movement full-time), RAM activists thought hard and long about the role of students and the petite bourgeoisie in the coming revolution. After charting the history and limits of black bourgeois reformism (e.g., the NAACP, the Urban League, the "so-called responsible Negro Leaders") and black bourgeois nationalism ("'Back to Africa' which is still struggling within the bonds of Western neo-colonialism, or asking for 'separate states' while White America sneers with scorn"), Askia Muhammad Toure suggested that the conditions that produced their generation also gave birth to a radical petite bourgeoisie who "identify strongly with the desires and aspirations of the black masses." This group was uniquely situated historically to "create a new synthesis from the militant, mass-oriented, universality of [Marcus] Garvey and the scientific, analytical scholarship of Du Bois"—a synthesis that would remain uncompromisingly anti-imperialist and anticapitalist. Max Stanford also recognized the revolutionary potential within certain segments of the black petite bourgeoisie, particularly among students. In his article "Revolutionary Nationalism and the Afroamerican Student," published in January of 1965, Stanford argued that black students of the "war baby" generation embodied several contradictions at once—contradictions that could lead them to embrace capitalism and white values, check out altogether, or join the revolutionary movement. The fact that racism still kept these well-educated and assimilated Negroes from fulfilling their aspirations could be either a wake-up call for the younger generation or an incentive to work harder within the system, or it could propel some into what Stanford called the "hip society." In other words, there was no guarantee that students would take the path of revolution, but the contradictions of racial capitalism and bourgeois democracy had led to the formation of a "revolutionary intelligentsia capable of leading black America to true liberation."[27]

At the same time, Stanford suggested that the most alienated segment of black working-class youth, the young men who coalesced in gangs, offered yet another rich reservoir for the revolution. "Gangs are the most dynamic force in the black community. Instead of fighting their brothers and sisters, they can be trained to fight 'Charlie.' They can be developed into a blood brotherhood (black youth army) that will serve as a liberation force in the black revolution." Like Robert Williams's musings on urban guerrilla warfare, Stanford anticipated the central themes in Greenlee's *The Spook Who Sat by the Door,* a novel (and later film) about a former black CIA agent who uses his training to turn gang members into a revolutionary army. While some might dismiss this position today as romantic, in 1965 it was entirely plausible. Stanford's piece appeared around the same time as *The Autobiography of Malcolm X,* which convinced unknown numbers of kids that even second-rate gangsters could become political radicals. Besides, the Black Panther Party in Los Angeles, founded less than two years after Stanford's article, recruited several ex-gang members into its ranks. Los Angeles Panther leaders Bunchy Carter and John Huggins were former Slausons, and their fellow banger, Brother Crook (also known as Ron Wilkins), founded the Community Alert Patrol to challenge police brutality in the late 1960s.[28]

Nevertheless, RAM itself had more success with those petit bourgeois youth willing, as African revolutionary Amilcar Cabral once put it, to commit "class suicide." These were the folks Stanford labeled "the Outlaws," the "Revolutionary black Nationalists" committed to world revolution. In May of 1964, dozens of these "outlaws" came together at the first Afro-American Student Conference on Black Nationalism on the Fisk University campus. The conference is significant, in part because it occurred before Malcolm X's address to civil rights activists in Selma—an event often regarded as a turning point in winning many young Southerners over to black nationalism. Conference participants boldly called for the development of a radical nationalist movement in the South and elsewhere, criticized civil rights leaders for "bourgeois reformism," and echoed W. E. B. Du Bois's sentiment that "capitalism cannot reform itself, a system that enslaves you cannot free you." A handful of Africans were also in attendance, including one young scholar who presented a paper on Pan-Africanism and called on black Americans to support the overthrow of "neo-colonialist puppet regimes" and the development of a socialist Africa.[29]

RAM activists wrote quite a bit about class, culture, and internationalism, but like many of their nationalist and left-wing counterparts, they had little to say about women. The revolution was clearly seen as a man's job since women barely figured in the equation. Indeed, one of the striking facts about the history of the antirevisionist Left is how male dominated it remained. Although Wanda Marshall had been one of the founding members of RAM, she apparently did not hold a national leadership post in

1964. Aside from promoting the creation of "women's leagues" whose purpose would be "to organize black women who work in white homes," RAM remained relatively silent on women's liberation.[30]

RAM's position should not be surprising given the masculinist orientation of black nationalist (not to mention the white New Left!) organizations in the 1960s, whether they were advocating civil rights or some incipient version of Black Power. The masculinism of RAM, however, was heightened by the fact that its leaders saw themselves as urban guerrillas, members of an all-black version of Mao's Red Army. Not all RAM members saw themselves this way, but those who did were deeply committed to a set of revolutionary ethics Mao laid down for his own party cadre and members of the People's Army. We see this very clearly in RAM's "Code of Cadres," a set of rules of conduct members were expected to live by. Here are some examples:

> A Revolutionary nationalist maintains the highest respect for all authority within the party. . . .

> A Revolutionary nationalist cannot be corrupted by money, honors or any other personal gains. . . .

> A Revolutionary nationalist will unhesitatingly subordinate his personal interest to those of the vanguard. . . .

> A Revolutionary nationalist will maintain the highest level of morality and will never take as much as a needle or single piece of thread, from the masses—Brother and Sisters will maintain the utmost respect for one another and will never misuse or take advantage of one another for personal gain—and will never misinterpret, the doctrine of revolutionary nationalism for any reason.[31]

The similarities with *Quotations from Chairman Mao Tse-tung* are striking. The last example comes straight out of Mao's "Three Main Rules of Discipline," which urges the cadre to "not take a single needle or piece of thread from the masses." Selflessness and total commitment to the masses is another theme that dominates *Quotations*. Again, the comparisons are noteworthy: "At no time and in no circumstances," says Mao, "should a Communist place his personal interests first; he should subordinate them to the interests of the nation and of the masses. Hence, selfishness, slacking, corruption, seeking the limelight, and so on are most contemptible, while selflessness, working with all one's energy, whole-hearted devotion to public duty, and quiet hard work will command respect."[32]

RAM's emphasis on revolutionary ethics and moral transformation, in theory at least, resonated with black religious traditions, and, like the Nation of Islam, its members preached self-restraint, order, and discipline. It is quite possible that, in the midst of a counterculture that embodied elements of hedonism and drug use, a new wave of student and working-class radicals found Maoist ethics attractive. Max Stanford offered a withering critique of what he called the "hip society," black youth caught between ghetto realities and white aspirations. Although he saw that these contradictions in black youth culture were produced by frustration and alienation, he characterized their world as "hedonistic" and "built on extreme pleasure seeking." He noted somewhat disdainfully that "Adherents of the hip society release themselves by being 'hard,' digging jams (listening to jazz records), 'getting off' (releasing frustration through dancing to rock 'n' roll), smoking pot, tasting (heavy drinking), 'doing the thing or taking care of business' (loose sex morals, sometimes sex orgies)."[33]

For many black revolutionaries, including those not directly linked to RAM, the moral and ethical dimension of Mao's thought centered on the notion of personal transformation. On his return from China in 1969, Robert Williams insisted that all young black activists "undergo personal and moral transformation. There is a need for a stringent revolutionary code of moral ethics. Revolutionaries are instruments of righteousness."[34] It was a familiar lesson embodied in the lives of Malcolm X and (later) George Jackson: each must possess the revolutionary will to transform *himself*. (These narratives are almost exclusively male despite the growing number of memoirs by radical black women.) Whether or not RAM members lived by the "Code of Cadres," Maoist ethics ultimately served to reinforce Malcolm X's status as a revolutionary role model.

Self-transformation through some kind of cultural revolution was a central tenet in RAM's ideology. As early as 1964, during the nationalist student conference at Fisk, activists in RAM agreed that "a fundamental cultural revolution or re-Africanization of black people in America was a prerequisite for a genuine Black Revolution." They spoke of "re-Africanization" in terms of a rejection of western materialism in favor of an essential African communalism, humanism, and spiritualism that, many insisted, was intrinsic to traditional African society.[35] Of course, the effort to "re-Africanize," at least in the post–World War II period, predates RAM. Black women singers such as Abbey Lincoln, Odetta, and Nina Simone not only began wearing short "Afros" or "naturals" during the early 1960s but identified with the African liberation movement and the African American cultural interest in Africa through the formation of groups such as the American Society of African Culture (AMSAC). Even *Ebony, Jet,* and *Sepia* magazines were covering Africa, and African publications such as *Drum* were being read by black people in the United States who could get their hands on it. An African American celebration of Africa found voice in pianist Randy Weston's album *Uhuru Afrika;* Max Roach's *We Insist: Freedom Now Suite* (featuring Abbey Lincoln, Roach's wife); Art Blakey's "Message from Kenya" and "Ritual"; and John Coltrane's "Liberia," "Dahomey Dance," and "Africa." Indeed, as early as 1962, Harold Cruse predicted that in the coming years "Afro-Americans . . . will undoubtedly make a lot of noise in militant demonstrations, cultivate beards and sport their hair in various degrees of la mode au naturel, and tend to be cultish with African- and Arab-style dress."[36]

Yet, while RAM's call for "re-Africanization" reflected a growing trend within elements of black youth culture, particularly among nationalist-minded intellectuals and artists, the very idea that culture was one of the most important terrains on which to make revolution was given a boost when China declared its own Great Proletarian Cultural Revolution in 1966. Of course, Mao meant something different when he launched the Cultural Revolution in China—he was proposing a vision of society where divisions between the powerful and powerless are blurred, where status and privilege don't necessarily distinguish leaders from the led. Thus while Mao's call for a Cultural Revolution meant getting rid of the vestiges (cultural and otherwise) of the old order, black radicals like Robert Williams (now publishing the *Crusader* from China) were talking about purging black culture of a "slave mentality." Less than a year into the Cultural Revolution, Williams published an article in the *Crusader* entitled "Reconstitute Afro-American Art to Remold Black Souls" which was widely circulated among RAM members. Williams's essay sought to build on the idea rather than on the ideology of the Cultural Revolution. He called on black artists to cast off the shackles of the old traditions and only make art in the service of revolution.[37] Likewise, *Some Questions concerning the Present Period,* an internal RAM document circulated in 1967, called for a full-scale black cultural revolution in the United States whose purpose would be to destroy the "conditioned white oppressive mores, attitudes, ways, customs, philosophies, habits, etc., which the oppressor has taught and trained us to have. This means on a mass scale a new revolutionary culture." It also meant an end to processed hair, skin lighteners, and other symbols of parroting the dominant culture. Indeed, the revolution targeted not only assimilated bourgeois Negroes but their accomplices—barbers and beauticians!

A Universal Dream That Haunts Their Wretched Nights

Although RAM persisted for years as an underground organization, it was brought into the public eye about 1966 when the mainstream press published a series of exposés. A particularly inflammatory piece in *Life* magazine identified RAM as one of the leading extremist groups "Plotting a War on Whitey." The "Peking-backed" group was not only considered armed and dangerous, but "impressively well read in revolutionary literature—from Marat and Lenin to Mao, Che Guevera and Frantz Fanon."[38] (The Harlem Branch of the Progressive Labor Party responded to the articles with a pamphlet entitled *The Plot against Black America,* which argued that China was not financing revolution, just setting a revolutionary example by its staunch anti-imperialism. The real causes of black rebellion, it insisted, could be found in the conditions of ghetto life.)[39] Not surprisingly, these highly publicized articles were followed by a series of police raids on the homes of RAM members in Philadelphia and New York City. In June of 1967, RAM members were rounded up and charged with conspiracy to instigate a riot, poison police officers with potassium cyanide, and assassinate Roy Wilkins and Whitney Young! A year later, under the repressive atmosphere of the FBI's Counter Intelligence Program (COINTELPRO), RAM transformed itself into the Black Liberation Party or the African American Party of National Liberation. By 1969, RAM had for the most part dissolved, though its members opted to "melt back into the community and infiltrate existing Black organizations," continue to push the twelve-point program, and develop study groups that focused on the "Science of Black Internationalism, and the thought of Chairman Rob [Robert Williams]."[40]

COINTELPRO operations only partly explain the dissolution of RAM. Some of its members moved on to other organizations, such as the Republic of New Africa and the Black Panther Party. But RAM's declining membership and ultimate demise can be partly attributed to strategic errors on its part. Indeed, its members' understanding of the current situation in the ghettos and their specific strategies of mobilization suggest that they were not very good Maoists after all. Mao's insistence on the protracted na-

ture of revolution was not taken to heart, evidenced by their pronouncement that a war for liberation might be won in ninety days. And because
RAM leaders focused their work on confronting the state head-on and attacking black leaders they deemed reformists, they failed to build a strong
base in black urban communities.

On the other hand, RAM was hardly a failure. While it never received
the glory or publicity bestowed on groups like the Black Panther Party, its
influence far exceeded its numbers—not unlike the African Blood Brotherhood (ABB) four decades earlier. Indeed, like the ABB, RAM's success
ought to be measured in terms of its theoretical contributions and its agit-
prop work; its publications and forums consistently placed the black freedom movement in an international context, drew powerful analogies
between the black condition in the United States and that of colonized
people throughout the world, offered incisive critiques of capitalism and
bourgeois democracy aimed at black urban communities, and elevated revolutionary black nationalism to a position of critical theoretical importance
for the Left in general. And by placing a critique of neocolonialism and imperialism at the center of their theory, RAM militants never agonized over
whether to support reactionary black regimes in Africa or the Caribbean.
They flatly rejected unconditional racial unity and developed a nationalism
built on a broader concept of revolutionary Third World solidarity. In
many respects, RAM served as a model for later radical black nationalist organizations, including the Black Panther Party, the African Liberation Support Committee, the Youth Organization for Black Unity, the All-African
People's Revolutionary Party, the Pan-African People's Organization, and
the Black Workers Congress.

More than anything, RAM contributed mightily to a nearly forgotten
tradition in black radicalism. This tiny group of young, mostly male, intellectuals insisted on putting the "inter" back into black nationalist discourse
and elevating it to a position of political importance. They fought for the
ghettos of North America but saw their struggle in terms of the entire
globe. Their Goliath was the entire western world, not just Kennedy and
Johnson or even the Rockefellers. And they entered into battle with a sense
that victory was inevitable, for not even the ruling class could control the
weather. "How long does the white 'Free World' have before the Gong of
History announces the Storm? Who knows in terms of days, months, in
terms of years? One thing is certain: it is coming as surely as the Great Sun
rises in the East and lights up the planet, dispelling the foggy mists and
murky darkness of the long, cold, miserable Night."[41]

NOTES

1. Of course, there are exceptions. Some excellent examples of scholarship that examines the international dimensions of the domestic black freedom struggle are Brenda Gayle Plummer, *Rising Wind: Black Americans and U.S. Foreign Affairs, 1935–1960* (Chapel Hill, N.C., 1996); Penny von Eschen, *Race against Empire* (Ithaca, N.Y., 1997); William Sales Jr., *From Civil Rights to Black Liberation: Malcolm X and the Organization of Afro-American Unity* (Boston, 1994); Azza Salama Layton, *International Politics and Civil Rights Policies in the United States, 1941–1960* (Cambridge, 2000).

2. The recent publication of Timothy B. Tyson, *Radio Free Dixie: Robert Williams and the Roots of Black Power* (Chapel Hill, N.C., 1999) represents one of the more significant book-length challenges to this narrative.

3. The impact of these events on African American politics is well documented. For a discussion of how these developments in Africa reshaped postwar black politics in the United States, see especially von Eschen, *Race against Empire;* Plummer, *Rising Wind;* Bernard M. Magubane, *The Ties That Bind: African-American Consciousness of Africa* (Trenton, N.J., 1987); Joseph E. Harris, ed., *Global Dimensions of the African Diaspora* (Washington, D.C., 1982); Immanuel Geiss, *The Pan-African Movement* (London, 1974); Robert Weisbord, *Ebony Kinship: Africa, Africans, and the Afro-American* (Westport, Conn., 1973); P. Olisanwuch Esedebe, *Pan-Africanism: The Idea and Movement, 1776–1963* (Washington, D.C., 1982).

4. Van Gosse, *Where the Boys Are: Cuba, Cold War America and the Making of a New Left* (London, 1993), pp. 147–48; LeRoi Jones [Baraka], "Cuba Libre," in his *Home: Social Essays* (1966; Hopewell, N.J., 1998), pp. 11–62; Komozoi Woodard, *A Nation within a Nation: Amiri Baraka (LeRoi Jones) and Black Power Politics* (Chapel Hill, N.C., 1998), pp. 52–63.

5. Harold Cruse, "Negro Nationalism's New Wave," *New Leader* (1962), reprinted in his *Rebellion or Revolution?* (New York, 1968), p. 73.

6. Most of the biographical material on Williams comes from Tyson, *Radio Free Dixie;* Marcellus C. Barksdale, "Robert Williams and the Indigenous Civil Rights Movement in Monroe, North Carolina, 1961," *Journal of Negro History* 69 (Spring 1984): 73–89; as well as Williams's own writings and interviews, particularly Robert F. Williams, *Negroes with Guns* (New York, 1962); Robert Williams, *Listen, Brother* (New York, 1968); "Interview: Robert Williams," *Black Scholar* 1, no. 7 (May 1970); Kalamu ya Salaam, "Robert Williams: Crusader for International Solidarity," *Black Collegian* 8, no. 3 (January–February 1978).

7. *Crusader* 2, no. 6 (August 20, 1960); *Crusader* 2, no. 21 (December 31, 1960).

8. Williams, *Negroes with Guns*, p. 120.

9. "Robert F. Williams: Interview," *Black Scholar* 1, no. 7 (May 1970): 5.

10. Harold Cruse, "Revolutionary Nationalism and the Afro-American," *Studies on the Left* (1962), reprinted in his *Rebellion or Revolution?*, pp. 74–75.

11. *Crusader* 8, no. 4 (May 1967); Maxwell C. Stanford, "Revolutionary Action Movement: A Case Study of an Urban Revolutionary Movement in Western Capitalist Society," master's thesis, Atlanta University, 1986, pp. 75–80.

12. Donald Freeman, "The Cleveland Story," *Liberator* 3, no. 6 (June 1963): 7, 18.

13. See also Gerald Horne, *Communist Front?: The Civil Rights Congress, 1946–1956* (London and Toronto, 1988).

14. Ernest Allen Jr., interview with author, June 8, 1997; Huey P. Newton, *Revolutionary Suicide* (New York, 1974), pp. 71–72.

15. *Crusader* 8, no. 4 (May 1967); Stanford, "Revolutionary Action Movement," 75–80.

16. Conversations with Michael Simmons and Tony Monteiro, October 24, 1998, Philadelphia.

17. Freeman, "The Cleveland Story," 18; Donald Warden, "The California Revolt," *Liberator* 3, no. 3 (March 1963): 15; Ernest Allen Jr., interview with author, June 8, 1997.

18. Stanford, "Revolutionary Action Movement," 197.

19. "Queen Mother" Audley Moore, interview with Mark Naison and Ruth Prago, Oral History of the American Left, Tamiment Library, New York University; Grace Lee Boggs, *Living for Change* (Minneapolis, 1997), p. 134; Stanford, "Revolutionary Action Movement," 40; interview with Tim Schermerhorn, conducted by Betsy Esch.

20. *Crusader* 5, no. 4 (May–June, 1964); *Crusader* 9, no. 2 (September–October 1967).

21. Cited in Stanford, "Revolutionary Action Movement," 79.

22. Ibid., 205–6.

23. Max Stanford, "The Colonial War at Home," *Monthly Review* (1964); Rolland Snellings (Askia Muhammad Toure), "Afro American Youth and the Bandung World," *Liberator* 5, no. 2 (February 1965): 4.

24. RAM, *The World Black Revolution,* pamphlet, 1966.

25. *Black America* (1965): 147.

26. RAM, *The World Black Revolution,* 5–7; on Roy's debate with Lenin, see Manabendra Nath Roy, *M. N. Roy's Memoirs* (Bombay and New York, 1964), pp. 378; John Haithcox, *Communism and Nationalism in India: M. N. Roy and Comintern Policy, 1920–1939* (Princeton, N.J., 1971), pp. 14–15; D. C. Grover, *M. N. Roy: A Study of Revolution and Reason in Indian Politics* (Calcutta, 1973), pp. 2–13. Roy's theses are available in V. B. Karnik, *M. N. Roy: A Political Biography* (Bombay, 1978), pp. 107–10. For Lenin's views on Roy's supplementary theses, see "The Report of the Commission on the National and Colonial Questions, July 26, 1920," in *Lenin on the National and Colonial Questions: Three Articles* (Peking, 1967), pp. 30–37.

27. Snellings (Askia Muhammad Toure), "Afro American Youth and the Bandung World," 6; Max Stanford, "Revolutionary Nationalism and the Afroamerican Student," *Liberator* 5, no. 1 (January 1965): 13–14.

28. Stanford, "Revolutionary Nationalism and the Afroamerican Student," 14–15; Mike Davis, *City of Quartz: Excavating the Future in Los Angeles* (New York and London, 1990), p. 297. We might also point out the role gang leaders played after the 1992 Los Angeles rebellion in drafting and proposing the first viable plan of action to rebuild South Central Los Angeles. Alexander Cockburn, "Beat the Devil," *Nation* 254, no. 21 (June 1, 1992): 738–39.

29. Don Freeman, "Nationalist Student Conference," *Liberator* 4, no. 7 (July

1964): 18; Stanford, "Revolutionary Action Movement," 91. Clearly, RAM conferees had been influenced by Julius Nyerere's "Arusha Declaration" of 1964, which proclaimed Tanzania an African socialist nation and attempted to establish a collectively run national economy based on communal villages. Three excellent critiques of "Ujamaa" and Nyerere's romantic notion of African communalism are Issa Shivji, *Class Struggles in Tanzania* (New York, 1976); A. M. Babu, *African Socialism or Socialist Africa?* (London, 1981); Arnold Temu and Bonaventure Swai, *Historians and Africanist History: A Critique* (London, 1983).

30. Stanford, "The Revolutionary Action Movement," 110.

31. Ibid.

32. Mao Tse-tung, *Quotations from Chairman Mao Tse-tung* (Peking, 1966), pp. 256, 269.

33. Stanford, "Revolutionary Nationalism and the Afroamerican Student," 13.

34. "Robert Williams: Interview," *Black Scholar* 1, no. 7 (May 1970): 14.

35. Freeman, "Nationalist Student Conference," 18; Stanford, "Revolutionary Action Movement," 91.

36. See Robin D. G. Kelley, "Nap Time: Historicizing the Afro," *Fashion Theory* 1, no. 4 (1997): 339–52; Cruse quote from his *Rebellion or Revolution?*, p. 73.

37. *Crusader* 9, no. 1 (July 1967).

38. R. Sackett, "Plotting a War on Whitey: Extremist Set for Violence," *Life* 60 (June 10, 1966): 100–100B.

39. Harlem Branch of the Progressive Labor Party, *The Plot against Black America* (New York, 1965), p. 147. See also A. B. Spellman, "The Legacy of Malcolm X," *Liberator* 5, no. 6 (June 1965): 13, which also challenges the press's attacks on RAM.

40. Washington, D.C., *Afro-American,* July 1, 1967; Stanford, "Revolutionary Action Movement," 210–15; "Robert Williams: Interview," *Black Scholar* 1, no. 7 (May 1970): 5–7, 14.

41. Snellings (Toure), "Afro American Youth and the Bandung World," 4.

4

Reflecting Black: Zimbabwe and U.S. Black Nationalism

Gerald Horne

Brian Raftopoulous was defined as "coloured" in Rhodesia, being of both African and European ancestry. "In the early '70s," he declared, "coinciding with the Black Power movement in America, there were many youngsters here who identified with that. The Afro, which I still wear today, the salute, the books—a lot of Malcolm X infiltrated into this community, I assure you. . . . We needed something like that to identify with, rather than the immediate black nationalism." "Brian's right," agreed Eugene Raftopoulous, who was also "coloured," though he quickly added, "Looking back [to the period before independence], the black power movement . . . created an identity for the guys. It was a tremendous thing in its time, and the Malcolm Xs of this world have a place in history, certainly. But now," he concluded tellingly, "the Lumumbas mean more to me than the Malcolm Xs do."[1]

John Ya-Otto, an African from Namibia, reflected the experience of many in the region. When he was growing up in this south Africa colony, he "knew only African singers such as Dorothy Masuka and Miriam Makeba but later . . . American pop music invaded Namibia. The Mills Brothers, the Everly Brothers, Pat Boone and Elvis; we played their records over and over again until we knew the words of every song, if not their meanings."[2]

While visiting south-central Africa in the 1950s, Doris Lessing found "sickening racial attitudes." Yet, somehow, this did not preclude many among this same European minority from loving Eartha Kitt: "they simply could not get enough of her."[3]

★

From its beginning as a colony in the 1890s, Rhodesia—a British colony that was rechristened Zimbabwe on its independence in 1980—had been influenced by currents flowing from the United States. Citizens from the United States had their most profound impact on the European minority of Rhodesia, with whom they shared anticommunism; racial solidarity and mutual unease with the pace of change on the racial front; a common language; a common "settler" project and traceable heritage—these factors and others bound many from the Pan-European world, most notably the United States, with Rhodesia. Their impact increased as the means of communication—television, trans-Atlantic telephone, short-wave radio, and so on—burgeoned.

However, the influence of the United States in southern Africa was not limited to the European minority. The images from films and magazines, the sounds from radios and records, the visits from touring artists and political figures—all this and more had significant impact on Africans.

Much of this impact was a result of the increasing role of African Americans in U.S. life and culture—a direct result of the civil rights movement. It had its positive effects, as the victories won by African Americans were suggestive of what Africans themselves could accomplish.[4] However, the African American struggle was evolving in a nation where anticommunism was prominent and inevitably impacted the trajectory of that struggle.[5] In the nation that became Zimbabwe, anticommunism frequently pushed the liberation forces away from natural allies in South Africa and elsewhere, thereby retarding the devolution of white supremacy. When the relationship of African Americans to liberation struggles in southern Africa is bruited, often much is made about the concord and mutual agreement between forces on both sides of the Atlantic. This is not necessarily inaccurate but it does not provide a complete picture. One purpose of this article is to correct this imbalance.

For the fact is that there have been peaks and valleys in the relationship between Africans and African Americans.[6] Having said that, the fact remains that an essential element of black nationalism in the United States—however defined—has been a relationship of some sort to Africa. This black nationalism has taken many forms and did so once more during the war that led to the creation of Zimbabwe. Two aspects of African Americans' relationship to Zimbabwe's struggle will be touched on here: one concerns the initiatives of more conservative African Americans who attempted to influence events across the Atlantic; the other touches on the concord between black nationalism and the forces that prevailed in the first all-race election in Zimbabwe in 1980.

★

The relationship of black nationalism in the United States to the African nation of Zimbabwe in particular provides a useful case study. Two primary independent movements formed in Rhodesia: the Zimbabwe African Peoples Union (ZAPU) and the Zimbabwe African National Union (ZANU), which came on the scene some years after the former. Like its comrade in arms, the African National Congress (ANC) of South Africa, ZAPU pursued a decidedly nonracial course. ZANU, on the other hand, was not averse to targeting "whites" qua "whites"; nor were they necessarily forthcoming toward other minorities. In October 1976, when negotiations commenced to end the war that had begun after an illegal declaration of independence by the European minority in 1965, all delegations present had "coloured" representation—including that of the outlaw regime—except for that of ZANU.[7]

ZANU was perceived in the United States as being more avowedly black nationalist and more in tune with proponents of this ideology in the United States than ZAPU. ZANU emerged triumphant in 1980 during the elections that led to independence; it absorbed ZAPU in a merger and has ruled Zimbabwe to this day. Strikingly, despite its antiwhite rhetoric, ZANU was seen by the U.S. government as less of a threat than ZAPU, not least because of the latter's relationship to the Cold War foe, the Soviet Union. This was not unlike the situation in southern California in the 1960s when the authorities seemed to harbor more hostility to the Black Panther Party, which rejected narrow nationalism and targeting whites qua whites, than to its antagonists, the cultural nationalists grouped around Maulana Ron Karenga.[8]

Thus, Sir Michael Palliser of Britain's Foreign Office agreed that "we had an objective beyond an immediate element. It was to limit the expanding Russian influence in that part of the world. In which case, even though [ZANU's] Mugabe himself was avowedly a Marxist-Leninist, you were inclined to discount that because of his 'difficult' relationship with the Russians." Lord Carrington, the chief British negotiator at the time of the war's conclusion, agreed that "Mr. Mugabe's coming to power, the man without Soviet patronage, actually helps to secure [British] interest[s]."[9] Another leading British official, Lord Soames, agreed, adding that "Mugabe's victory was the best thing that could have happened, since . . . [ZAPU] would have let the Russians in."[10]

Like its black nationalist counterparts in the United States, ZANU was quite critical of Communists; ironically this tendency made it more acceptable to many whites who its members otherwise vilified. Also like its U.S. counterparts, ZANU had a reputation for hypermasculinity, a tendency that has manifested itself repeatedly during the tenure of President Robert Mugabe in his frequent references to gays and lesbians as "pigs" not deserving of equal rights.[11]

Still, as the remarks of Brian and Eugene Raftopoulous suggest, there are differences between the struggles of an African minority in the United States and an African majority in Africa. In the former case, American unions were on the decline and, as a partial result, a heavy emphasis evolved on "race" and "guys."[12] This trend shows in the popularity of the sect Malcolm X helped to build, the Nation of Islam, which demonized whites; it is also apparent in a decided masculinist emphasis that reinforced a tendency in southern Africa—which was helped along by the cruelty of the war that gripped Zimbabwe in the 1960s and 1970s—to exalt armed struggle to the detriment of other tactics, such as the kind of mass mobilization seen in neighboring South Africa.[13]

In Rhodesia, the number of Europeans who would ally with the liberation forces was quite small, so it was not as if African American nationalism diverted potential allies from the liberation movement; however, this ideology did complicate relations, in particular with the multiracial African National Congress of South Africa and its principal backers.

American "Negroes" did not appear in this part of Africa for the first time in the 1960s. Black American missionaries had been present from the colony's beginnings, and in 1897, Peter Jackson, "an American Negro" born in Philadelphia, somehow wound up guarding a chain gang in Rhodesia— his plight indicating that African Americans too had continued moving west after the closing of the frontier in their country.[14] The Council on African Affairs, led by Paul Robeson, W. E. B. Du Bois, and W. A. Hunton, concentrated heavily on southern Africa for over two decades until the council's demise in the mid-1950s, a victim of the United States's harassment of "communist fronts."[15] Still, it was clear that there was a synergy between the struggles in the United States and the region: a 1964 "discussion meeting" at the elite Council on Foreign Relations in New York City cautioned that "the extent to which the rest of the world believes that American policy is guided by . . . [democratic] values is influenced by, among other things, the status of the Negro within the United States. The African and the American Negro are taking greater interest in the status of one another. This creates pressures on the U.S. government from both Africans and American Negroes."[16]

Still, the ouster of Robeson, Du Bois, and others from influence on African Americans set the stage for the rise of those more in tune with the rightward shift that the United States was experiencing. More African Americans took more interest in the African states, and more of them both traveled and moved there permanently in the final decades of the twentieth century. But not all exploits of African Americans in Africa were helpful to the cause of liberation.

After Mozambican independence in 1975 and Rhodesia's formation of an army to overthrow the Maputo regime there, even the mercenary journal *Soldier of Fortune* was struck by "the appearance for the first time—of several American blacks within the ranks of the Mozambique based *terrorist army.*"[17] But as early as 1964 Leo Aldridge, "an American citizen . . . born in Pittsburg, Texas," who had been "wreaking havoc" in the ranks, was expelled from the Front for the Liberation of Mozambique (FRELIMO); he claimed that he was of Mozambican origin.[18] The CIA also "had penetration of the U.S.-educated Mozambicans. One of the key people in this regard was Jose Massinga, who would later admit in 1981 . . . to being a CIA agent." A key anti-FRELIMO operative, Luis Serapiao, was a professor at the historically black Howard University in Washington, D.C.[19] Typical of U.S.-backed agents, Serapiao and his comrades focused heavily on the race and color question in Mozambique, ironically targeting Janet Mondlane, the Euro-American widow of national hero Eduoard Mondlane. The "fact that a number of FRELIMO's leaders were white, Asian or [mestizo]" was used to "discredit the leadership . . . with black nationalist students." Serapiao's group, RENAMO (Mozambican National Resistance), collaborated closely with an "American Robert MacKenzie, a mercenary serving as one of the top commanders of Rhodesia's Special Air Service" who was in charge of "support operations" for them. MacKenzie, typically, was a Vietnam War veteran and a *Soldier of Fortune* correspondent.

One of the six founding members of RENAMO was Leo Milas, an African American: a "mysterious figure who had infiltrated FRELIMO in the early 1960s."[20] This Mozambican intrigue was an extension of what some African Americans had done in Rhodesia. J. A. Parker, another African American, was often found in Salisbury, dining with Ian Smith and his wife. In addition to heading a U.S. group called "Friends of the FBI," he labored for Pretoria as a "public relations agent for the unrecognized 'independent' South African homeland of Transkei" and, later, Venda.[21]

Parker's activity was equaled, if not surpassed, by that of Ralph Moss—yet another pro-Salisbury African American. He was quite conservative and found even Bishop Abel Muzorewa, who collaborated with Rhodesian leader Ian Smith, too radical for his tastes. "He wants to [be] the head of some new state Zimbabwe," sniffed Moss in a Durban interview.

"Waal," he drawled, "if the good Bishop ever does come to power that's what Rhodesia will be—a ruin like Zimbabwe." He was a self-professed freelance journalist—though he rarely seemed to publish anything—and political consultant. By the autumn of 1977 Moss—who had been born in the United States in 1945—had been living in Rhodesia for nine months. He had come there due to a "chance meeting" with a Rhodesia information officer in Washington. After this encounter he flew to Geneva to meet with Ian Smith; "he and I got on very well together," said Moss, so he packed his bags and moved to Salisbury.[22]

There he became a propagandist for the rebel regime. He released a 45 rpm record, "It's Rhodesia . . . Please Listen," which was released in Salisbury. On this recording, Moss spoke in his thick U.S. accent against sanctions and with high praise for the Smith regime. It is uncertain if there was any profit from this venture, which was aimed at a U.S. audience.[23]

Why would African Americans support a regime that symbolized to many the highest stage of white supremacy? Moss, Parker, and those of that ilk felt they were backing a regime that symbolized the highest stage of anticommunism. The virtue of this latter ideology was that it offered a broader base of support and did not carry the obvious downside of a racially based ideology.

As a consequence, these African Americans were also useful to the Smith regime in helping to assail Andrew Young and the Carter administration; thus, Clay Claiborne, "national director of the Black Silent Majority Committee, an anti-communist pro-American group" was especially critical of the U.S. administration during his sojourn in Salisbury.[24] When African Americans attacked Young and Carter, their criticisms carried more weight in the eyes of some than those made by Euro-American conservatives.

Thus Salisbury was buzzing when Bayard Rustin, a former aide to Dr. Martin Luther King Jr., arrived in 1979 with a delegation from Freedom House in New York City to place their imprimatur on the internal settlement that temporarily created the hybrid "Zimbabwe-Rhodesia" government. Rustin's sympathetic biographer noted that they "were about the only observers who thought the elections were free and fair."[25] Of course, Rustin, who had his own disputes and difficulties with black nationalists in the United States, was hardly predisposed to provide support for their counterparts in Zimbabwe.

Still, Rustin was one of many African Americans who traveled to Rhodesia, often in the face of fierce opposition from liberation forces. This list included Imam Abdul Malik Bashir Rushiddin of the World Community of Islam in the West—an offshoot of the Nation of Islam—who came to meet with Ndabaningi Sithole, a leading Zimbabwean nationalist.[26]

American entertainers also began to travel to Africa, for example, Percy Sledge, the singer best known for the song "When a Man Loves a Woman." The liberation forces felt he did not show his "love" for their nation when he toured Bulawayo in 1972. Sledge was puzzled as to why the concert promoters were seeking to keep him away from Africans. "I don't know why they are hiding me. I want to see my people," he said, referring to Africans, not the minority population. Born in Alabama in 1942, Sledge confessed that he had not broken the "cultural boycott" of Rhodesia because of his desperation for money. "I have been a multimillionaire," he said with pride. In any event, Sledge did manage to make contact with the Africans during his stay; while a reporter was interviewing him, his telephone kept ringing with—apparently—fans of his on the line.[27]

Of course, Sledge, Moss, Parker, and all the rest were far from representing the mainstream of African American opinion on Rhodesia; African Americans had voted en masse for Jimmy Carter in 1976, and their organizations fully expected him to pressure Salisbury relentlessly until majority rule became a reality. Still, there were reasons for the liberation forces to be somewhat dubious of even the best intentioned in the United States. In 1979 Henry Richardson, a progressive African American lawyer, was forced to depart from the White House's National Security Council after clashing with Zbigniew Brzezinski; Richardson was disappointed with the low level of pressure his government had exerted on Rhodesia.[28] Shortly after that, it was reported that "the CIA was attempting to staff its African operations by soliciting the support of black psychologists at Howard."[29] In sum, it was more than rank paranoia that caused some liberation forces to look suspiciously at the growing numbers of African Americans who were flooding into south-central Africa in the late 1970s.

At the same time, it was apparent that the United States was also seeking to use its belated opposition to second-class citizenship for Negroes in order to impress Africans; this sly tactic was clear even before November 1965, when the white minority in "Rhodesia" made a Unilateral Declaration of Independence (UDI) from British colonial rule. In a typical example, when American civil rights leader James Farmer was hosted by the U.S. consul-general at a luncheon at the Jameson Hotel in Salisbury, he was touted as a "Methodist leader" by a Methodist journal. It displayed a large picture of him pointing his finger as he proclaimed that racial segregation was "doomed."[30]

Early on Washington recognized not only that it could use the publicity generated by the civil rights movement to its credit but, likewise, could use it to positively differentiate its policy from those of its erstwhile allies— Western Europe—and actual antagonists—the Soviet Union. As early as 1963, ZAPU noticed that, as more African students were traveling to Eastern Europe to receive higher education, the United States stepped up its campaign to offer scholarships to Africans. This, warned ZAPU, has "superceded [*sic*] even [American] considerations on economic development."[31]

ZAPU members had personal reasons to be aware of this policy. Joshua Nkomo, a leader of the liberation forces, himself had two children enrolled in school in the United States; he also worked closely with the African American Institute in New York City, which was known to maintain close ties with the U.S. government.[32] Gordon Chavunduka, a leading intellectual who later headed the University of Zimbabwe, attended mission schools until 1962 when he received a Rockefeller Foundation scholarship that allowed him to spend three years at the University of California.[33]

Of course, southern African intellectuals' receiving education in the United States was nothing new. Alfred B. Xuma, a leading South African oppositional figure, had attended Tuskegee Institute in Alabama, the University of Minnesota, Marquette University in Wisconsin, and Northwestern University in Illinois; his first wife was Liberian—probably Americo-Liberian—and his second wife was from North Carolina.[34] Stanleke Samkange, the leading Zimbabwean intellectual, attended Indiana University, and his wife too hailed from the United States.[35] Obtaining education and a spouse in the United States was reflective of a time when the United States was seen as being more advanced—relatively—than its European counterparts in its attitude toward Africans.

This perception gave Washington an advantage over London in the eyes of many Africans. Even before World War I, U.K. firms had a pointed "dread that certain British commercial firms in the Gold Coast" would have to face "commercial competition" from African American and other competitors.[36] Nevertheless, other factors came into play too. Before the 1952 Mau-Mau rebellion in Kenya, "the Kenyan government tried to prohibit any more students from [going] to the United States where they would be subject to 'Communist subversion.'"[37]

During that same period, U.S. religious authorities also worried that Africans—like Ndabaningi Sithole—who were coming to North America for religious training would become "deliberate target[s] of the very small proportion of American Negroes who are Communists." Mentioned specifically was Paul Robeson, who was a founder of the soon-to-be-vanquished Council on African Affairs.[38]

American-British tension rose again during the latter stages of the war in Rhodesia when London accused Washington of going behind its back to devise plans to buy out farmers.[39] This incident exposed how times had changed from the days when the United States was seen as trailing behind Britain.

Though a number of leaders of the liberation forces attended university in South Africa, particularly Fort Hare, and the United Kingdom, others did cross the Atlantic for higher education. Among these students was Nathan Shamuyarira—the former journalist—who earned a doctorate from Princeton (and developed close ties with Rockefeller interests), as well as Shelton Siwela, who took a degree at Boston University.[40] Both became leaders of ZANU. Bernard Chidzero, one of the leading economic theorists among the liberation forces, had close ties in the United States.[41] Educating Africans was seen by U.S. elites as a long-term investment that could pay dividends if majority rule were to occur.

A number of African leaders also attended churches that had affiliates in the United States. Ndabaningi Sithole was trained at Andover Seminary in Massachusetts; he spent three and a half years in the United States, where he worked with the American Board of Commissioners for Foreign Missions. While there he preached in Congregational churches—the church of Andrew Young—in Boston, New York City, and Chicago. Like Young, he was a staunch critic of communism and a self-proclaimed moderate. Like some moderates in the United States, he spoke glowingly of the "positive role of colonialism."[42] Sithole—a founder of ZANU in 1963 who was expelled subsequently—was cultivated carefully by the U.S. religious authorities, who plied him with scholarships and funding: perhaps, not surprisingly, because his ideas were well within the ambit of mainstream discourse in Washington. Likewise, Sithole's articulation of cultural nationalism reflected ideological currents then flowing in the African American community. At a time when the United States was being questioned severely about its racial practices, on his return to Rhodesia in 1958 Sithole noted proudly that he was "glad . . . to correct some of the wrong impressions about the States." Indeed, "for the whole of June" he spent "most" of his "time talking about the U.S.A."[43] This was no minor matter, for by that point Sithole had attained some prominence. After his book, *African Nationalism,* was published in 1959, he claimed that "one bookshop in Salisbury . . . sold 50 copies in 2 days. In Umtali they were sold out in less than four days."[44]

The leading Zimbabwean figure, Abel Muzorewa, was a bishop in the United Methodist Church and had attended school in Columbia, Missouri, and at Central Methodist College in Fayette, Missouri, during a time when this state was pockmarked with racial segregation.[45]

This common religious background formed a basis for Andrew Young—a cleric himself—to meet such leaders. The U.S. ambassador to the United Nations during the Carter years tended to be treated harshly by liberation forces, who viewed him as something of a Trojan horse whose dark face was designed to deflect their attention away from the shortcomings of U.S. policy. But Young was not embraced by enemies on the Right either; Robin Moore felt that Carter had been induced to sell out Salisbury "in return for America's black vote which only the President's Marxist ambassador . . . could deliver."[46] From the other shore, ZAPU charged that Young, "the imperialist agent who pretends to talk our language," averred that "the solution he conceives of is that whereby the Blacks have political power" in Zimbabwe, "the Whites [*sic*] have the [economic] power."[47]

Actually, ZAPU did not distort Young's words. He had intimated such a division of power with the proviso that an independent Zimbabwe "would have the strongest economy in Africa immediately after the settlement" and the surrounding nations would be "dependent" on Harare. In such a situation, the United States, with its relationships with both educated and religiously inclined Africans and the European minority alike, would be in an advantageous position compared to its European allies and socialist antagonists alike.[48]

During the period of UDI, Muzorewa's prominent position in Rhodesia was indicative of how influential Methodists had become in the country. The Methodists were critics of the Smith government *and* supporters of Muzorewa. "The church must be the guide and critic of the State, says [Martin] Luther King," they announced, and this was an edict they sought to follow.[49]

In September 1965 in an eruption of racial militance, the Rhodesian Methodists even questioned the basis of their faith, noting, "it seems clear that the white people have no sympathy [for] us Africans. Since Jesus was a white person how can he listen and save the African race which his race hates. Is it not wise to turn to our ancestral spirits and worship them as our forefathers used to do?"[50] As a result of their challenges to the status quo, they were subjected to censorship by the government. Their view of religion through a racial lens reflected a larger trend in the nation, which also made it easier for the words of Malcolm X to resonate there.

The centrality of religion in south-central Africa and its impact on nationalism was simply one aspect reflecting U.S. influence in that part of the world. The larger question is to what extent did ideological currents from the United States sustain ethnic divisiveness.

Rhodesia—much more than South Africa—was fertile ground for the flowering of black nationalist notions ascending in the United States as the war in south-central Africa was unfolding; trade unionism was stronger historically in South Africa than Rhodesia, and the European minority there—which was substantially larger than in the northern neighbor—was more involved in liberation struggles.[51] Malcolm X was killed in 1965—as independence was proclaimed by the European minority in Rhodesia—but black nationalism in the United States did not die with him.[52]

Popular magazines directed at the African population in Rhodesia did tend to focus heavily on African Americans, disseminating ideological currents that Washington would not have found particularly objectionable. This was not true only of Rhodesia but of neighboring South Africa as well. In the latter country, *Drum* became one of the most prominent publications among Africans; during its heyday in the 1950s, it "created an impression of a highly romantic age decked out in American clothing, American drawls, American gangsterism."[53] *Parade,* published in Rhodesia, was similar to its counterpart across the Limpopo River; like *Drum* it targeted Africans though it was not controlled by them. More than this, the ideas expressed in *Parade* would have been familiar to those who followed black nationalist publications in the United States.[54]

Parade posed the conflict between the Soviet Union and China as a racial conflict;[55] played up Islam to the detriment of Communist parties in Sudan, Indonesia, and elsewhere;[56] and espoused anticommunism generally.[57] It trumpeted frequently the accomplishments of African Americans like Duke Ellington,[58] Jesse Owens,[59] George Foreman, Joe Frazier,[60] Percy Sledge,[61] and Diana Ross;[62] in fact, it tended to discuss African Americans more than Africans in other parts of Africa. Surely this was partially a function of U.S. global cultural hegemony, but that does not obscure the point that African American influence in Rhodesia was not negligible.

In South Africa, the black nationalist organization—the Pan Africanist Congress (PAC)—was an ally of ZANU, while ZAPU was allied with the ANC; yet, the PAC has performed miserably in post-1994 elections while ZANU emerged triumphant in Zimbabwe. Many of the U.S. citizens in the region at the time of the Boer War had opposed the Afrikaaners who came to dominate South Africa and found more compatibility with the

English speakers who were hegemonic in Rhodesia. This development facilitated an increase in U.S. influence—including African American influence—in Rhodesia, which accelerated during the liberation.

The *Zimbabwe News,* which reflected mainstream ZANU opinion, also reflected concepts that would have been well received in certain African American precincts. Whereas ZAPU received substantial assistance from the Soviet Union, this paper was quite critical of Moscow and what it saw as the USSR's "endless collaboration with American imperialism."[63] While Washington did not appreciate the ANC's alliance with the South African Communists, the *Zimbabwe News* was critical of the ANC for basking "in the comfort of multiracial pacifism since its foundation in 1912"; using U.S. references that some of its audience might not have understood, the newspaper expressed outrage that the ANC—"Southern Africa's oldest Uncle Tom"—would dare to attack the U.S. activist Stokely Carmichael.[64] This paper as well had high praise for "our Afro-American brothers."[65]

The nationalism of the *Zimbabwe News* was akin to its counterparts among its "Afro-American brothers." It reported on Black Power and H. Rap Brown, and its ethnocentrism meant that it could allege without qualification that "Asians themselves are to blame for the plight in which they find themselves in Kenya."[66] The paper was explicit in asserting that "Afro-Americans" were "showing innocent Africa the road to UHURU—through Black Power."[67] This nationalism merged with an admiration for China, as the paper frequently cited Chairman Mao and his assertion that "political power grows out of the barrel of a gun."[68]

From its inception, the *Zimbabwe News* was critical of the multiracial nature of ZAPU and complimentary of the "committed African Socialist" approach of ZANU.[69] ZAPU was "scared to fight," the paper suggested, while ZANU had taken advantage of the "antiwhite" attitudes of the "masses" and had been "the only liberation movement to have caused evil settlers to lose their lives."[70] This attitude was fueled among ZANU supporters by the simple fact that there were few among the European minority courageous enough to identify staunchly with majority rule. Hence, it became easier to allege that not only were there no radicals among the Europeans, there were "no liberals among settlers" either.[71]

The identification of the *Zimbabwe News* with African Americans did not arise in a vacuum. When coloureds in Rhodesia organized in 1968, their central grouping—the NACP (National Association of Coloured People)—mirrored its counterpart of a similar name in the U.S, the NAACP (National Association for the Advancement of Colored People).[72] ZANU was quite close to anti-ANC elements in South Africa, which in turn were influenced by political streams flowing from the United States, including the writings of Richard Wright.[73]

The decline of working-class organization in the United States led to the rise in influence of the African American middle-class—particularly the rise of middle-class nationalism, which was not outraged by exploitation per se but more by the fact that it was Euro-Americans and not themselves that were exploiting the masses of African Americans.[74] There was arable soil in Rhodesia for such a trend to grow. Not only were trade unions weak but, as Angela Cheater has suggested, for years Salisbury had been building an African middle class through land ownership allotted to a few, particularly during the time when the European population was comparatively tiny. Thus, by 1973 one African farmer had an "annual turnover . . . [of] Z$1 million" and "approximately 130 employees staffed [his] eight businesses."[75] When UDI occurred, there was an African middle class of some heft—particularly compared to neighboring nations.[76]

ZAPU charged frequently that ZANU's appeal was to middle-class intellectuals.[77] Of course, this stratum could also be found in the leadership ranks of ZAPU itself, but that does not obscure the differences—particularly in foreign policy—that distinguished the two groups. The contemporary Zimbabwean intellectual Ibbo Mandaza has concurred with this analysis. "African nationalism" in his homeland, he has written, "was part of the liberal-capitalist ideology"; it was "essentially the ideology of the African petit[e] bourgeoisie," which "finds it easier to mobilize the masses effectively on the basis of the racist or cultural aspects of imperialist and colonialist domination."[78]

Influencing "African nationalism" in Zimbabwe were trends flowing from the United States. The "imagination" of many coloureds and Africans "during the late 1960s" was "captured by the Black Power Movement"; it was "quite common," particularly among coloureds, to "identify 'Black' with Black Americans rather than with indigenous Africans. . . . The Black American was regarded as someone enjoying equality and affluence"; this trend was facilitated by the fact that the "physical appearance" of many African Americans was "somewhat akin to that of the Coloureds themselves." The coloureds became a prime vector for the transmission of nationalist thinking from the United States—however, they were far from being alone in this.[79]

The characterization "middle-class intellectual" befits ZANU founder Sithole and also does justice to the man most closely identified with the organization over the years, Robert Mugabe. He was born in Zvimba Reserve in

1926 and was regarded as a "true Mission boy." He was a "blue blood" and belonged to the "Zvimba chiefly clan." He was "entitled to contest for the chieftainship." He was a "real intellectual" but, until he went to Ghana, "he never knew that there was nothing wrong in fighting for your country even if you are educated," claimed one anti-ZANU organ, perhaps inaccurately. Interestingly, ZAPU, which wrestled with its own "middle-class intellectual" problem, used this label to attack Mugabe.

Mugabe, it was reported, had been a victim of "Boer" education and believed that the struggle "belonged to those who had failed in life—the uneducated, the unemployable, the spivs [sic]." At Fort Hare, he did not identify with the anticolonial struggle either, it was said—but now he knew better. When he returned home from Nkrumah's Ghana on a holiday in July 1960, he did not intend to stay, but when the voice of one of the main speakers became hoarse, the articulate Mugabe had the opportunity to address the crowd of 100,000, according to this account. Thus began his ascendancy to the highest levels of African politics. But even then he was called "proud" and "aloof. . . . He terribly lacks the common touch. He can hardly carry out a friendly conversation with people who are not of his educational level. . . . His most deadly weakness is that he looks at the struggle as a means to project his self-pride and personality." On the other hand, unlike many of his comrades, he was not "ambitious." In fact, he was "the least ambitious of all the political vultures" of ZANU; however, he would "not hesitate to wreck the organization, if his self-pride is hurt or if he is hurt personally."[80]

Though Mugabe was a Catholic, he defined himself as a Marxist-Leninist. However, ZANU's hostility toward Moscow and closeness to Beijing meant that Washington viewed him as the lesser of evils. Hence, in the spring of 1979, as elections loomed, *New York Times* columnist Anthony Lewis's report from Maputo sought to convince his readers of ZANU's legitimacy by reminding them that Moscow not only allegedly considered their leader—Mugabe—an "upstart" but backed Nkomo as well.[81]

At this juncture, China and the United States were allied against the Soviet Union and those perceived as being Moscow's surrogates. They collaborated in trying to halt the rise to power of those alleged surrogate states. Thus, in the summer of 1976 the *Washington Post* reported an extraordinary development: Chinese soldiers decamped in Tanzania—perhaps Beijing's closest ally on the continent—were helping ZANU murder opposing ZAPU cadres.[82] ZAPU itself was more explicit, charging that "Chinese military experts fired light machine guns and automatic rifles and set their dogs on the panic-stricken former ZAPU reservists." Seven died, scores were wounded. Worse, "Tanzania in delaying the investigation for so long, had in actual fact connived with ZANU to destroy material evidence. The investigation should also probe the Chinese military instructors' involvement in the massacre." Eventually, "13 bodies were exhumed. Twenty-eight . . . are still unaccounted for."[83]

The multifaceted aid that ZANU received from China and the stumbles of ZAPU itself guaranteed that the former would emerge triumphant in the elections of 1980. Repeatedly, ZAPU was accused of husbanding its forces. It claimed in response that it did not want to recklessly toss them into battle against the more experienced Rhodesian troops, but this charge stung and stuck; it reinforced ZANU's assertion that it was more willing to wield the barrel of the gun and, thus, oust the recalcitrant Rhodesians from power. ZAPU probably had less appeal in the countryside than ZANU, where the bulk of the population resided. Perhaps because of this, ZAPU disastrously engaged in negotiations at various times with Ian Smith's government—which was backed heavily by farmers.

In this ZAPU mirrored its South African ally, the ANC. Govan Mbeki has written that "in spite of the awakening of the peasants in reserves throughout the country, both the ANC and the Communist Party gave scant attention to organisation of the peasants."[84] He also has noted that the ANC's chief rival, the Pan Africanist Congress—like their ZANU ally—was led by "intellectuals" such as "Robert Sobukwe, Potlako Leballo, Peter Raboroko and Z. B. Molete."[85] Moreover, like the ANC, ZAPU was more prone to accept members from the European minority, and, in a nation where this group was largely identified with oppression and reaction, this did not necessarily endear ZAPU with the wider population.[86]

Nkomo's forces did not help themselves when they reportedly assaulted ZANU members and sympathizers after the latter's founding in 1963.[87] Viewing ZANU as a nascent PAC of South Africa, Nkomo and his allies assailed the newcomers as "tribalists and opportunists," as "political informers," and as the functional equivalent of a "snake."[88] Early in 1965 a pro-Nkomo paper wondered why he, but not ZANU's Sithole, had been banned and why the latter could hold meetings but the former could not. Why did Hastings Banda of Malawi, an ally of the United States and apartheid South Africa, back ZANU? they asked plaintively.[89]

The perception that ZAPU was allied with the chief Cold War antagonists of the United States did not help Nkomo's cause in the long run. Particularly after the defeat of U.S. allies in Angola, a hysteria arose about supposed Soviet global advances, and inevitably this hysteria became fixated on Rhodesia; that the kith and kin of Euro-Americans were implicated in this battle made this "advance" all the more sensitive—and important. In this context, the triumph of ZANU became an acceptable consolation.

Eventually ZANU and ZAPU allied in the "Patriotic Front," which became involved in talks with Rhodesia in both Switzerland and the United Kingdom—talks that led to a negotiated settlement. Still, the parties ran separately in the 1980 elections, and Washington no doubt was not displeased that ZAPU did not prevail.

It was becoming increasingly evident that the chief antagonist of the United States—the socialist bloc—favored ZAPU. Though the memorandum was not unveiled until years later, the U.S. State Department would not have been surprised by the summary of a spring 1979 meeting in Havana between the counselor of the Soviet embassy there and Cuban Communist leader Raul Valdes Vivo, whose portfolio included relations with Africa. The Cuban leader, in between noting the presence in Rhodesia of "2 thousand . . . [white] mercenaries," mentioned that his nation was "unable to satisfy [ZAPU's] request to send pilots for the repulsion of air attacks on the training camps for the Patriotic Front armed forces."[90] They were not able to come to ZAPU's aid this time by sending their own armed forces, but Cuba and the Soviet Union did not hesitate in providing all manner of military materiel—and this was not viewed benignly in Washington either.

The ANC of South Africa had similar global ties and this too irked the United States. Thomas Nkobi, the ANC treasurer, had been born in Rhodesia, which facilitated his close working relationship with ZAPU. ZAPU militants often were trained in Eastern Europe, and after independence these relationships were expected to continue.[91] Nkomo himself was in and out of the Cold War trip wire, East Berlin, quite frequently and often was photographed with Communist leader Eric Honecker.[92] That he was also known to meet frequently with executives of the U.K.-based transnational corporation Lonrho did not assuage doubts about him in Washington. The dilemma faced by ZAPU was revealed with clarity when an ally of the liberation forces, Sister Janice McLaughlin, ascribed "recent anti-Catholic tendencies" in "some groups" to the "training received in some countries," among which were the Soviet Union, Cuba, and Ethiopia.[93] When this sympathetic U.S. nun raised queries about ZAPU's alliance with the socialist bloc, it was indicative of the uphill climb that this group had to endure.

Despite these trends, the rumor persisted that Washington *favored* Nkomo over the supposedly more militant Mugabe. Thus, in the summer of 1977 it was reported that "the Anglo-American aim is that Mr. Nkomo should emerge as Zimbabwe's Prime Minister."[94] That the "Anglo-American" alliance, which had colonized Rhodesia in the first instance, backed Nkomo was not news that would help him among Africans—or with the bulk of African Americans for that matter. Such rumors may have contributed to ZAPU's smashing defeat in the elections of 1980, which led to Robert Mugabe becoming the nation's first post-independence leader—a development that effectively liquidated colonial rule. The Catholic Commission for Justice and Peace reported that physical "intimidation" had been a factor in his victory, and that ZANU had allegedly claimed that if Mugabe did not prevail, the war would continue.[95]

However, Rhodesia did not die after the election: it moved to South Africa. There, despite the historic Anglo-Boer enmity, Rhodesia was able for a while to help stave off majority rule—with the aid of old friends in the United States.

The triumph of "ZANU-PF" in Zimbabwe was remarkably congruent with contemporaneous black nationalist trends in the United States. Both carried antipathies toward multiracial alliances, both were skeptical of Nelson Mandela's African National Congress and, particularly, its alliance with the South African Communist Party. Both have had difficulty adjusting to a world where the Soviet Union no longer exists and, thus, the necessity for certain Pan-European elites to favor them in their conflicts with their domestic left-wing antagonists (e.g., the Black Panther Party or ZAPU) has been eroded. This latter tendency has been particularly evident in Zimbabwe, where black nationalism actually has held state power and, thus, has had further to fall. Yet, what has occurred in south-central Africa is of interest on this side of the Atlantic, not least because black nationalism here and there flourished at the same time. Likewise, as the future is assayed, it is sobering to realize that with the discrediting of the socialist ideal and the more troubling aspects of black nationalism, ideological options are becoming ever more narrow. On the other hand, this sobering situation may lead both Africans and African Americans to forge newer ideological options that embrace the best of the socialist and nationalist traditions, while setting aside the lamentable weaknesses of both.[96]

NOTES

1. Julie Frederiske, *None but Ourselves: Masses vs. Media in the Making of Zimbabwe* (New York, 1982), p. 239; see also John Day, *International Nationalism: The Extra-*

Territorial Relations of Southern Rhodesia African Nationalists (London, 1967); Lila Ammons, "The Consequences of War on African Countries," Ph.D. diss., University of Maryland, 1989; Peter B. Clarke, *West Africans at War, 1914–1918, 1939–1945: Colonial Propaganda and Its Cultural Aftermath* (London, 1986).

2. John Ya-Otto, *Battlefront Namibia* (Harare, 1982), p. 28.

3. Doris Lessing, *Walking in the Shade: My Autobiography, 1949–1962* (New York, 1997), p. 200.

4. In the Rhodesian Parliament in 1971 in a debate on "integration," members were told that "the Negroes" were protesting because they had been deprived for so long and there was a lesson for Salisbury to draw from this. See "Rhodesia Parliamentary Debates," March 26, 1971; see also "Rhodesia Parliamentary Debates," September 16, 1970, September 4, 1969, September 16, 1969, Box 73, *Lewis Gann-Peter Duignan Collection*.

5. See generally Gerald Horne, *Communist Front? The Civil Rights Congress, 1946–1956* (London, 1988); Gerald Horne, *Black Liberation/Red Scare: Ben Davis and the Communist Party* (Newark, Del., 1994).

6. Tunde Adeleke, *UnAfrican Americans: Nineteenth-Century Black Nationalists and the Civilizing Mission* (Lexington, Ky., 1998); Valentin Y. Mudimbe, *The Invention of Africa* (Bloomington, Ind., 1988); K. Anthony Appiah, *In My Father's House: Africa in the Philosophy of Culture* (New York, 1992).

7. Ibbo Mandaza, *Race, Colour, and Class in Southern Africa: A Study of the Coloured Question in the Context of an Analysis of the Colonial and White Settler Racial Ideology, and African Nationalism in Twentieth Century Zimbabwe, Zambia, and Malawi* (Harare, 1997), p. 750.

8. See generally Gerald Horne, *Fire This Time: The Watts Uprising and the 1960s* (Charlottesville, Va., 1995).

9. Michael Charlton, *Diplomacy and the Independence of Rhodesia* (Cambridge, 1990), pp. 9, 119, 138. The British high commissioner in Mozambique was astonished by the "conspicuous absence of the Eastern bloc" at the 1980 independence celebration of Zimbabwe: "No Russians, no Czechs, no Poles, no East Germans, no Bulgarians."

10. Hugo Young, *The Iron Lady: A Biography of Margaret Thatcher* (New York, 1989), p. 182.

11. *Los Angeles Times,* July 27, 1998.

12. See generally Horne, *Fire This Time.*

13. Claude Andrew Clegg, *An Original Man: The Life and Times of Elijah Muhammad* (New York, 1997); see also Robert Singh, *The Farrakhan Phenomenon: Race, Reaction, and the Paranoid Style in American Politics* (Washington, D.C., 1997).

14. "Criminal Court Records," 1897, D3/3/1, *NAZ.*

15. Penny von Eschen, *Race against Empire: Black Americans and Anti-Colonialism, 1937–1957* (Ithaca, N.Y., 1997).

16. "Discussion Meeting Group," February 5, 1964, *Council on Foreign Relations Archives.* See also "Records of Conferences, 'Anglo-American Conference on Southern Africa,'" 1964, *Council on Foreign Relations Archives.*

17. Al J. Venter, "Zimbabwe-Rhodesia: State of the Nation," December 1979, MS 308/44/6, *IDAF Papers, NAZ;* emphasis in original.

18. Iain Christie, *Machel of Mozambique* (Harare, 1988), p. 35. Roy Innis, an African American, and "three other CORE [Congress of Racial Equality] members . . . received Ugandan citizenship for their services" to Idi Amin's regime; see Mahmood Mamdani, *Imperialism and Fascism in Uganda* (Nairobi, 1983), p. 78. See also *New York Times,* June 27, 1973; *International Herald Tribune,* March 24–25, 1973; *Christian Science Monitor,* February 23, 1973. Amin also worked with Salisbury in training black private armies; see *Catholic Herald,* November 3, 1978, MS 308/57/7, *IDAF Papers, NAZ.*

19. Abiodun Alao, *Brothers at War: Dissidence and Rebellion in Southern Africa* (London, 1994), p. 69.

20. William Minter, *Apartheid's Contras: An Inquiry into the Roots of War in Angola and Mozambique* (London, 1994), pp. 109, 132–33, 157. It is unclear if "Leo Milas" used the name "Leo Aldridge" as a pseudonym—or vice versa.

21. Ibid.; and Frederiske, *None but Ourselves,* p. 344.

22. Clipping, October 2, 1977, MS 308/35/2, *IDAF Papers, NAZ.*

23. Ralph Moss, "It's Rhodesia . . . Please Listen," MS 536/2/3, *NAZ.*

24. *The Herald,* March 30, 1979; *The Herald,* March 31, 1979.

25. Jervis Anderson, *Bayard Rustin: The Troubles I've Seen* (New York, 1997), p. 342.

26. *The Herald,* February 2, 1978.

27. *Moto,* September 16, 1972, MF 398, *NAZ.*

28. *Africa Confidential,* January 31, 1979, MS 308/35/2, *IDAF Papers, NAZ.*

29. *Africa Confidential,* June 6, 1979, MS 308/35/4, *IDAF Papers, NAZ.*

30. *Umbowo* 24, no. 1 (February 1965): 1, *NAZ.*

31. *Zimbabwe Review* 2, no. 1 (August–September 1963): 1, *NAZ.*

32. *Daily Telegraph,* August 16, 1977.

33. *Moto,* April 29, 1972, MF 398, *NAZ;* see also Gordon Chavunduka, *Traditional Medicine in Modern Zimbabwe* (Harare, 1994).

34. Steven D. Gish, "Alfred B. Xuma, 1893–1962: African, American, South African," Ph.D. diss., Stanford University, 1994; Christopher Nyangoni, ed., *Zimbabwe Independence Movements: Select Documents* (London, 1979).

35. *Moto,* July 1965, *NAZ.*

36. Robert Hill, "Before Garvey: Chief Alfred Sam and the African Movement, 1912–1916," in *Pan-African Biography,* ed. Robert Hill (Los Angeles, 1987), pp. 57–77; quote at p. 66.

37. St. Clair Drake, "Mbiyu Koinange and the Pan African Movement," in ibid., pp. 161–207, quote at p. 184.

38. John A. Reuling to Rev. John C. Heinrich (Mt. Silinda), September 1, 1954, Box 5:20, Rhodesian Mission, 1950–1960, HL, 15.6, *American Board of Commissioners for Foreign Missions Papers.*

39. File, "Strategic Mid-East and Africa," MS 308/5/4, *IDAF Papers, NAZ.*

40. Nathan Shamuyarira, "National Liberation through Self-Reliance in Rhodesia, 1956–1972," Ph.D. diss., Princeton University, 1976.

41. *Moto,* December 1964, *NAZ.*

42. Ndabaningi Sithole, *African Nationalism* (Cape Town, 1959). See the reviews

of this book in *Central African Examiner*, July 18, 1959, and *The Herald*, August 5, 1959. Per usual, the reviewer does not refer to "whites" in this review but to "the European in Africa." In 1992 Sithole returned to Zimbabwe after "eight years of self-imposed exile in the United States." *Boston Globe*, January 26, 1992.

43. Ndabaningi Sithole to Dr. and Mrs. J. A. Rueling, July 14, 1958, Box 7:33, Rhodesia Mission, 1950–1960, HL, 15.6, *American Board of Commissioners for Foreign Missions Papers.*

44. Ndabaningi Sithole to Dr. Reuling, August 11, 1959, Box 7:33, Rhodesia Mission 1950–1960, HL, 15.6, *American Board of Commissioners for Foreign Missions Papers.*

45. Abel Muzorewa, *Rise Up and Walk: An Autobiography* (Houghton, South Africa, 1978), p. 48.

46. Advertisement for a new book by Robin Moore, October 1980, MS 536/8/2, *Julie Frederiske Papers, NAZ.*

47. *Zimbabwe Review* 7 (January 1978): 3, *NAZ.*

48. "Confidential" Intelligence Report from Rhodesia, September 1, 1977, Box 1, *Kent Crane Papers.*

49. *Umbowo,* September 1966, *NAZ.*

50. *Umbowo,* September 1965, *NAZ.*

51. Alan Mabin, ed., *Organisation and Economic Change: Southern African Studies,* vol. 5 (Johannesburg, 1989); Ronnie Kasrils, *"Armed and Dangerous": My Undercover Struggle against Apartheid* (Portsmouth, N.H., 1993).

52. Peter Goldman, *The Death and Life of Malcolm X* (Urbana, Ill., 1979); Michael Eric Dyson, *Making Malcolm: The Myth and Meaning of Malcolm X* (New York, 1995); William W. Sales Jr., *From Civil Rights to Black Liberation: Malcolm X and the Organization of Afro-American Unity* (Boston, 1994).

53. Mike Nicol, *A Good-Looking Corpse: The World of Drum—Jazz and Gangsters, Hope and Defiance in the Townships of South Africa* (London, 1995), p. 34; see also Angela Caccia, ed., *The Beat of Drum* (Johannesburg, 1983); Anthony Sampson, *Drum: An African Adventure—and Afterwards* (London, 1983).

54. Clovis E. Semmes, ed., *Roots of Afrocentric Thought: A Reference Guide to Negro Digest/Black World, 1961–1976* (Westport, Conn., 1998).

55. *Parade,* April 1966, N/S/AF 63, *NAZ.*

56. *Parade,* June 1966, N/S/AF 63, *NAZ.*

57. *Parade,* February 1979, 3, N/S/AF 63, *NAZ:* here "Marxist Islamic Iran" was denounced as a "Soviet Satellite."

58. *Parade,* May 1971, N/S/AF 63, *NAZ.*

59. *Parade,* October 1970, N/S/AF 63, *NAZ.*

60. *Parade,* March 1973, N/S/AF 63, *NAZ.*

61. *Parade,* September 1972, N/S/AF 63, *NAZ.*

62. *Parade,* June 1972, N/S/AF 63, *NAZ.*

63. *Zimbabwe News* 3, no. 15 (August 17–31, 1968), MF 460, *NAZ.*

64. *Zimbabwe News* 3, no. 19 (October 12, 1968), MF 460, *NAZ.*

65. *Zimbabwe News* 3, no. 20 (October 26, 1968), MF 460, *NAZ.*

66. *Zimbabwe News* 3, no. 4 (March 3, 1968), MF 460, *NAZ.*

67. *Zimbabwe News* 3, no. 7 (April 13, 1968), MF 460, *NAZ.*

68. *Zimbabwe News* 3, no. 8 (April 27, 1968), MF 460, *NAZ.*

69. *Zimbabwe News* 1, no. 1 (February 1965), MF 460, *NAZ.*

70. *Zimbabwe News* 1, no. 10 (August 20, 1966); see also *Zimbabwe News* 1, no. 2 (April 16, 1966), MF 460, *NAZ.*

71. *Zimbabwe News* 2, no. 8 (April 15, 1967), MF 460, *NAZ.*

72. Bridget Machine, "A Political Biography: Herbert Joseph Foya-Thompson," history honours diss., University of Cape Town, 1994, p. 95.

73. Doreen Musson, *Johnny Gomas, Voice of the Working Class: A Political Biography* (Cape Town, 1989), p. 118.

74. Ibid.; and Horne, *Fire This Time,* passim.

75. Angela P. Cheater, *Idioms of Accumulation: Rural Development and Class Formation among Freeholders in Zimbabwe* (Gweru, 1984), p. 104.

76. Michael Oliver West, "African Middle Class Formation in Colonial Zimbabwe, 1890–1965," Ph.D. diss., Harvard University, 1990.

77. Maurice Nyagumbo, *With the People: An Autobiography from the Zimbabwe Struggle* (London, 1980), p. 180. See also Patrick O'Meara, "Aspects of African Political Opposition and Political Conflict in Rhodesia with Particular Emphasis on the Period, 1961–1968," Ph.D. diss., Indiana University, 1970, p. 138.

78. Mandaza, *Race, Colour and Class,* pp. xxiv, 528, 685, 730, 731.

79. Ibid.

80. *Zimbabwe Sun,* February 15, 1964. See also David Smith et al., eds., *Mugabe* (London, 1981); Robert Mugabe, *Our War of Liberation: Speeches, Articles, Interviews, 1976–1979* (Gweru, 1983); Liberation Support Movement, ed., *Zimbabwe: The Final Advance: Documents on the Zimbabwe Liberation Movement* (Oakland, Calif., 1978).

81. *New York Times,* February 8, 1979.

82. *Washington Post,* September 17, 1976.

83. *Zimbabwe Review* 5, no. 5 (September–October 1976), *NAZ.* See also Colin Legum and Geoffrey Mmari, eds., *Mwalimu: The Influence of Nyerere* (Trenton, N.J., 1995); Josiah Magama Tongogara, *Our Struggle for Liberation* (Gweru, 1984).

84. Govan Mbeki, *South Africa: A Short History* (Bellville, South Africa, 1992), p. 56.

85. Ibid., p. 72.

86. Interview, Paul Brickhill, February 2, 1988, #252, *NAZ.*

87. *Moto,* September 1964, MF 398, *NAZ;* see also Reg Shay, *The Silent War: The Fight for Southern Africa* (Salisbury, 1971).

88. *Zimbabwe Sun,* February 1, 1964.

89. *Zimbabwe Sun,* January 18, 1965.

90. "Memorandum of Conversation between Minister Counselor of the Soviet Embassy in Havana M. Manasov and Cuban Communist Party Member Raul Valdes Vivo," May 7, 1979, *Cold War International History Project Bulletin* 1, nos. 8–9 (Winter 1995–97), pp. 36–37, quote at p. 36.

91. Andrew Nyathi with John Hoffman, *Tomorrow Is Built Today: Experiences of War, Colonialism, and the Struggle for Collective Cooperatives in Zimbabwe* (Harare, 1990), p. 10.

92. *Zimbabwe People's Voice* 2, no. 8 (February 24, 1979), *NAZ;* see also *Commonwealth Political Ephemera from the Institute of Commonwealth Studies, University of London* phase 1, *Africa:* part 2, *Central Africa, Zimbabwe Political Parties, Trade Unions and Pressure Groups,* fiche 32. London, 1988.

93. Janice McLaughlin, *On the Frontline: Catholic Missions in Zimbabwe's Liberation War* (Harare, 1996), p. 44.

94. Clipping, July 25, 1977, MS 308/35/2, *IDAF Papers, NAZ.*

95. Catholic Commission for Justice and Peace in Rhodesia, "The Meaning of Intimidation: Some Notes on the Problem of Intimidation in the Rhodesian Elections of 1980," "Strictly Confidential," February 22, 1980, MS 308/58/10, *IDAF Papers, NAZ.*

96. Organized in Chicago in June 1998, the Black Radical Congress avowedly seeks to meld the socialist and nationalist traditions while incorporating feminism; see http://www.blackradicalcongress.com.

Conflict and Chorus: Reconsidering Toni Cade's *The Black Woman: An Anthology*

Farah Jasmine Griffin

1

I first encountered The Black Woman: An Anthology in the early 1970s (certainly before March 24, 1972, the day my father died), when I was seven or eight years old. My father and I would alternate trips to the Free Library of Philadelphia with trips to our favorite bookstore—Robins. In the early seventies Robins was a vibrant place where you could purchase books, especially those by radical writers and by writers of color, and a bevy of underground newspapers, among them the *Panther Newspaper* and *Rolling Stone.* Works by Thomas Jefferson and Thomas Paine sat next to those by Mao Tse-tung and Frantz Fanon. There were displays of the latest offerings of Amiri Baraka, Jerry Rubin, Abbie Hoffman, and Eldridge Cleaver. In these days of Barnes and Noble and Borders, Robins is fighting the good fight for its life. But back then, it was a place where you went not only to purchase books but also to find out where the meetings and rallies were going to be held, and where you were sure to find ongoing political debates and dialogues as well.

On one of these trips I spotted *The Black Woman.* Staring from the cover directly at me was a beautiful brown woman with a large Afro that merged with the black background of the book's cover. I had to have that book. At home, huge pictures of Kathleen Cleaver—perfect Afro, light glistening eyes, beauty mark in the middle of her forehead—and of Angela Davis—huge Afro and round granny glasses—graced my bedroom wall. I loved these women, they were my idols, they populated my fantasy world; and my parents' stories of them helped me to learn the geography of northern Africa, the politics of race in the United States, facts about Vietnam and Cuba, definitions of communism and socialism. Because of Angela I knew who Ronald Reagan was a decade before he became president of the United States. Those photographic images of Angela and Kathleen were my iconography for what it meant to be a revolutionary black woman.

However, one crucial thing stood between me and the golden beauties who graced my wall. In the still color-conscious black world of McDaniel Elementary School in South Philadelphia, I was constantly reminded that I was "black" (which always seemed to be qualified by phrases such as "and ugly," "and shiny," "and crispy"), not at all like Angela or Kathleen who were light-skinned. So, you see, I was in desperate need of a browner, Afro-ed revolutionary image. I didn't mind if she wasn't as dark as me, just as long as she was brown. Nina Simone, Roberta Flack, and Abbey Lincoln did not meet my purposes because I could not and did not sing. Assata Shakur's autobiography with her own chocolate face gracing the cover had not yet appeared. I needed a rapping sister, a poet or journalist or writer. And this anonymous sister on the Cade anthology was going to be the one. Lacking name or voice, she could become what I was going to make of her, of us— revolutionary, writer, lawyer, and world traveler. By possessing the book, I could possess the woman, could become the woman—or so I reasoned.

Now, my father would buy me books on my asking, but I always had to tell him why I wanted a particular title. Because it had a pretty woman on the cover was not going to sit well with him.

I looked through the book. There were names I recognized—Nikki Giovanni and Abbey Lincoln. And a lot I did not recognize: for instance, who was this Toni Cade (was that her on the cover?) and what did it mean to "edit" something?

> Me: Daddy, daddy will you buy me this book?
> Daddy: Why do you want it?
> Me: There is poetry in it. Some by Nikki.
> Daddy: Well, I will make a deal with you. I will buy it for you if
>   you promise to remember one of the poems and recite it to me.

Now that was almost too easy. I was always remembering poems and reciting them. Hadn't I just remembered Nikki Giovanni's "Revolutionary Dreams" and recited it to him and all those friends of his on the corner of the bar?

i used to dream militant
dreams of taking/over america to show
these white folks how it should be done
i used to dream radical dreams
of blowing everyone away with my perceptive
powers/of correct analysis
i even used to think i'd be the one
to stop the riot and negotiate the peace
then i awoke and dug/that if i dreamed natural
dreams of being a natural/woman doing what a woman
does when she's natural
i would have a revolution.

I got lots of quarters and "That little sister sure is something."

Within a week I had imagined myself as that woman on the cover and created a whole life for us. There were two new poems by Nikki in there, but I decided to add a new poet to my repertoire. I loved the Audre Lorde poem ending "Nor give a damn whose wife I am." But I was afraid that would count as cursing, and I wasn't allowed to curse, so I picked "Poem" by Kay Lindsey. Then, much to his delight, I recited both "Revolutionary Dreams" and "Poem" for my father:

Anyway I gave birth twice
And my body deserves a medal for that
But I never got one.

Mainly because they thought
I was just answering the call of nature.

But now that the revolution needs numbers
Motherhood got a new position
Five steps behind manhood.

And I thought sittin' in the back of the bus
Went out with Martin Luther King.

After I finished my proud recitations—having actually understood little about the last poem except the back of the bus stuff and women walking behind men like the Muslims do sometimes—my father applauded and kissed me and then asked, "Which one of those women are you going to be, baby girl?" And I, thinking he meant the poets and not the personas, said confidently, "Why both, Daddy, I am going to be both."

2

The tension implied in these two poems and in my father's question is one of the internal tensions of Toni Cade's anthology, and it is this which makes it such a unique and still important document. The current political moment calls for a reconsideration of this founding text of contemporary black women's thought. By "reconsideration" I mean we need to reconsider *The Black Woman* as a text, but also to reconsider the mission of black feminist thought and its relationship to black feminist politics, black women's lives, and related struggles for black liberation.

At its inception black feminist thought (including fiction, literary criticism and theory, the social sciences, and polemics) claimed a relationship to political struggle. As more black women began to enter the academy, black feminists sought legitimacy there—a seeking that led to a movement away from blatantly political commitments to black freedom. Here, I am primarily concerned with the arena of black women's writing which has received unprecedented recognition by the mainstream literary establishment in the three decades following the publication of Bambara's anthology. And while black women still make up few of the American professoriate, black women academics are among our most significant intellectuals.

Audre Lorde and Toni Cade Bambara are two black women who did not abandon activism for their writing, nor did they separate the work of writing from their activism. And they both managed to create exquisitely beautiful works of art as they did so—works of art that articulated not only the conditions of black women and black people in general but also a vision of hope and possibility. In their very different ways, they each provided a guide for reimagining our reality. Both women were present in the important anthology to which I want to turn my attention now.

The Black Woman: An Anthology is one of the first major texts to lay out the terrain of black women's thought that emerged from the civil rights, Black Power, and women's liberation movements. *The Black Woman* was published in 1970, in the same era that produced Toni Morrison's *The Bluest Eye* (1970) and Alice Walker's *The Third Life of Grange Copeland* (1970).[1] In May of that year the first issue of *Essence—A Magazine for Today's Black Woman*—hit the newsstands. Finally, it was the year that a bril-

liant Marxist professor of philosophy, Angela Davis, was placed on the
FBI's ten most wanted list; and it was one year after Kathleen Cleaver joined
Eldridge in exile in Algeria (1969).

In this anthology we find the vibrancy, excitement, politics, and
rhetoric of the time, and we have the articulation of the dilemma confronting black women activist intellectuals. In the preface Cade notes the
need for the anthology:

> The "experts" are still men, Black or white. And the images of the
> women are still derived from their needs, their fantasies, their second-
> hand knowledge, their agreement with the other "experts." . . .
> [White woman have also] produced the canon of literature fondly re-
> ferred to as "feminist literature." . . . And the question for us arises:
> how relevant are the truths, the experiences, the findings of white
> women to Black women? Are women after all simply women? I don't
> know that our priorities are the same, that our concerns and methods
> are the same, or even similar enough so that we can afford to depend
> on this new field of experts white, female.[2]

Here Bambara situates the anthology at the nexus of two oppositional
discourses—black nationalism and feminism—both of which were profoundly limited by their failure to acknowledge sexism and racism respec-
tively. She articulates the critique launched by black women that challenged
the normalization of women as white and middle class and of blacks as
male. In so doing, she anticipates the title of another important anthology,
All the Women Are White, All the Blacks Are Men, But Some of Us Are Brave
(1982).[3] In fact, she sends out the call to which two decades of black
women's creative and critical writings would respond.

Ironically, the blindness that Bambara points to in her preface is reproduced in the *New York Times* review of the book. In February 1972 the
Times published two book review sections, one specifically for paperback
books. The editors explained: "Because so many important recent paper-
backs address themselves to the overriding issues of the day, a large portion
of this section is devoted to critical appraisals of leading works in these
fields: Women's Lib, Blacks, Ecology, Law and Order, Vietnam, Youth and
Cities." Alan Dershowitz wrote the "Law and Order" review essay. Martin
Kilson wrote the essay on recent books by blacks. There are no books by
women in his essay. In the essay on books by women, Anne Gottlieb makes
one mention of a book by a black woman: "The women's movement which

emerged from the militant new left has produced substantial anthologies: *Sisterhood Is Powerful* and *Voices from Women's Liberation*. To these in militancy and beauty and selfhood must be added an excellent anthology of black women's writings: *The Black Woman Anthology* edited by Toni Cade." Gottlieb surbordinates the Cade anthology to the other two and offers no real analysis of its contents.

The book was widely reviewed in contemporary black publications, including *Black Scholar* and *Black World*. It seems to have immediately opened doors for the publication of other books by black women, and it clearly met black women's hunger for works of intelligence, beauty, and rigor. In the early nineties Ann duCille wrote that *The Black Woman* "stands as a pivotal text," a "founding text of contemporary black feminist studies," and E. Frances White notes, "Toni Cade's *The Black Woman* reached out to early black feminists as we emerged battle-scarred from our confrontation with cultural nationalists."[4]

The Black Woman is not a black feminist text as we have come to understand that term. Nonetheless, it is a text that paved the way for an emerging black feminism that came to flower in the late seventies and early eighties—a black feminism that I want to suggest has found a greater life in the literary marketplace and the academy than it has in the lives of far too many African American women (a topic to which I will return).

Unlike so many of the anthologies on black women that followed it, Bambara's text was not only concerned with articulating a black feminist ideology; nor was it primarily concerned with the establishment of an academic field of black women's studies. Clearly, she recognized that the establishment of the field was necessary for drawing attention to the life and works of black women and for providing analyses, critiques, and visions for a liberation movement that made black women's freedom from racism, sexism, and poverty central to its goals.

In editing *The Black Woman,* Toni Cade Bambara also recognized that the book would identify a market to publishers. In an interview that appears in the posthumously published *Deep Sightings and Rescue Missions,* edited by Toni Morrison, Bambara notes:

> I put together this anthology that I felt would open the door and
> prove that there was a market. Sure enough, within the second
> month that the book came out, it went into a new edition. The book
> was everywhere. There were pyramids of *The Black Woman* in every
> bookstore. All I knew in the beginning was that it had to fit in your

pocket and be under a dollar. I didn't know anything about publishing, but I stuck to that.[5]

Imagine that motivation: to open the door for others while making sure the people about whom you care the most can read, carry, and afford the book. In this day and time, that in and of itself is enough to give one the credentials of a "politically engaged" or "public" intellectual.

Nonetheless, the identification of a market and the establishment of an academic field were not Bambara's primary concern. Again, in the preface to *The Black Woman* she writes:

> The work grew out of impatience: . . . an impatience with the half-hearted go-along attempts of Black women caught up in the white women's liberation groups around the country. Especially out of an impatience with all the "experts" zealously hustling us folks for their doctoral theses or government appointments. And out of an impatience with the fact that in the whole bibliography of feminist literature, literature immediately and directly relevant to us wouldn't fill a page.[6]

Most significantly, she notes of the contributors: "Many are professional writers. Some have never before put pen to paper with publication in mind. Some are mothers. Others are students. Some are both. All are alive, are Black, are women. And that, I should think, is credentials enough to address themselves to issues that seem to be relevant to the sisterhood."[7]

The anthology includes a diverse collection of writings that seek to address these questions. Among these are poems by Nikki Giovanni, Kay Lindsey, and Audre Lorde, fiction by Paule Marshall, Alice Walker, Sherley Ann Williams, essays by Abbey Lincoln, Jean Carey Bond, and three by Toni Cade herself among at least a dozen others. Most interestingly, the anthology also includes excerpts from the Poor Black Women's Study Papers, a group working paper on black women in cities, and the transcript of a rap session of women students from City University of New York. I find the latter especially fascinating because the dialogue shows the contest over the direction of young black women's self-definition, their strategies for empowerment. One finds phrases like "Why do we have to wait for the man supposedly to do something before we make a move?" followed by "Men are our leaders, you know." Here is a true dialogue, debate between black women, talking to each other.

3

The chorus of voices in *The Black Woman* shares a sense of political urgency, a sense of the importance of internal critique, a sense of the diversity of black women and their ties to black nationalism, feminism, and black men. If the chorus of voices lends to its vibrancy, so too does the conflict inherent in its contents. A struggle is going on here, and it is an exciting and important one. One need only read the classic piece by Abbey Lincoln, composer, intellectual, actress, singer, poet, "Who Will Revere the Black Woman?" republished from *Black World*. Lincoln writes:

> Who will revere the Black woman? Who will keep our neighborhoods safe for innocent Black womanhood? Black womanhood is outraged and humiliated. Black womanhood cries for dignity and salvation. Black womanhood wants and needs protection and keeping and holding. . . . Who will keep her precious and pure? Who will glorify and proclaim her beautiful image? To whom will she cry rape?[8]

Similarly, Fran Saunders's essay, "Dear Black Man," is a plea for understanding and support from black men. She asks, "Are we to be told what to do and how to do it, without benefit of being able to sit back and be lovely and feminine and delicate and to be taken care of in the bargain?"[9] This question implies black women will accept black men as the leaders of family and community in exchange for the benefits of femininity: protection and security. The dominant emotions of these two essays are disappointment, pain, and yearning. There is no critique of patriarchy or of femininity. Instead they fit within a long-standing tradition of African American thought and politics of protection and respectability. The call for reverence and protection stems from a sincere concern for black women's psychic and physical safety; however, the pure and protected black woman of this vision will also be obligated to obey her protector—the black man.[10]

Nonetheless, many black women continue to be willing to accept the terms of this contract. The promise of patriarchal protection is certainly much better than the methodical abuse suffered by black women throughout much of their history in the New World. It also seems to offer a solution to the problems faced by so many heterosexual black women who find themselves struggling to raise families without the economic and emotional support of a male partner. Even many women who find themselves in abusive relationships would trade in physical and emotional violence for protection and reverence. This continues to be a reality for a great many black women.

Lincoln and Saunders gave voice to these desires in a way that few black women publically articulate today; this is in spite of the fact that the large number of women who supported the Million Man March and who attend Rev. T. D. Jakes's sermons and purchase his books—such as *Woman, Thou Art Loosed! Healing the Wounds of the Past*—clearly seem to desire a form of black patriarchy.[11]

Of course, protection is not in and of itself a bad thing. Patriarchal societies such as ours foster misogyny from which all women need protection. A racist patriarchal society is particularly dangerous for black women. Nonetheless, it is one thing to protect an individual so that she may actually live with a greater degree of freedom. It is another thing entirely to "protect" someone and in so doing to limit their freedom and mobility. We must be careful to distinguish offers of protection that are made in a context that limits women's freedom and mobility.

In contrast to the calls for protection articulated by Saunders and Lincoln, other contributors to *The Black Woman* clearly recognize the danger of such notions. Their essays begin to theorize a black feminist politics and praxis. Most of these share the pain of the two essays discussed above, but the pain has turned to frustration and anger. As such this change begins to lay the ground for the emergence of a black feminist politics. Among the essays that fall into this category are those by Jean Carey Bond, Kay Lindsey, Toni Cade, and Frances Beale. Beale's essay, "Double Jeopardy: To Be Black and Female," is one of the first to articulate a theory of multiple oppression suffered by black women.

In one of her own contributions to the volume, Toni Cade Bambara argues against the stance presented by Lincoln and Saunders:

> There is a dangerous trend observable in some quarters of the movement to program [black women] out of their "evil" ways into a cover-up, shut-up, lay-back-and-be-cool obedience role. . . . She is being encouraged—in the name of the revolution no less—to cultivate "virtues" that if listed would sound like the personality traits of slaves. . . . We rap about being correct but ignore the danger of having one-half of our population regard the other with such condescension and perhaps fear that half finds it necessary to "reclaim his manhood" by denying her peoplehood. We have much, alas, to work against. . . . [We must] face the task of creating a new identity, a self, perhaps an androgynous self, via commitment to the struggle.[12]

Here, Bambara not only offers a critique but also an alternative, a vision for
moving forward. She may be one of the first black women to suggest that an
identity of androgyny might help further black struggle, long before current critiques of black "masculinity" by black men, gay and straight, and
black feminists.[13] Indeed, many of the essays seem to ask "What kind of
women are we going to be? What kind of movement is ours going to be?
What does our fiction, poetry, sociology, theory, look like? What does it
mean to be a black woman in the United States? What is our role in the continuing struggle for black liberation?"

Bambara's anthology also demonstrates the kind of political and cultural work that publications can accomplish.[14] Its chorus of voices reminds
us of the extra-academic origins of black women's intellectual work and of
its concern with something other than curriculum, canons, fields, careers,
and academic publication. And while the academy is certainly an important
site of struggle, it is not the only one where socially and politically engaged
intellectuals ought to find themselves. In no way do I mean to belittle our
academic and professional endeavors; I for one have greatly benefited intellectually, personally and professionally from the presence of black intellectuals in the academy. Here I want to suggest the ways that social and
political contexts shape the conception, publication, and reception of books.
The social and political context out of which *The Black Woman* emerged—
and out of which Toni Cade Bambara emerged as a public figure—was one
which held intellectuals accountable for their writings and actions. Many
people engaged in diverse political movements; an even larger group knew
that something was at stake for oppressed peoples. This is not the case in the
predominantly white academy. We must ask of intellectuals both inside and
outside the academy, to whom are you accountable? Who is your constituency? In the absence of a social movement this is a difficult question to
answer.

4

In the years after the publication of *The Black Woman,* something crucial
happened. First, the political climate of the country shifted to the Right;
with this change, any program to alleviate the conditions of poor people
and black people was swept off the national agenda. Black feminists tended
to retreat from the hostility and homophobia they often encountered when
they tried to raise feminist concerns in all-black settings, be they black
churches or cultural nationalist venues. Black women academics and critics

continued to talk to and argue with white feminist and black male scholars, but they have not continued the dialogue among black women who shared different gender politics—a dialogue so evident in *The Black Woman*. One need only look at the anthologies which followed *The Black Woman*. *Homegirls: A Black Feminist Anthology* (1983), edited by Barbara Smith, provided a safe discursive space for black feminists—heterosexual and lesbian—to present their ideas. *Women in Africa and the African Diaspora* (1996), edited by Rosalyn Terborg-Penn, Andrea Rushing, and Sharon Harley, attempted to forge a relationship between black nationalism and black women's struggles against sexism. Similarly there is an emerging discourse of Africana Womanism within Afrocentrist intellectual arenas and publications. Among these Clenora Hudson-Weems's *Africana Womanism: Reclaiming Ourselves* (1995) is perhaps best known. Finally, Beverly Guy-Sheftall's *Words of Fire: An Anthology of African-American Feminist Thought* (1995) contains historical writings by "academics, activists, artists, community organizers, mothers . . . race women, socialists, communists, Christians, atheists, lesbian and straight, traditional and radical." However, today we are hard-pressed to find written evidence that these groups of black women intellectuals continue a contemporary dialogue in print.

Black nationalist women have accused leftist and left-liberal black feminists of being too influenced by white feminism and thus remaining marginal to the concerns of most black women. Black leftist and left-liberal feminists, too often wounded from encounters with certain black nationalists, have had little desire to continue a dialogue with anyone articulating a nationalist perspective. In *The Black Woman* there was still a possibility for dialogue; a possibility that also existed in the person and work of Toni Cade Bambara. Not only did Bambara's anthology contain essays from various standpoints, it also presented the proceedings from actual dialogues and debates. Furthermore, the book became a catalyst for reading and discussion groups around the issues it raised.

I think many self-identified black feminists have assumed that the notion of a nationalist feminist was oxymoronic. Black feminist historians Deborah Grey White and Paula Giddings have argued convincingly that black nationalism and black feminism have historically been "like oil and water."[15] In the course of all this, we all lost something very significant: the opportunity to really impact the lives of large numbers of black women. I also think that the disconnection between black women who are feminists and black women who are nationalists is often based on class as much as it is on ideological differences.

While most black women will never accept complete domination by black men, many are far more open to the promises of protection and support offered by many forms of black nationalism. Similarly, while the majority of black women are not cultural nationalists—willing to live in polygamous households, cover their hair, and change their names—many are attracted to the affirmation of blackness and the open confrontation with white supremacy offered by black nationalist ideologies. Finally, many black women recognize what so many black feminist intellectuals fail to see: the diversity within black nationalism itself. While certain forms of cultural nationalism, perhaps the most visible forms, are conservative on gender relations, other strains of nationalism range from the politically conservative to liberal to radical. Many black women see room to negotiate gender roles within this continuity. Unfortunately, women and their rights are rarely more than symbolic in even the most radical strains; but we ought not conflate all of them.

I cannot help but think that if black feminist intellectuals, black nationalist women intellectuals, and black women who identified themselves as neither nationalist nor feminist had maintained an ongoing dialogue, black feminists might not have been so caught off guard by such developments as the publication and popularity of Shahrazad Ali's *The Black Man's Guide to Understanding the Black Woman* or the tremendous support of black women for Clarence Thomas, Mike Tyson, O. J. Simpson, and the Million Man March. Furthermore, had we continued to engage in dialogue with black women who are not in the academy or in feminist organizations, we might have had a greater impact on the ways these events were viewed and analyzed by many black women.

Had black nationalist women been less hostile to black feminists, including black lesbian feminists, perhaps the platform of the historic Million Woman March held in Philadelphia in October 1997 would have reflected a more sustained engagement with black feminism. This is a march that many black feminists, including myself, did not attend because of the lack of an explicit feminist politics. (I think Toni Cade Bambara would have been there because that is where so many black people were.) While that platform does not appear to be a feminist one, it is especially representative of the concerns of many poor black women. Among these issues were black women in the penal system, black families' access to quality health care, and black women drug addicts and those in recovery. There is no reason why these issues should not be black feminist issues. On the other hand, any event organized to give voice to the concerns of black women ought to have included the issues of rape and domestic violence on the platform—both absent from that of the Million Woman March. These absences call into question the impact of the march, beyond that of symbolism and momentary euphoria, on the lives of black women.

A rereading and reconsideration of *The Black Woman* by black feminists would stress the importance of an ongoing dialogue and debate between black women in spite of ideological differences. We have proved willing to continuously debate with white feminists in spite of the stubborn persistence of racism. The desire and need to speak with other black women does not preclude the desire or need for an ongoing dialogue with white feminists and other women of color. In spite of what many of our nonblack allies might argue, intraracial solidarity is not racist.[16]A rereading and reconsideration of *The Black Woman* by black nationalist women would expose the pitfalls of certain elements of black nationalist ideology for women's freedom. For instance, women such as Abbey Lincoln no longer ask for protection and reverence in the same way, because they have learned that it comes at too high a cost.

As a black feminist, I believe it is urgent that we acknowledge and attempt to come to terms with the continuing appeal of black nationalism to large numbers of black people, particularly black women. Had the Million Woman March been organized by black feminists, would we have had the same turnout? Unless we seek to come to terms with black nationalism, it is highly unlikely that we will be successful in attempts to create a mass movement. The Black Women in the Academy Conference of January 1994 at MIT and the Million Woman March are evidence that, across class and ideological boundaries, black women are seeking the terms and plans by which we will organize our lives and our struggles in the next century. Both events left us wanting for a program, a political or intellectual agenda, an organization that addresses the struggles of African American women. Only the Black Feminist Caucus of the Black Radical Congress seems to be attempting to address this void.

I am in agreement with Beverly Guy-Sheftall's astute observation:

> Black feminist discourse is inherently oppositional because it runs
> counter to mainstream points of view both within and without
> African American communities. Being oppositional, especially if
> you're black and female, requires courage and tenacity. Being feminist
> exposes you to criticism, hostility, and even outright misogyny.[17]

However, at the end of the twentieth century, when the class divide in the black community is wider than our ancestors ever could have anticipated, at a time when young black women are the fastest growing segment of the prison population and of those contracting HIV, it is of utmost importance that we initiate the kind of dialogue evident in *The Black Woman*. Such a dialogue would allow for a black feminism that E. Frances White describes:

> Because I value the contributions of nationalists . . . I want to engage them seriously. Yet, it is the kind of feminism that demands attention to internal community relations that leads me to interrogate this discourse even while acknowledging its ability to undermine racist paradigms. This kind of black feminism recognizes the dangers of criticizing internal relations in the face of racist attacks but also argues that we will fail to transform ourselves into a liberated community if we do not engage in dialogue on the difficult issues that confront us.[18]

White's brilliant essay, "Africa on My Mind: Gender, Counter Discourse, and African American Nationalism," from which the above quotation is taken, is exemplary of the kind of dialogue about which I write.

5

By including essays representative of the diversity of black women's thought, Toni Cade Bambara did not avoid contest, controversy, and debate. She did not avoid the messiness involved in laying the groundwork for social struggle. Instead, she seems to have seen it as essential to the integrity of the volume. One of Bambara's primary characteristics as a "political intellectual" is that she was willing to jump right into the mess and provide a space for its articulation, all the while maintaining her own stance as a feminist greatly influenced by black nationalism, without compromise. She maintained a vision of black people that took for granted their capacity for growth, change, and long-term struggle.

The sites of intellectual work are always shifting. There is nothing inherently wrong about the move that took place when the academy opened its doors ever so slightly. Bambara, however, chose not to enter completely into the academy. She taught college classes but she also became an independent filmmaker, directing the documentary "The Bombing of Osage Avenue." She nurtured the founding of the ImageWeavers, a collective of young black women independent filmmakers who carry on her mission of making interventions in black women's lives through film. Most of the works to emerge from this collective have an explicit black feminist agenda, but this work is not fearful of being labeled "black nationalist" because its concerns are primarily with black women—heterosexual as well as lesbian—and because its desire is to encourage and provide a ground for intraracial dialogue.

Toni Cade Bambara and her groundbreaking anthology remind us to aspire toward the important tasks before us, regardless of the institutional settings we occupy. Among these tasks, three of the most important are (1) Articulate the struggles of the underrepresented; (2) Raise the consciousness of and provide alternative visions for the communities to whom we are dedicated; (3) Continuously offer internal criticism and analysis.

Toni Cade Bambara's life and work insist that we write books and essays, edit anthologies, do archival work, maintain tradition or, for that matter, even construct canons. However, she insists that we do this for something other than, or in addition to, degrees, tenure, and celebrity status. And she insists that we keep talking to and arguing with each other in order to clarify our goals and our visions. The stakes are too high for us to abandon this kind of commitment. In closing, I want to turn to Bambara's own words from her novel *The Salt Eaters*. Bambara's important but underread novel is the story of a black woman activist, Velma Henry, defeated by the sexism of her black male comrades and the decimation of the revolutionary fervor of the movement by infiltration. Bambara writes:

> She thought she knew that. At some point in her life she was sure Douglass, Tubman, the slave narratives, the songs, the fables, Delaney, Ida Wells, Blyden, Du Bois, Garvey, the singers, her parents, Malcolm, Coltrane, the poets, her comrades, her godmother, her neighbors, had taught her that. Thought she knew how to build immunity to the sting of the serpent that turned would-be cells, could-be cadres into cargo cults. Thought she knew how to build resistance, make the journey to the center of the circle, stay poised and centered in the work and not fly off, stay centered in the best of her people's traditions and not be available to madness, not become intoxicated by the heady brew of degrees and career and congratulations for nothing done, not become anesthetized by dazzling performances with somebody else's aesthetic, not go under. Thought the workers of the sixties had pulled the Family safely out of the range of the serpent's fangs so the workers of the seventies could drain the poisons, repair damaged tissues, retrain the heartworks, realign the spine. Thought the vaccine offered by all the theorists and activists and clear thinkers and doers of the warrior clan would take. But amnesia had

set in anyhow. . . . Something crucial had been missing from the po-
litical/economic/social/cultural/aesthetic/military/psychosocial/
psychosexual mix. And what could it be? And what should she do?

The Salt Eaters is a feminist text; it encourages coalitions between other
women of color as well as other progressive causes. And it never loses sight
of the goal of freedom for all black people. The protagonist is healed not in
order to retreat, but in order to continue in struggle.

In the above paragraph, Bambara provides an alternative use of tradition and cultural canon building—one that is inseparable from political
struggle. Note the various, sometimes conflicting voices of this chorus. The
paragraph serves as a warning against allowing terms we did not set to
define us for ourselves. We need turn to the kind of intellectual practice
described by cultural critic Herman Gray, who calls on other black intellectuals to

> expand our horizons, to make connections between the global and
> the local, to resist the seductions of professional preoccupation and
> disciplinary stability, to continue to understand specifically just how
> culture matters in the lives of people, and ultimately to make inter-
> ventions that matter . . . [to] offer the intellectual substance, the visi-
> bility and access to produce an effective and consequential discourse
> and intervention in the public sphere that transcends limited and
> limiting academic and professional preoccupations.[19]

Bambara's anthology continues to offer this kind of challenge for all of us.
She continues to ask: What kind of women are we going to be? What are we
going to do?

NOTES

1. This was the beginning of the contemporary renaissance of black women's writing. Maya Angelou's *I Know Why the Caged Bird Sings* appeared in 1969, Toni Morrison's
Sula in 1973, and Gayle Jones's *Corregidora* in 1975. Bambara's own collection of short stories, *Gorilla My Love,* was published in 1972.

2. Toni Cade, preface to *The Black Woman: An Anthology,* ed. Toni Cade (New
York, 1970), p. 9.

3. See Gloria T. Hull, Patricia Bell Scott, and Barbara Smith, eds., *All the Women*

Are White, All the Blacks Are Men, But Some of Us Are Brave: Black Women's Studies (New York, 1982).

4. E. Frances White, "Listening to the Voices of Black Feminism," *Radical America* (1984).

5. Toni Cade Bambara, *Deep Sightings and Rescue Missions,* ed. Toni Morrison (1996), p. 230.

6. Toni Cade, preface to *The Black Woman,* ed. Cade, pp. 10–11.

7. Ibid., pp. 11–12.

8. Abbey Lincoln, "Who Will Revere the Black Woman?" in *The Black Woman,* ed. Cade, p. 84.

9. Fran Saunders, "Dear Black Man," in *The Black Woman,* ed. Cade, pp. 73–79.

10. Twenty years after the publication of her essay, Abbey Lincoln discussed her opposition to this cost for protection. See *You Gotta Pay The Band* (video documentary, 1992).

11. The National Association of Colored Women was formed in 1896 in part to protect the name and image of black women. Leaders like W. E. B. Du Bois and Alexander Crummell both called for the protection of black women from rape, physical abuse, and economic poverty. Large numbers of the urban women to whom Malcolm X spoke were the daughters of or themselves women who fled the South in an attempt to escape the threat of rape from white males. Black women also found themselves the victims of economic exploitation, unfair employment practices, medical experimentation, and domestic violence. Who was deemed better to play the role of protector than the black man? This, of course, is a role that had been denied black men throughout history. I discuss the "promise of protection" at length in my essay "Ironies of the Saint: Malcolm X, Black Women, and the Price of Protection," forthcoming in Bettye Collier-Thomas and V. P. Franklin, eds., *Black Women in the Civil Rights Movement.*

12. Toni Cade, "On the Issue of Roles," in *The Black Woman,* ed. Cade, pp. 102–3.

13. See, e.g., Don Belton, *Speak My Name: Black Men on Masculinity and the American Dream* (Boston, 1995); Hazel Carby, *Race Men* (Cambridge, Mass., 1998); and Marcellus Blount and George Cunningham, *Representing Black Men* (New York, 1996).

14. Even those with no explicit political or cultural agenda perform cultural work.

15. Deborah Grey White, lecture at the Mid-Atlantic African American Studies Seminar, Princeton University, Princeton, N.J., October 3, 1998.

16. See Lewis Gordon, "In a Black Antiblack Philosophy," in *Her Majesty's Other Children* (New York, 1997), pp. 115–34.

17. Beverly Guy-Sheftall, *Words of Fire: An Anthology of African-American Feminist Thought* (1995), p. 487.

18. E. Frances White, "Africa on My Mind: Gender, Counter Discourse, and African American Nationalism," *Journal of Women's History* 2 (Spring 1990): 74; reprinted as chap. 6 in this volume.

19. Herman Gray, "Is Cultural Studies Inflated? The Cultural Economy of Cultural Studies in the United States," in *Disciplinarity and Dissent in Cultural Studies,* ed. Cary Nelson and Dilip Parameshar Gaonkar (New York, 1996), pp. 203–16.

6

Africa on My Mind: Gender, Counter Discourse, and African American Nationalism

E. Frances White

Equality is false; it's the devil's concept. Our concept is complementarity. Complementarity means you complete or make perfect that which is imperfect.

The man has the right that does not destroy the collective needs of his family.

The woman has the two rights of consultation and then separation if she isn't getting what she should be getting.

—M. Ron Karenga

The African past lies camouflaged in the collective African American memory, transformed by the middle passage, sharecropping, industrialization, urbanization. Few material goods from Africa survived this difficult history, but Africans brought with them a memory of how social relations should be constructed that has affected African American culture to the present. Although the impact of these African roots is difficult to assess, few historians today deny the importance of this past to African American culture.

But the memories I seek to interrogate in this essay have little to do with "real" memories or actual traditions that African Americans have passed along through blood or even practices. Rather, I am concerned with the way African Americans in the late twentieth century construct and re-construct collective political memories of African culture to build a cohesive group that can shield them from racist ideology and oppression. In particular it is the political memories of African gender relations and sexuality that act as models for African American social relations that will serve as this paper's focus.

Below I will focus on black nationalism as an oppositional strategy that both counters racism and constructs conservative utopian images of African American life. I will pay close attention to the intertwined discussions on the relationship of the African past to present-day culture and to attempts to construct utopian and repressive gender relations. After situating my work theoretically in the next section, I return to an examination of Afrocentric paradigms that support nationalist discourse on gender and the African past. Finally I look at the emergence of a black feminist discourse that attempts to combine nationalist and feminist insights in a way that counters racism but tries to avoid sexist pitfalls.

Throughout the essay, I choose examples from across the range of nationalist thinking. Some of this writing is obviously narrow and sexist. Other works have influenced my thinking deeply and have made significant contributions to understanding African American women's lives. I argue, however, that all fail to confront the sexist models that ground an important part of their work. I imagine that my criticisms will be read by some as a dismissal of all Afrocentric thinking. Nothing could be further from my intentions. It is because I value the contributions of nationalists that I want to engage them seriously. Yet it is the kind of feminism that demands attention to internal community relations that leads me to interrogate this discourse even while acknowledging its ability to undermine racist paradigms. This kind of black feminism recognizes the dangers of criticizing internal relations in the face of racist attacks but also argues that we will fail to transform ourselves into a liberated community if we do not engage in dialogue on the difficult issues that confront us.[1]

African American nationalists have taken the lead in resurrecting and inventing African models for the African diaspora in the United States. They recognize that dominant, negative images of Africa have justified black enslavement, segregation, and continuing impoverishment.[2] Accordingly, nationalists have always argued persuasively that African Americans deny their connections to Africa at the peril of allowing a racist subtext to circulate without serious challenge. At the same time, nationalists have recognized that counterattacks on negative portrayals of Africa stimulate political mobilization against racism in the United States. The consciously identified connections between African independence and the U.S. civil rights movements and, more recently, between youth rebellion in South Africa and campus unrest in the United States stand out as successful attempts to build a Pan-African consciousness.

The construction of Pan-African connections can have its problems, however. At times it depends on the search for a glorious African past while accepting dominant European notions of what that past should look like. As I have argued elsewhere,[3] proving that Africans created "civilizations" as sophisticated as those in Europe and the Near East has concerned nationalists too much.[4] In the process of elevating Egypt, for example, they have often accepted as uncivilized and even savage primitives the majority of Africans who lived in stateless societies but whose past deserves respect for its complex relationship to the world around it.[5]

Perhaps more importantly, the nationalist or Afrocentric construction of a political memory attempts to set up standards of social relations that can be both liberating and confining. The quotation at the beginning of this essay by the "inventor" of Kwanza traditions, Ron Karenga, illustrates this point. Building off conservative concepts of "traditional" African gender relations before colonial rule, he argues that the collective needs of black families depend on women's complementary and unequal roles. As I shall make clear below, Karenga has significantly modified his sexist ideas about gender relations, but the ideology of complementarity and collective family needs continues to work against the liberation of black women.

In addition, many nationalists, both male and female, remain openly hostile to any feminist agenda. In a paper arguing that black people should turn to African polygamous and extended family forms to solve the "problem" of female-headed households, Larry Delano Coleman concludes:

> The "hyper-liberated" black woman is in fact so much a man that she has no need for men, however wimpish they may be; and the "hyper-emasculated" black man is so much a woman, that he has no need for women. May each group of these hyper-distorted persons find homosexual heaven among the whites, for the black race would be better served without them.[6]

Coleman defines "the race" in a way that excludes feminists, lesbians, and gay men from community support—a terrifying proposition in this age of resurgent racism.[7]

In advocating polygamous families, Nathan and Julia Hare, the influ-

ential editors of *Black Male/Female Relationships,* link homosexuality with
betrayal of the race:

> Just as those black persons who disidentify with their race and long to
> alter their skin color and facial features to approximate that of the
> white race may be found to suffer a racial identity crisis, the homo-
> sexual individual who disidentifies with his/her biological body to
> the point of subjecting to the surgery of sex-change operations simi-
> larly suffers a gender identity confusion, to say the least.[8]

Both the Hares and Coleman's standards of appropriate gender relations depend on a misguided notion of African culture in the era before "the
fall"—that is, before European domination distorted African traditions.
These nationalists have idealized polygamous and extended families in a
way that stresses both cooperation among women and male support of
wives but ignores cross-generational conflict and intrafamily rivalry also
common in extended, polygamous families. They have invented an African
past to suit their conservative agenda on gender and sexuality.

In making appeals to conservative notions of appropriate gender behavior, African American nationalists reveal their ideological ties to other
nationalist movements, including European and Euro-American bourgeois
nationalists over the past two hundred years. These parallels exist despite
the different class and power bases of these movements. European and Euro-
American nationalists turned to the ideology of respectability to help them
impose the bourgeois manners and morals that attempted to control sexual
behavior and gender relations. This ideology helped the bourgeoisie create
a "private sphere" that included family life, sexual relations, and leisure
time. Respectability set standards of proper behavior at the same time that
it constructed the very notion of private life. Nationalism and respectability intertwined as the middle class used the nation-state to impose its notions of the private sphere's proper order on the upper and lower classes.
Through state-run institutions, such as schools, prisons, and census bu-
reaus, the bourgeoisie disciplined people and collected the necessary information to identify and control them.[9]

Often African Americans have served as a model of abnormality against
which nationalism in the United States was constructed. White bourgeois
nationalism has often portrayed African Americans as if they threatened respectability. Specifically, white nationalists have described both black men
and women as hypersexual. Moreover, black family life has consistently

served as a model of abnormality for the construction of the ideal family life. Black families were matriarchal when white families should have been male dominated. Now they are said to be female-headed when the ideal has become an equal heterosexual pair.[10]

As I have suggested, black people have developed African American nationalism as an oppositional discourse to counter such racist images. Ironically, though not surprisingly, this nationalism draws on the ideology of respectability to develop a cohesive political movement. The African American ideology of respectability does not always share the same moral code with western nationalism. Some Afrocentric thinkers, such as Larry Coleman, turn to Africa for models of gender relations and call for polygamy as an appropriate form of marriage between black men and women. More crucially, black nationalists did not and cannot call on state power to enforce their norms. Their opposition to abortion carries very different weight from the campaign of the Christian Right whose agenda includes making a bid for control of state institutions.

It is this lack of access to state power and African American nationalists' advocacy of an oppressed people that gives Afrocentric ideology its progressive, radical edge and ultimately distinguishes it from European and Euro-American bourgeois nationalism. Paradoxically, then, Afrocentric ideology can be radical and progressive in relation to white racism and conservative and repressive in relation to the internal organization of the black community. Clearly, nationalists struggle in a way that can deeply threaten white racism. Both the open repression of and the ideological backlash against nationalists indicate that their discourse strikes at the heart of black oppression. Yet I often find too narrow black nationalist efforts to define what the community or nation should be. In particular many nationalists attempt to construct sexist and heterosexist ideal models for appropriate behavior.

The Dialectics of Discursive Struggle

How does one prove strength in oppression without overstating the case, diluting criticism of the system and absolving the oppressor in the process? Likewise, the parallel dilemma is how does one critique the system and state of things without contributing to the victimology school which thrives on litanies of lost battles and casualty lists, while omitting victories and strengths and the possibilities for change inherent in both black people and society?[11]

Karenga has identified a key dilemma facing black scholarship: how do black scholars take into account the possibilities of liberation at the same time that they balance a sense of strength against the realities of victimization? One strategy for moving beyond this dilemma to what Karenga calls an "emancipatory Black science" is to examine the ideological battles in which black people engage, exploring both the racist discourse that they struggle against and the oppositional language constructed in the process of this struggle. As a site of ideological battles, discourses intertwine with the material conditions of our lives. They help organize our social existence and social reproduction through the production of signs and practices that give meaning to our lives.[12] Closely tied to the socioeconomic and political institutions that enable oppressive relations, discourses are often reflected in a variety of forms. For example, the dominant discourse on Africa includes multilayered interventions that are knitted together from scholarly literature, fiction, art, movies, television, media, travel books, government documents, folklore, jokes, and more. The discourse that relies on these interventions creates an image of Africa that reinforces the continent's subordinate power relations to the West. Dominant discursive practice depends on more than lies and myths, although misrepresentation and deception do have roles to play in its strategy. Instead, the West's will to knowledge about Africa has been inextricably bound up with imperialist relations.

It is impossible for people's thoughts on Africa to be unencumbered by this discourse. None of us—not even Africans—can come to the study of Africa without being influenced by its negative image. Accordingly, dominant discourse attempts to blind both the oppressor and the oppressed by setting up smokescreens between people and reality. As Edward Said argues for the Middle East, "for a European or American studying the Orient there can be no disclaiming the main circumstance of his actuality: that he comes up against the Orient as a European or American first, as an individual second."[13] One way that dominant discourse sets up a smokescreen is to make arbitrary categories appear natural and normal. For example, it makes us think that race is a natural category by taking minor biological differences and infusing them with deep symbolic meanings that affect all our lives. Race, then, is a social construction that feels real to us and has significant consequences.

The popular literature that influences even nationalists is peppered with images of primitive natives confronting European civilization. These natives build huts rather than houses, while in England similar-looking

structures are called picturesque cottages. By nature natives divide themselves into tribes while more sophisticated people form ethnic groups. These
words—"tribe," "hut," "native," "civilization," and "primitive"—form a
cluster of words that helps build a discourse on Africans that places them in
a time warp outside our present time. Not surprisingly, this cluster of words
has a history in the anthropological vocabulary that supported imperialism,
a vocabulary that anthropology has discarded but that remains in popular
usage. Many of these words can be found in Raymond Williams's 1976
Keywords: A Vocabulary of Culture and Society, since the western discourse
on Africa is as much about Europe as it is about Africa—an exploration of
what Africa is and, therefore, what Europe is not.[14]

As Johannes Fabian has argued, the cluster of words surrounding
Africa fixes "natives" in a time other than our own complex, contemporary
time. Natives are primitive in the sense that they came first, living as western ancestors lived in a simpler age.[15] Even the word "tribe" suggests an earlier time, since Europeans were said to have lived in them only in the distant
past. The *Oxford English Dictionary* reminds us that a tribe is "a primary ag-
gregate of people in a primitive or barbarous condition, under a headman
or chief." Tribe, then, suggests a notion of ethnicity that is more fixed than
social relations have ever been in Africa.

The concept of fixed, static tribes suited the interests of colonial
rulers who sought to categorize and control Africans. It continues to suit
the interests of white South Africans who engage in deadly ideological warfare. As long as we believe in the existence of isolated, primitive tribes, white
South Africans will find a market for their racist ideology of separate development. They continue to claim that separate development protects tribes
from the ravages of civilization and allows each tribe/nation to evolve from
different starting points to its fullest potential. "Tribe" feeds off the racist
cluster of words that speak to us through films (*Tarzan* and its recent imitation, *The Gods Must Be Crazy*); magazines (*National Geographic* and related
PBS specials); and newspapers (the *New York Times*'s reports on tribal mas-
sacres in Burundi and South Africa). The smokescreen created by words
central to this racist discourse casts a thick pall over Africa.

And yet alternative voices do emerge. Unfortunately, many influential
works on discourse, such as Said's *Orientalism,* have failed to account adequately for the development of the oppositional strategies that reveal
contradictions in the dominant discourse. Admittedly even those who consciously reject hegemonic ideology or who appear to live unencumbered by
it cannot go untouched by its power. But the existence of resistance suggests
a need to recognize the interrelationship between dominant and counter

discourse. I have followed Richard Terdiman's lead in focusing on the inseparably intertwined nature of hegemonic and oppositional discursive practices. In his "celebration" of counter discourse he suggests, "we might thus posit something like a Newton's Law in the discursive realm: for every dominant discourse a contrary and transgressive counter discourse."[16] More tersely: "No discourse is ever a monologue."[17]

The very nature of dominant discourse leads it to be contested by subordinate groups whose daily experiences help penetrate and demystify its hegemony.[18] This "dialectic of discursive struggle" reveals the vulnerabilities of hegemonies.[19] As part of the same dialectic, counter discourses operate on the same ground as dominant ideology. James Scott argues:

> The crucial point is rather that the very process of attempting to legitimate a social order by idealizing it always provides its subjects with the means, the symbolic tools, the very ideas for a critique that operates entirely within the hegemony. For most purposes, then, it is not at all necessary for subordinate classes to set foot outside the confines of the ruling ideals in order to formulate a critique of power.[20]

As I will argue below, African American nationalist contestation over the image of Africa often unconsciously accepts many of the terms of dominant discursive strategies, even when it attempts to move beyond the limits set by racist ideology.

In *Marxism and the Philosophy of Language*, V. N. Volosinov examines the struggles between dominant and counter discourses as a contest over ideological signs. A sign represents, depicts, or stands for something lying outside itself. It does not "simply exist as a part of a reality—it reflects and refracts another reality. Therefore, it may distort that reality or be true to it, or may perceive it from a special point of view, and so forth."[21] For Volosinov, language and words were often a starting place to understand social relations. Unlike other ideological signs,

> The entire reality of the word is wholly absorbed in its function of being a sign. A word contains nothing that is indifferent to this function, nothing that would not have been engendered by it. A word is the purest and most sensitive medium of social intercourse.[22]

Words, like all signs, evolve only on "interindividual territory," that is, between individuals. Thus, he stresses the "multiaccentuality" of the ideological sign. Caryl Emerson explains:

Each social group—each class, profession, generation, religion, region—has its own characteristic way of speaking, its own dialect.
Each dialect reflects and embodies a set of values and a sense of
shared experience. Because no two individuals ever entirely coincide
in their experience or belong to precisely the same set of social
groups, every act of understanding involves an act of translation and
a negotiation of values. It is essentially a phenomenon of interrela-
tion and interaction.[23]

As Volosinov, Richard Terdiman, and others have argued, language
reflects the struggles between dominant and dissident discourses. Hazel
Carby expresses this view: "The sign, then, is an arena of struggle . . . ; the
forms that signs take are conditioned by the social organization of the participants involved and also by the immediate conditions of their interac-
tions."[24] In the case of interest to us, the meaning of Africa—the
ideological sign, Africa—is contested on discursive terrain. Dominant discourse assigns a plethora of negative images to Africa while those influenced
by nationalist impulses in Africa and its diaspora struggle to replace these
images with their own positive meanings.

The writings of certain feminists of color reveal the Janus-faced nature of counter discourse as these women search for allies among the male-
dominated nationalist and white-dominated feminist movements. For example, women of color offered challenges within the feminist movement
that forced women to acknowledge the problems with an undifferentiated
category, Woman. Many of these theorists highlighted the complexities of

human identity in recognition of the reality that women have ethnic/race and class positions, *inter alia,* that interact with gender and sexuality to influence their lives. Accordingly, feminists of color pushed for a movement whose discursive practices opposed sexism and racism simultaneously.[26] For example, Audre Lorde has asked, how does horizontal hostility keep women from ending their oppression? She argued that women need to celebrate their differences and use difference for creative dialogue.[27] Outside a narrow band of bourgeois or separatist feminists, few U.S. white feminists today write without giving at least token acknowledgement to Lorde's call to recognize difference.[28]

At the same time, women of color challenged their various ethnic communities to become conscious of sexism at home. Cherríe Moraga problematizes the meaning of home and community as she sensitively explores the way her education and light skin pushed her away from other Chicanos. "I grew white," she acknowledged.[29] But she also stressed that her community forced her to leave home because of her feminism and lesbianism. Feeling betrayed by a mother who accepted the ideology that males were better than females, she fled from those who told her, you are a traitor to your race if you do not put men first. She watched the rise of the Chicano nationalist movement, La Raza, alienated on the sidelines. Yet she found herself increasingly uncomfortable in her nearly all-white surroundings.

Ultimately, she concluded that to be critical of one's race is not to betray it. She joined with other Chicana feminists to turn around the traditional interpretation of Malinche's life, which traces the birth of the Mexican people to Malinche's betrayal of her people. Instead, Moraga and others expose a prior betrayal of Malinche who had been sold into slavery by her own people.[30] By refusing to accept the terms of a Chicano nationalist movement that brands her a traitor because she publicly criticizes gender relations, Moraga demands a place for herself and other lesbians within Chicano communities.

It is not surprising that feminists such as Audre Lorde and Cherríe Moraga challenge both feminist and nationalist communities. As women with strong lesbian political consciences, they confront homophobia in nationalist movements. Locked in struggle against heterosexism in their own communities, it is very difficult for them to maintain an image of their communities as harmonious. Cheryl Clarke has specifically accused nationalists of increasing the level of homophobia in African American communities during the 1960s and 1970s. She argues persuasively that homophobia limits the political struggle of African Americans:

The expression of homophobic sentiments, the threatening political postures assumed by black radicals and progressives of the nationalist/communist ilk, and the seeming lack of any willingness to understand the politics of gay and lesbian liberation collude with the dominant white male culture to repress not only gay men and lesbians, but also to repress a natural part of all human beings, namely the bisexual potential in us all. Homophobia divides black people as political allies, it cuts off political growth, stifles revolution, and perpetuates patriarchal domination.[31]

In *Reconstructing Womanhood,* Hazel Carby goes even further when she finds fault with some African American feminists for failing to recognize that even their writings form part of a multiaccented counter discourse. She cautions black feminist literary critics to be historically specific when they write about black women's fiction and to recognize competing interests among African American women. She asserts, "in these terms black and feminist cannot be absolute, transhistorical forms (or form) of identity."[32] Black feminists do not have an essential, biologically based claim on understanding black women's experience since we are divided by class, region, and sexual orientation. Even we have multiple identities that create tensions and contradictions among us. We need not all agree nor need we all speak with one voice. As with all counter discourses, the assumption that there exists one essential victim suppresses internal power divisions. To Terdiman's "no discourse is ever a monologue," we should add, the site of counter discourse is itself contested terrain.

Inventing African Tradition

The contemporary African-American woman must recognize that, in keeping with her African heritage and legacy, her most important responsibilities are to the survival of the home, the family, and its children.[33]

It is out of the feminist tradition of challenging the oppositional discourses that are meaningful to women of color that I interrogate the significance of black nationalism for African American women's lives. Like Sylvia Yanagisako, "I treat tradition as a cultural construction whose meaning must be discovered in present words no less than past acts."[34] As I have suggested, the traditions revealed in nationalist discursive practices are Janus-faced—

turned toward struggle with oppressive forces and contesting for dominance within black communities.

This discourse can be represented by Molefi Kete Asante's writings and the journal he edits, *Journal of Black Studies.* Asante recognizes the importance of developing a counter discourse within the privileged arena of academia and has consistently published a high quality journal. He is also responsible for developing the first Ph.D. program in African American Studies at Temple University.

The focus of his work and his journal is an Afrocentric one because it places "Africans and the interest of Africa at the center of our approach to problem solving."[35] By African, he means both people from the African continent and its diaspora. Although he has collapsed the distinction between African Americans and Africans, he avoids the traps many nationalists fall into when they posit a simplistic, mystical connection between Africa and African Americans. Unlike earlier nationalists who appealed to a natural, essential element in African culture, he argues that culture "is the product of the material and human environment in which people live."[36] In an editor's note introducing a special issue of the *Journal of Black Studies,* "African Cultural Dimensions," he continues:

> As editor I seek to promulgate the view that all culture is cognitive. The manifestations of culture are the artifacts, creative solutions, objects, and rituals that are created in response to nature. Thus, the manuscripts which have been scrupulously selected for this issue are intended to continue the drama of cultural discussion of African themes.[37]

Africans, he argues, have constructed a culture that stands in opposition to Eurocentric culture. He develops a convincing critique of a Eurocentric worldview. For Asante, Eurocentric culture is too materialistic, and the social science that has evolved from this culture in academe too often assumes an objective, universal approach that ultimately suffers from positivism. He argues that neither Marxism nor Freudianism escape from this shortcoming though he acknowledges that the Frankfurt School's criticisms of positivism have influenced his work.

According to Asante, the task for African Americans is to move beyond the Eurocentric idea to a place where transcultural, Afrocentric analysis becomes possible. He cautions against using a Eurocentric mode that accepts oppositional dichotomies as a reflection of the real world.[38] His critique of the positivist tendency to split mind and body is cogent. Unfortunately, his theory also relies on a false dichotomy. Essentially, his categories, Afrocentric and Eurocentric, form an untenable binary opposition: Europeans are materialistic while Africans are spiritual; Europeans abort life while Africans affirm it.

He is quite right to recognize the existence of a protest discourse that counters racist ideology. But he denies the way that these discourses are both multivocal and intertwined. As suggested above, the dialectic nature of discursive struggle requires that counter and dominant discourses contest the same ideological ground.

This point can be better understood by examining the roots of Asante's Afrocentric thought. He consciously builds off Negritude and authenticity, philosophies devised explicitly to counter racist ideology and develop nationalist cohesion. V. Y. Mudimbe has exposed the nature of the binary opposition used by cultural nationalists of the 1930s and 1940s who explored their difference as blacks. Léopold Senghor and Aimé Césaire and other Francophone Africans and African Caribbeans relied on the spiritual/materialistic dichotomy. Turned on its head, this is the opposition used against Africans during the late nineteenth century. As many have pointed out, this reversal of paradigms owed much to the celebration of the "noble savage" by such interwar European writers as J.-P. Sartre. Ironically, western anthropologists, whom nationalists often disparage, also took an active role in this ideological "flip." It was anthropologists such as Michel Griaule and Melville J. Herskovits who revealed to western-educated intellectuals the internal coherence of African systems of thought.[39] Equally important was the cross-fertilization of ideas between Africans, African Caribbeans, and African Americans. As a result of these three influences, "African experiences, attitudes, and mentalities became mirrors of a spiritual and cultural richness."[40] Far from cultureless savages, Africans had built the essence of spiritual culture.

This reversal of the racist paradigms on Africa accompanied and contributed to the growth of the nationalist movements that ultimately freed the continent from formal colonial rule. The nature of African independence reflects the double-edged character of this nationalism. On the one hand, nationalism helped build the political coherence necessary to threaten European rule; on the other hand, it obscured class and gender divisions in a way that prevented them from being addressed fairly. Clearly, this nationalism shared much with a European brand of nationalism that envisioned a culture unequally divided along gender and class lines.

Similarly, Asante does little to take us beyond the positivism that he criticizes, and his schema assumes a universality as broad as the Eurocentric discourse he shuns. Moreover, the Afrocentric ideology he uses depends on an image of black people as having a culture that has little or nothing to do with white culture. This is one of its major contradictions. On the one hand, nationalists like Asante have to prove to African Americans that Afrocentric ways are different from and better than Euro-American ways. Nationalists try to convince black people that they should begin to live their lives by this Afrocentric ideology. For example, some nationalists argue that African Americans should turn away from materialism to focus on the spiritual needs of the black community. Yet on the other hand, Asante and others argue that black culture is already based on an Afrocentric worldview that distinguishes it from Euro-American culture. Rather than being an ideology that African-Americans must turn to, Afrocentric thought becomes inherent in black culture, and black people already live by these ways in opposition to dominant culture.

I would argue instead that African American culture constantly interacts with dominant culture. Of course, black people do have their own ways not only because they protect themselves from penetration by white culture but also because they are creative. Nonetheless, blacks and whites all live together in the same society, and culture flows in both directions. Like the dominant culture, most African Americans believe that spirituality has a higher value than materialism at the same time that most of these people pursue material goals. If materialism were not considered crass by dominant society, Afrocentric critique would have little value. It is also important to note the extent to which white culture is influenced by African Americans. At an obvious level, we see black influence on white music with the most recent appearance of rap music on television and radio commercials. At a less obvious level, Afrocentric critiques compel hegemonic forces to work at covering the reality of racist relations. Far from being an ideology that has no relationship to Eurocentric thought, nationalist ideology is dialectically related to it.

What I find most disturbing about Asante's work is his decision to collapse differences among black people into a false unity that only a simplistic binary opposition would allow. The focus on similarities between Africans and African Americans at the expense of recognizing historical differences can only lead to a crisis once differences are inevitably revealed. Moreover, his binary opposition cannot account for differences among Africans. Many eloquent African writers have warned us about the problems that came from accepting a false unity during the decolonization phase that has led to the transfer of local power from an expatriate elite to an indigenous one. Ngugi wa Thiongo, Sembene Ousmane, and Chinua Achebe would all warn us against such pitfalls.

And, of course, we cannot face sexism with this false unity, as Buchi Emecheta, Sembene Ousmane, and Mariama Bâ movingly show. Asante does tell us that along with the move beyond the Eurocentric idea, we can develop a "post-male ideology as we unlock creative human potential."[41] Yet he has nothing more to say about gender in the entire book. It is hard to believe that this gesture toward black feminists needs to be taken seriously. It is to other Afrocentric thinkers that we must turn to understand more clearly what this discourse has to say about women.

Among the most important nationalists the *Journal of Black Studies* publishes is Ron Karenga, the founder of US. Some readers will remember him for his leadership role among cultural nationalists in ideological battles against the Black Panthers in the 1960s and 1970s and for his pamphlet, *The Quotable Ron Karenga.* In *Black Awakening in Capitalist America,* Robert Allen quoted a critical excerpt from Karenga's book, exposing its position on women and influencing many young black women (including myself) to turn away from this nationalist position.[42]

Perhaps the key word in Karenga's early analysis of utopian gender relations is complementarity. In this theory, women should complement male roles and, therefore, share the responsibilities of nation building. Of course, in this formulation, "complementary" did not mean "equal." Instead, men and women were to have separate tasks and unequal power. Indeed, in much of Africa today, women give more to men than they get in return in their complementary labor exchange. This is not to suggest that African women are only victims in their societies; nonetheless, sexism based on a complementary model severely limits the possibilities of many women's lives.

It is important to note that Karenga has reformed his position on women. Apparently, he used the time he spent in jail during the 1970s effectively by spending much of his time studying. It is from his jail cell that he published influential pieces in *Black Scholar* and the *Journal of Black Studies.* He began to articulate more clearly a critique of hegemonic culture, showing the impact of reading Lukács, Gramsci, Cabral, and Touré. And though he does not say so explicitly, he begins to respond to black feminist critics of his work. Indeed, I find the change in his position on women impressive. Although he remains mired in heterosexist assumptions and never acknowledges his change of heart, he drops his explicit arguments supporting the subordination of women. The new Ron Karenga argues for equality in the heterosexual pair despite his continued hostility to feminists.[43]

Unfortunately, too few nationalists have made this transition with him. Male roles remain defined by conventional, antifeminist notions that fail to address the realities of black life. For example, articles in Nathan and Julia Hare's journal, *Black Male/Female Relationships,* consistently articulate such roles. Charlyn A. Harper-Bolton begins her contribution, "A Reconceptualization of the African-American Woman," by examining "traditional African philosophy, the nature of the traditional African woman, and the African-American slave woman."[44] She uses African tradition as her starting point because she assumes an essential connection between the African past and African American present:

> The contemporary African-American woman carries within her very
> essence, within her very soul, the legacy which was bequeathed to her
> by the traditional African woman and the African-American slave
> woman.[45]

She leaves unproblematic the African legacy to African Americans as she presents an ahistorical model of African belief systems that ignores the conflict and struggle over meaning so basic to the making of history. This model assumes a harmonious spirituality versus conflicting materialism dichotomy that grounds the work of Asante and her major sources, John Mbiti and Wade Nobles.[46]

It is a peculiarly Eurocentric approach that accepts conflict and competing interests in a western context but not in an African one. Harper-Bolton never moves beyond the mistaken notion that Africans lived simply and harmoniously until the evil Europeans upset their happy life. Ironically, as I have been arguing, such an image of Africans living in static isolation from historical dynamics supports racist ideals and practices and conveniently overlooks the power dynamics that existed in precolonial Africa like anywhere else in the world. In addition, her model portrays African women as a monolithic and undifferentiated category with no competing interests, values, and conflicts. The power of older women over younger women that characterizes so many African cultures becomes idealized as a vision of the elders' wisdom in decision making. It accepts the view of age relations presented by more powerful older women whose hidden agenda often is to socialize girls into docile daughters and daughters-in-law.

When Harper-Bolton turns to the legacy of slave women for contemporary life she owes a large, but unacknowledged, debt to the social science literature on African survivals in African American culture. In particular, her work depends on the literature that explores the African roots of African American family patterns. Writers such as Gutman, Blassingame, and Kullikoff have attempted to build off Melville J. Herskovits's early work on African survivals. This literature has been crucial for forming our understanding of black women's roles during slavery with particular reference to the African roots of these roles.

Unfortunately, this literature also shares certain problems that have clouded our understanding of this African heritage. What concerns me most are the sources that these historians use to compare African and African American slave families. Two major sources have been used uncritically that are particularly problematic when studying African women's roles in the precolonial era. First, historians have relied on precolonial travelers' accounts written by Westerners exploring the African continent. These accounts are important sources to turn to—and I have used them myself. But they must be used with great care because it is precisely at the point of describing African women and gender relations that these accounts are most problematic. Often these travelers' debates over whether or not African women were beasts of burden and whether or not African women were sexually loose spoke to debates in Europe. Rosalind Coward has explored the obsession of eighteenth- and nineteenth-century Westerners with gender relations around the world, assuming as they did that these relations were a measure of civilization.[47] Needless to say, these travelers brought the sexist visions of their own society to bear on African gender relations, and, therefore, their writings must be used carefully.

But I am more troubled by the second major source used by historians looking for African legacies, that is, anthropological reports written between the 1930s and 1950s. My interest here is not in being a part of "anthropology bashing"—accusing it of being the most racist of the western disciplines. (Historians, after all, did not believe that Africa even had a history; they rarely turned their attention to its study until the 1960s.) But the use of anthropological accounts in the study of African history is very troubling to me. Used uncritically, as they most often are, these accounts lead historians into the trap that assumes a static African culture. Anthropology can give us hints about the past; but given the dynamic cultures that I assume Africa had in the past, these hints must be treated carefully.

Moreover, there is a particular problem in the use of these accounts for understanding African women's history. Most of the reports relied on were written in the mid-twentieth century, a time when anthropologists and the colonial rulers for whom they worked were seeking to uncover "traditional" African social relations. They were responding to what they saw as a breakdown in these relations, leaving the African colonies more unruly and, most importantly, more unproductive than they hoped. Young men and young women ran off from the rural areas to towns, escaping the control of their elders. Divorce soared in many areas. The elders, too, were concerned with what they saw as a breakdown in their societies. Both elders and colonial rulers worried that young people made marriages without their elders' approval and then, finding that they had chosen partners with whom they were no longer compatible, the uncontrollable youth divorced without approval and made new, short-term marriages.

The anthropologists set out to find out what led to this "breakdown" and to discover the customary rules that they felt had restricted conflict in "traditional" Africa. Once again we see the concept of a harmonious Africa before colonial rule emerging. In his introduction to the seminal collection *African Systems of Kinship and Marriage,* A. R. Radcliffe-Brown expressed this concern:

> African societies are undergoing revolutionary changes, as the result
> of European Administrators, missions, and economic factors. In the
> past the stability of social order in African societies has depended
> much more on the kinship system than on anything else. . . . The an-
> thropological observer is able to discover new strains and tensions,
> new kinds of conflict, as Professor [Meyer] Fortes has done for the
> Ashanti and Professor Daryll Forde shows for the Yakö.[48]

In part, Radcliffe-Brown and his coeditor, Daryll Forde, offered this set of essays as a guideline to colonial administrators so that the colonialists could counteract the destabilizing influences of westernization. Such anthropologists obviously felt the need for a better understanding of people under colonial rule.

Not surprisingly, it was the male elders whom the anthropologists asked about these customary laws, not the junior women and men who now divorced at an increased rate. Martin Chanock points out in "Making Customary Law: Men, Women, and Courts in Colonial Northern Rhodesia" that customary law was developed out of this alliance between the colonial rulers and the elders' interests. Of course, African elders were unequal partners in this alliance. Yet since both elders and colonial rulers viewed the increasing rates of divorce and adultery as signs of moral decline, they collaborated to develop customary laws that controlled marriages. "For this purpose claims about custom were particularly well-suited as they provided the crucial and necessary legitimation for the control of sexual behavior."[49] Chanock shows the way customary laws in Northern Rhodesia represented increased concern with punishing women to keep them in control. Therefore, in many cases such as adultery what got institutionalized as "tradition" or "custom" was more restrictive for women than in the past.

It is with the concern of maintaining male control over women and elders' control over their juniors that many anthropologists of the 1940s and 1950s explored "traditional" African culture. To read their sources into the past could lead us to very conservative notions of what African gender relations were about. Yet Harper-Bolton accepts these views uncritically when she presents as unproblematic a model of gender relations that fails to question women's allocation to a domestic life that merely complements male roles.[50] And, by extension, she buys into an antifeminist ideology. She warns that rejection of African tradition leads women into two directions that are antithetical to healthy developments in African American family life. In one direction, women can fall into loose sexual behavior by accepting Euro-American conceptions of woman and beauty. In the other direction, women become trapped in aggressiveness in the workplace and rejection of motherhood. Harper-Bolton argues:

> What happened to this African-American woman is that she ac-
> cepted, on the one hand, the Euro-American definition of "woman"
> and attempts, on the other hand, to reject this definition by behaving
> in an opposite manner. Her behavior becomes devoid of an African
> sense of woman-ness. In her dual acceptance/rejection of the Euro-
> American definition of woman, this African-American woman, in
> essence, becomes a "white man."[51]

Can Nationalism and Feminism Merge?

Not all Afrocentric thinkers need be so blatantly antifeminist. Some African American women have attempted to combine nationalism and feminism. As black feminists have sought an independent identity from dominant white, bourgeois feminism, some have explicitly turned to Afrocentric ideology for their understanding of these gender relations. These efforts stressed that African American women grew up in families that had roots in African experiences and, therefore, were fundamentally different from the ones described by white feminists. Such arguments recognized the need to search for solutions to sexism in black families that are based on their own experiences and history.

One of the most successful attempts to rely on Afrocentric thinking comes from a newly evolving school of thought known as African women's diaspora studies. This school of thought is represented best by *Black Woman Cross-Culturally*, edited by Filomina Chioma Steady, and *Women in Africa and the African Diaspora*, edited by Rosalyn Terborg-Penn, Andrea Benton Rushing, and Sharon Harley, and tries to reclaim the African past for African American women. These works have significantly raised the level of understanding of the connections among women in Africa and its diaspora. A number of the scholars published in these books have read extensively about black women around the world and have drawn bold comparisons. For them, women from Africa and the African diaspora are united by a history of "economic exploitation and marginalization manifested through slavery and colonization and . . . [in the contemporary period] through neocolonialism in the U.S."[52] Influenced by nationalist impulses, they criticize much of the earlier literature on black women for using a white filter to understand African culture. Further, they persuasively argue that too often black women are presented as one-dimensional victims of patriarchy or racism.[53] Instead, these women use African feminist theory as described by Steady to remove this white filter on African American lives and to identify "the cosmology common to traditional African women who lived during the era of the slave trade" and who provided a common cultural source for all black women today.[54]

Steady is careful to point out that she does not want to romanticize African history as she acknowledges that tensions and conflicts existed in Africa as they did elsewhere. Unfortunately, none of these authors explores any of these tensions and conflicts, and, thus, they present an overwhelmingly harmonious picture. Nor do they clearly articulate the ways that they will unearth the cosmology of Africans living in the era of the Atlantic slave trade. Their footnotes do not reveal any sources on this cosmology that go beyond the problematic anthropological reports that give a male-biased view of the past.

While African women's disapora studies takes us a long way, it reveals some of the same shortcomings I have criticized in the nationalist writings of Asante and Harper-Bolton. These feminists accept the ideology of complementarity as if it signified equality. They rely on a notion of African culture that is based on biased anthropological reports of a static, ahistorical Africa. Finally, they construct a dichotomy between African feminism and western feminism that depends on the Afrocentric spirituality/materialism dichotomy. Clearly, these women advocate women's equality, but they find it much easier to address racism in the women's movement than sexism in black liberation struggles. In their attempt to combine Afrocentric and feminist insights, they recognize the importance of nationalist discourse for countering the hegemonic ideology that seeks to confine African American lives. But I would go beyond the conservative agenda that nationalists have constructed and, thus, strengthen their advocacy of a feminist discourse.

In the fine special issue of *Signs* on women of color, Patricia Hill Collins has produced one of the most persuasive attempts to combine Afrocentric thought and feminism. In the tradition of Molefi Asante, she recognizes the need to struggle for increased space within the academy for African American scholars. Although she does not say so explicitly, I read her article in the light of the narrow-minded failure of many academic departments to take Afrocentric scholars seriously and to give African Americans tenure. In recognition of the serious work many women's studies programs must do to make their classrooms appeal to more than white middle-class students, she tries to sensitize feminists to the worldview that their black students may bring with them to classes but that may be at odds with narrow academic training.

She may have gone too far, however, when she tries to identify an essential black women's standpoint. For Collins, the black women's standpoint has evolved from the experiences of enduring and resisting oppression. Black feminist thought is interdependent with this standpoint as it formulates and rearticulates the distinctive, self-defined standpoint of African American women.[55] At the same time, black feminist theory intersects with Afrocentric and feminist thought.

For Collins, both Afrocentric and female values emerge out of concrete experience:

> Moreover, as a result of colonialism, imperialism, slavery, apartheid, and other systems of racial domination, Blacks share a common experience of oppression. These similarities in material conditions have fostered shared Afrocentric values that permeate the family structure, religious institutions, culture, and community life of Blacks in varying parts of Africa, the Caribbean, South America, and North America.[56]

Similarly:

> Women share a history of patriarchal oppression through the political economy of the material conditions of sexuality and reproduc-

tion. These shared material conditions are thought to transcend divisions among women created by race, social class, religion, sexual orientation, and ethnicity and to form the basis of a women's standpoint with its corresponding feminist consciousness and epistemology.[57]

Thus, the contours of Afrocentric feminist epistemology include black women's material conditions and a combination of Afrocentric and female values. Collins's Afrocentric feminist values share much with the essentialist cultural feminism of Carol Gilligan, including the ethic of caring and the ethic of personal accountability.[58]

Collins builds from the black feminist insight that black women experience oppressions simultaneously. Unfortunately, she remains mired in a false dichotomy that limits the value of this insight. For example, while she recognizes the importance of discussing class, she is unable to keep class as a variable throughout her analysis. At times, she assumes that all white women are middle class and all black women are working class. She sets up working-class black women to comment on the lives of privileged white women:

> Elderly domestic Rosa Wakefield assesses how the standpoints of the powerful [white middle-class women] and those who serve them [poor black women] diverge: "If you eats these dinners and don't cook 'em, if you wears these clothes and don't buy or iron them, then you might start thinking that the good fairy or some spirit did all that. . . . Blackfolks don't have no time to be thinking like that. . . . But when you don't have anything else to do, you can think like that. It's bad for your mind, though."[59]

Missing in such accounts is the position of middle-class black women and working-class white women. In Collins's view, all white women have class privilege, although she does recognize that some black women have obtained middle-class status. She admits that "African-American women do not uniformly share an Afrocentric feminist epistemology since social class introduces variations among Black women in seeing, valuing, and using Afrocentric feminist perspectives."[60] She even acknowledges that black women's experiences do not place them in a better position than anyone else to understand oppression.[61] Yet the quintessential black woman is one who has "experienced the greatest degree of convergence of race, class, and gender oppression."[62] Collins certainly does not raise the possibility that class differences may create tensions within the black sisterhood that she takes as unproblematic.

Ultimately, she falls prey to the positivist social science that she seeks to critique. She links positivist methodology to a Eurocentric masculinist knowledge-validation process that seeks to objectify and distance itself from the "objects" of study.[63] Like Asante, she recognizes many of the shortcomings with mainstream social science research such as the tendency to create false objectivity. Yet also like Asante, she falls into a positivist trap. In her case, she brings her readers back to the possibility of universal truths.

> Those Black feminists who develop knowledge claims that both
> [Afrocentric and feminist] epistemologies can accommodate may
> have found a route to the elusive goal of generating so-called objec-
> tive generalizations that can stand as universal truths.[64]

Like most positivists, she never asks, "whose universal truths are these anyway?" Collins's quest for universal truth will be doomed to failure as long as she accepts as unproblematic an Afrocentric sisterhood across class, time, and geography. Her truths depend on an Afrocentric ideology that suppresses differences among African Americans.

Like all oppositional discourses, the Afrocentric feminisms of Collins, Steady, and Terborg-Penn have multisided struggles. They compete for ideological space against the dominant discourse on Africa, its diaspora, and within feminist and nationalist movements. The dialectics of discursive struggle links their work to dominant discourse and other competing oppositional voices. Both dominant and counter discourses occupy contested terrain. Afrocentric feminists may reveal an almost inescapable tendency in nationalist discourse that ties it to conservative agendas on gender and sexuality. At the same time, they reveal the strengths of nationalist ideology in its counterattack against racism.

NOTES

This essay benefited from the careful readings given it by a number of people. I especially want to thank Paulla Ebron, Evelynn Hammonds, Margaret Cerullo, Marla Erlien, and Frank Holmquist.

1. See Cheryl Clarke, "The Failure to Transform: Homophobia in the Black Community," in *Home Girls: A Black Feminist Anthology,* ed. Barbara Smith (New York, 1983), pp. 197–208; Audre Lorde, *Sister Outsider: Essays and Speeches* (Trunmansburg, N.Y., 1984).

2. They only need point to the racist scientific theories that AIDS began in Central

Africa from people who ate [subtext: had sex with] green monkeys to prove this point. Spread by the popular and scientific media, this theory appealed to a white culture that still believes that black sexuality is out of control and animalistic. The scientific evidence contributed to the racist subtext of the anti-AIDS hysteria. See Evelynn Hammonds, "Race, Sex, AIDS: The Construction of 'Other,'" *Radical America* 20, no. 6 (1986); and Evelynn Hammonds and Margaret Cerullo, "AIDS in Africa: The Western Imagination and the Dark Continent," *Radical America* 21, nos. 2–3 (1987).

3. E. Frances White, "Civilization Denied: Questions on *Black Athena*," *Radical America* 18, nos. 2–3 (1987):5.

4. See, e.g., Cheikh Anta Diop, *The African Origins of Civilization: Myth or Reality*, trans. Mercer Cook (New York, 1974).

5. Chancellor Williams, *Destruction of African Civilization: Great Issues of a Race from 4500 B.C. to 2000 A.D.* (Chicago, 1974).

6. Larry Delano Coleman, "Black Man/Black Woman: Can the Breach Be Healed?" *The Nile Review* 2, no. 7:6.

7. Clarke, "The Failure to Transform," has raised similar objections in this thoughtful essay. She argues that leftist male intellectuals have helped to institutionalize homophobia in the black community. I refer to this essay in more detail below.

8. Nathan Hare and Julia Hare, "The Rise of Homosexuality and Other Diverse Alternatives," *Black Male/Female Relationships* 5 (1981):10.

9. George Mosse, *Nationalism and Sexuality: Respectability and Abnormal Sexuality in Modern Europe* (New York, 1985).

10. According to George Mosse (ibid.), German nationalists defined certain people as "outsiders" who did not live up to the norms set up by nationalism and respectability. By labeling homosexuals, prostitutes, Jews, etc. as perverts who lived outside the boundaries of acceptable behavior, nationalists helped build cohesion. Jewish men, for example, were said to epitomize all that was unmanly and unvirile. By contrast, a good, manly German looked on suspiciously at Jewish men. Many of the newly evolving negative identities and classifications fused with the stereotypes of Jews. In this way the rise of National Socialism was inextricably tied to the increase in anti-Semitism.

11. M. Ron Karenga, *Introduction to Black Studies* (Los Angeles, 1982), p. 213.

12. See Richard Terdiman, *Discourse/Counter-Discourse: The Theory and Practice of Symbolic Resistance in Nineteenth-Century France* (Ithaca, N.Y., 1985).

13. Edward W. Said, *Orientalism* (New York, 1978), p. 11.

14. Raymond Williams, *Keywords: A Vocabulary of Culture and Society* (London, 1976).

15. Johannes Fabian, *Time and the Other: How Anthropology Makes Its Objects* (New York, 1983).

16. Terdiman, *Discourse/Counter-Discourse*, p. 65.

17. Ibid., p. 36.

18. See James C. Scott, *Weapons of the Weak: Everyday Forms of Peasant Resistance* (New Haven, Conn., 1985). Scott, however, may underemphasize the extent to which people are influenced by dominant hegemonies.

19. Terdiman, *Discourse/Counter-Discourse*, p. 68.

20. Scott, *Weapons of the Weak*, p. 338.

21. V. N. Volosinov, *Marxism and the Philosophy of Language*, trans. Ladislav Matejka and I. R. Titunik (New York and London, 1973), p. 10.

22. Ibid., p. 14.

23. Caryl Emerson, "The Outer World and Inner Speech: Bakhtin, Vygotsky, and the Internalization of Language," *Bakhtin: Essays and Dialogues on His Work*, ed. Gary Saul Morson (Chicago, 1986), p. 185.

24. Hazel V. Carby, *Reconstructing Womanhood: The Emergence of the Afro-American Woman Novelist* (New York and Oxford, 1987), p. 17.

25. Emerson, "The Outer World and Inner Speech," p. 185.

26. For further exploration of these ideas, see E. Frances White, "Racisme et sexisme: La confrontation des féministes noires aux formes conjointes de l'oppression," *Les Temps Modernes* 42, no. 485 (December 1986): 173–84.

27. See Lorde, *Sister Outsider.*

28. For examples of white feminists who have been influenced by Audre Lorde's insights, see Barbara Johnson, *A World of Difference* (Baltimore and London, 1987); Teresa de Lauretis, "Feminist Studies/Critical Studies: Issues, Terms, and Contexts," in *Feminist Studies/Critical Studies*, ed. T. de Lauretis (Bloomington, Ind., 1986), pp. 1–19; and de Lauretis, *Technologies of Gender: Essays on Theory, Film, and Fiction* (Bloomington, Ind., 1987).

29. Cherríe Moraga, *Loving in the War Years: lo que nunca pasá por sus labios* (Boston, 1983), p. 99.

30. See also Gloria Anzaldúa, *Borderlands/La Frontera: The New Mestiza* (San Francisco, 1987); Norma Alarcón, "Chicana's Feminist Literature: A Re-vision through Malintzin or Malintzin: Putting Flesh Back on the Object," in *This Bridge Called My Back: Writings by Radical Women of Color,* ed. Cherríe Moraga and Gloria Anzaldúa (Watertown, Mass., 1981), pp. 182–90.

31. Clarke, "The Failure to Transform," p. 207.

32. Carby, *Reconstructing Womanhood,* p. 17.

33. Charlyn A. Harper-Bolton, "A Reconceptualization of the African-American Woman," *Black Male/Female Relationships* 6 (1982): 42.

34. Sylvia Junko Yanagisako, *Transforming the Past: Traditions and Kinship among Japanese Americans* (Stanford, Calif., 1985), p. 18.

35. Molefi Kete Asante, *The Afrocentric Idea* (Philadelphia, 1987), p. 8 n. 3.

36. Molefi Kete Asante, "Editor's Note," *Journal of Black Studies* 8, no. 2 (1977): 123.

37. Ibid.

38. See Asante, *Afrocentric Idea,* p. 8.

39. V. Y. Mudimbe, *The Invention of Africa: Gnosis, Philosophy, and the Order of Knowledge* (Bloomington, Ind., 1985), pp. 75–92.

40. Ibid., p. 89.

41. Asante, *Afrocentric Idea,* p. 8.

42. Robert L. Allen, *Black Awakening in Capitalist America: An Analytic History* (Garden City, N.J., 1970).

43. See Karenga, *Introduction to Black Studies.*

44. Harper-Bolton, "Reconceptualization of the African-American Woman," 32.

45. Ibid., 40.

46. See John Mbiti, *African Religion and Philosophy* (Garden City, N.J., 1970), and Wade Nobles, "Africanity: Its Role in Black Families," *Black Scholar* 5, no. 9 (1974).

47. Rosalind Coward, *Patriarchal Precedents: Sexuality and Social Relations* (London, 1983).

48. A. R. Radcliffe-Brown and Daryll Forde, eds., *African Systems of Kinship and Marriage* (London, 1950), pp. 84– 85.

49. Martin Chanock, "Making Customary Law: Men, Women, and Courts in Colonial Northern Rhodesia," *African Women and the Law: Historical Perspective,* ed. Margaret Jean Hay and Marcia Wright (Boston, 1982), 60.

50. See Harper-Bolton, "Reconceptualization of the African-American Woman," 38.

51. Ibid., 41.

52. Filomina Chioma Steady, "African Feminism: A Worldwide Perspective," in *Women in Africa and the African Diaspora,* ed. Rosalyn Terborg-Penn, Sharon Harley, and Andrea Benton Rushing (Washington, D.C., 1987), p. 8.

53. Rosalyn Terborg-Penn, "African Feminism: A Theoretical Approach to the History of Women in the African Diaspora," in *Women in Africa and the African Diaspora,* ed. Terborg-Penn, Harley, and Rushing, p. 49.

54. Ibid. See also Steady, "African Feminism"; and Steady, "The Black Woman Cross-Culturally: An Overview," in *The Black Woman Cross-Culturally,* ed. Steady (Cambridge, 1981), pp. 7–48.

55. Patricia Hill Collins, "The Social Construction of Black Feminist Thought," *Signs: Journal of Women in Culture and Society* 14, no. 4 (1989):750.

56. Ibid., 755.

57. Ibid.

58. See Carol Gilligan, *In a Different Voice* (Cambridge, Mass., 1982).

59. Collins, "Social Construction of Black Feminist Thought," 748-49.

60. Ibid., 758.

61. Ibid., 757.

62. Ibid., 758.

63. Ironically she shows how difficult it is to separate out knowledge-validation processes when she argues that we have to use different techniques to study Black women than to study the powerful at the same time that much of her analysis depends on the insights of white men such as Peter L. Berger and Thomas Luckmann, *The Social Construction of Reality* (New York, 1966).

64. Collins, "Social Construction of Black Feminist Thought," 773.

7

Standing In for the State: Black Nationalism and "Writing" the Black Subject

Wahneema Lubiano

What is blackness? I present this question as it relates to a specific moment of black literary theory whose content is reproduced in the terms of the larger discourse of black common sense. Understanding the black nationalist terms of "blackness" is preliminary to figuring out what that black common sense means for political analysis and strategies in the United States. I'm interested here in the ways that black nationalism makes its presence known and its effects felt. It is articulated in various kinds of black writing and film, and in commentary by writers, filmmakers, and critics, in hip hop generally, and specifically in interviews with hip hop cultural producers such as Ice Cube. While black literary criticism may have receded as a form, its content is everywhere. It is less important as a producer of a market or even as a guarantor of aesthetic value, but it has been incredibly important as a producer of some other kinds of understandings; it has been central in the production of consciousness as part of the ongoing war against racist significations of blackness.

I have three ambitions here. I want to explicate: a general sense (albeit brutally reduced) of black nationalism's relation to and difference from more general notions of nationalism; its statelike cultural "work"; and its articulation in literary criticism. For the purpose of this discussion, I define nationalism as the activation of a narrative of identity and interests. Whether or not it is concrete in the form (or even the possibility) of a state, this narrative is one that members of a social, political, cultural, ethnic, or "racial" group tell themselves, and that is predicated on some understanding—however mythologized or mystified—of a shared past, an assessment of present circumstances, and a description of or prescription for a shared future. Nationalism articulates a desire—always unfulfillable—for complete representation of the past and a fantasy for a better future.

Nationalism is a social identification. My definition is Weberian in that it draws on his notions of a "community of memories" and a community of shared values, but it also draws on various nineteenth-century black intellectuals' descriptions of their group's political imperatives (I have in mind here Henry Highland Garnet, Martin Delaney, and the early W. E. B. Du Bois). I insert this brief and highly concentrated definition as a reminder that black nationalism is a form of generally understood nationalism, something easily forgotten if it is thought of only as a form of racial separatism.

Black nationalism in its broadest sense is a sign, an analytic, describing a range of historically manifested ideas about black American possibilities that include any or all of the following: racial solidarity, cultural specificity, religious, economic, and political separatism (this last has been articulated both as a possibility within and outside of U.S. territorial boundaries). Black nationalism has most consistently registered opposition to the historical and ongoing racism of the U.S. state and its various institutions and apparatuses, and has been deployed to articulate strategies of resistance. It is particularized as a constantly reinvented and reinventing discourse that generally opposes the Eurocentrism of the U.S. state, but neither historically nor contemporaneously depends upon a consistent or complete opposition to Eurocentrism; as conservative thinker Wilson Moses argues, black nationalism does not necessarily entail a complete rejection of the Euro-American cultural tradition. In fact, one consistent black feminist critique of black nationalist ideology is that it insufficiently breaks with patriarchical modes of economic, political, cultural (especially familial), and social circulations of power that mimic Euro-American modes and circulations.

Moses is correct when he describes black nationalism as "seeking to 'unite' the entire black 'family' and assuming that the entire race has a collective destiny and a 'message' for humanity comparable to that of a nation" (Moses, 17). That "message," I think, has been described variously as either an example of a "better" world directed at the rest of the actually existing world and/or as a meaning available only within the group. Since the late eighteenth and early nineteenth century, the message has been circulated as resistance by black nationalists who have detailed for black Americans an origin and a destiny outside the myth of "America" (including America's reimagining of its own national "self"), if not outside its territorial boundaries.

I will return to black nationalism, but first I want to explain that when I say "the state," I mean not only the system of formal governmental and economically influential entities of executive mandate, legislation, policy making, and regulation—the president, the cabinet and administration, Congress—but also what Tim Mitchell refers to as the "common ideological and cultural construct [that] occurs not merely as a subjective belief, incorporated in the thinking and action of individuals [but as] represented and reproduced in visible everyday forms" (Mitchell, 81). I agree with Mitchell's assertion that the state's "boundary within society appears elusive, porous, and mobile" (Mitchell, 77), and that it is no less efficient for all that it is difficult to describe in its presence and effects.

Within the terms of black nationalism, how do we understand the state and its function? Its role in imagining and representing the nation is of paramount importance in managing social structure if, despite the state's "elusive and porous" mobility, we understand its various entities to have the power and access to forums—civic, institutional, formally and informally political—that allow it to describe and circulate representations of what our social structure is and ought to be. The education system, for example, is of primary importance in the circulation of the state's idea of its subjects. And while black Americans are subject to, as well as negative subjects of, that circulation, historically, black nationalism has been the articulated consciousness of black Americans' awareness of their place in the state's intentions.

With this in mind, it seems to me that black nationalism resists the U.S. state and its social and racialized ethnic domination—including what black social theorist Oliver Cox described as the tendency of the white bourgeoisie to proletarianize the entire black American group (Cox, 19). In the eyes of the dominant group, there are no easily discernible class differences among the black American group members. Within the terms of its resistance to racism, black nationalism resists racialized domination for all classes of the group. But while it functions as resistance to the state on one hand, it reinscribes the state in particular places within its own narratives of resistance. That reinscription most often coheres within black nationalist narratives of the black family. (Black feminist cultural commentators across two centuries have developed a critique of this familial narrative.)

I bring these articulations on race and its classed nature into play here because black nationalism establishes itself as counter to the narrativizing of race as class within this social order. While black nationalism has not always, under all circumstances, understood the black struggle to focus on redistribution of wealth, its strategies for "liberation" in the U.S. context have cohered around the "fact" that within the discourse of white supremacy, all blacks are equally debased, and that for the most part class has not mediated many of the effects of racism. Black nationalism is predicated on the notion of racial solidarity across class lines.

But it is to the narrative site of black cultural nationalism, described in black literary criticism as "autonomy," "authenticity," or even as attention to the black "masses," that I turn now. In the present moment, it might be difficult to remember the pervasiveness, indeed, the ubiquity and force of black American literary critical discourse during the civil rights movement and the Black Power era. Not only were black poetry and poets everywhere (including campuses, churches, street corner soap boxes, community organizing, prisons and jails, theaters, clubs, radio, and albums), but many of the writers and critics of the era were involved in local racial activist politics. Amiri Baraka was only the most highly profiled figure and one of those most responsible for articulating both the criteria by which to evaluate cultural production and the substance of black nationalist politics.

Literary critics made literary production the "proof" or "reality" of black cultural coherence and the desire for a wished-for reality. Authenticity functions within the terms of this economy as the way to counter what might otherwise be a possible destiny of cultural "disappearance." Claims of authenticity or criticism of its lack are the last defenses against cultural imperialism. Cultural imperialism becomes the black nationalist cultural equivalent to actual imperialism (land seizure) because, lacking a homeland and a sovereignty, culture is all we can "own." Cultural imperialism, then, equals the destruction of black nationalist desire.

In part of its work fighting the forces of cultural imperialism, black nationalism articulates what is "best" for "the people," and that articulation stands in for the work of the state. In other words, to the question "what replaces the state within black nationalism?" the answer is cultural production and its consumption, and its adherence to black nationalist evaluative criteria as well as black patriarchal familial prescriptions. If, for example, the black slave mother, as Hortense Spillers argues, was the "bearer" of the U.S. national political economy during the era of the "peculiar institution," black nationalism postslavery "corrects" that historical nightmare; that is, while the black mother bears the contradiction of African American ontology in U.S. history, she is both the material and metaphoric site of our collective "past," or she is an image that evokes that "past" (Spillers, 79–80). To reclaim her is to reclaim the site of black potentiality, black futurity.

It is in the work of cultural commentary—including literary criticism's black aesthetic (the cultural arm of Black Power) theorizing—that black nationalism implicitly articulates its romanticizing of nonstate resistance and fills that nonstate void by playing the state's role in delimiting and representing acceptable or liberatory forms and images, including the means by which the black nationalist versions of the black American past, present, and future can be authorized and disseminated.

One of the most powerful and interesting examples of black aesthetic theorizing is summarized by David Lionel Smith: "The emphasis on vernacular performance implies that literature should become an immediate, communal form to be experienced in public as a 'definitive characteristic'" (Smith, 101). Performance equals the wished-for destiny but it also equals the strategy by which that destiny literally comes into being at the moment of consumption of cultural production. Interestingly enough, hip hop currently functions in this regard, and the discourse around hip hop is finally a site where the content of black literary criticism can be found. It is the site where the black nationalist "subject making" imperative is being fought out.

Smith accurately explicates the black nationalist anti-middle-class bias found in, for example, Leroi Jones/Amiri Baraka's early black aesthetic critique of black writing; it is a bias, Smith points out, that could only read as "true" a particular class perspective—that of the imagined black proletariat. A bias, I add, that "reads out" of black American history the production of a particular hybrid within that history: the middle-class black American cultural producer. Such a reading is an example of the limitation of a political imagery that tries to do the work of "creating" the potential black revolutionary subject, but which cannot account for any possible middle-class black agency—including its own. Whether or not articulated as an explicitly anti-middle-class bias, theories of the black aesthetic privileged the most oppressed of the group as being those for whom the black aesthetic must speak. This insistent focus on only the most economically and politically marginal was both evidence of concern for inscribing a critique of U.S. class harm (of blacks as a proletarian group generally, and specifically of the most economically oppressed within the group) into black nationalist reimaginings of the world and an added incentive for cultural workers to see their middle-class selves as political warriors on behalf of "the people" against the domination of a white American bourgeoisie.

This romanticizing of themselves gave and continues to give added impetus to black middle-class cultural workers "making" a (generally) masculinist and heterosexist black national subject who is always working-class or poor. Such a subject, once created, reflects his (and I use the pronoun advisedly) politically resonant glow back onto the non-working-class warriors who articulate him and his agenda. In other words, the middle-class black cultural workers whose articulations create the black subject not only ally themselves with the economically and politically most dominated of the group, they use that subject to stand in for the whole group. Doing so allows them to avoid coming to terms with the complexity of their own class standing and its history. They "become" what they articulate.

In 1971, Julian Mayfield addressed this combination of black vanguardism and romantic shouldering—across class lines—of the burden of black aesthetic theory:

> For me the Black Aesthetic is in a photograph in the book *Harlem on My Mind* of two old black women . . . their faces, especially their eyes, are tired and worn, and their backs are bent, for they and their mothers before them have been working for centuries for nothing, . . . tired old men and women working, working, working, and then dying and leaving nothing because they hadn't earned anything, . . . the murdered hope one sees on the faces of these same children, now barely out of adolescence, as they are routinely shuffled off to prison careers, because everything else—school, parents, protest movement—has failed them, drowsy, blinking addicts on the subway and the young winos sitting on the doorsteps waiting for the juice joints to open.
>
> My Black Aesthetic is Bobby Seale, bound and gagged and straining at his leash in a Chicago courtroom. . . . My Black Aesthetic is the image of the beautiful Malcolm the last time I saw him in Africa, driven by his own recalled images, determined to return to what he knew was a certain early death because he must try to make a revolution in this white American hell-pit. (Mayfield, 28–29)

This language of poverty, prison, violence, undereducation (or none at all), addiction, and black male rage against oppression as the defining commentary of blackness returns to us now in hip hop and in the discourse around it.

With this kind of language, then, it is no wonder that the black middle-class producer and his romanticized cultural commentary move in to fill the space that the state would otherwise occupy. This production generates a momentum that speeds black nationalist intellectuals and activists over the rough spots that might otherwise draw attention to any flaws in their paradigm, or the lack of such a paradigm's self-critique. And with these words, "It is in our racial memory, the unshakable knowledge of who we are, where we have been, and springing from this, where we are going" (Mayfield, 27), Mayfield not only stated his sense of the black aesthetic but at the same time produced the bare bones of the basic definition of nationalism in its most historically general sense—nationalism as a narrative of desire about the past, the present, and a possible future.

Larry Neal's retrospective essay, "The Social Background of the Black Arts Movement" (published posthumously), compiles some of the most explicit and succinct imperatives to produce black nationalist subjectivity:

> You have to remember that there was contention over which way to go. . . . In the readings that we were doing we were always trying to make sure that the form we were evolving was a form that could include the people, the community. We were looking at black national culture for things that would be useable for national liberation or for nationhood. . . . The question was how to convey to blacks the strength and values of Afro-American culture and politics through culture. (Neal, 16–19)

Black literary criticism, then, has been of primary and specific importance in "creating" blackness. I do not want to be misunderstood: I am not implying necessarily that such creation is only and inevitably falsification or fantastical manipulation. I mean that it pulls together or suggests an understanding of what black specificity has meant in the past, how it operates in the present, and what its possible future is in a narrative that represents or imagines blackness—under the rubric of the black aesthetic, for example. Such imagining, however, is never an isolated event; the moment of imagining is ongoing—we are witnessing such a contested reimagining within hip hop's production and reception (see Decker, 53–84)—and, as is the case with any imagining of the character of a specific group's resistance, it leaves certain things unsaid and perpetuates existing omissions—for example, women's marginalization.

What I am describing is more than a simple context. The Black Arts movement and its theoretical arm, black aesthetic criticism, were realizations of particular imperatives. In that regard, the nature of the object— book or rap—is not as important as its potential use for statelike activity in the cultural realm. In other words, if the state produces and reinforces an "authentic" American subject by virtue of its presence in the cultural realm, and the social weight given to its representations, and if black nationalism articulates, for better and for worse, resistance to that particular state as well as alternatives (some resembling state representations, some not), and further, if opposition to white racial hegemony legitimizes and privileges black nationalist imaginings, then we have before us the formation of a resisting subjectivity with awareness of history and cynicism about the usual authorities. In short, a nonstate romanticized subject. Further, it is a subjectivity that resists self-criticism precisely because it presents itself as a need to fill the vacuum resulting from our abandonment by and resistance to the state.

I don't mean to suggest that acting in lieu of the state in producing national subjects can only be a bad thing. We could also see black nationalism's intervention against state-manufactured subjectivity as a disruption of the totalizing production of public consciousness. An efficacious oppositional strategy requires a new hegemony, a new cultural "common sense." But what those of us interested in the areas marginalized by a patriarchal, masculinist, and heterosexist black nationalism are doing is contesting the terms of that hegemony. In short, black nationalism produces a nonstate romanticized subject but not necessarily a critique, for example, that would lead to the overthrow of global capitalism and/or homophobic patriarchy.

Nonetheless, black cultural nationalism has almost always blocked resistance within its ranks. And black straight and lesbian feminism has functioned as a site for resistance against its hegemony. At the height of Black Aesthetic hegemony, Toni Cade's anthology *The Black Woman* both explicitly and implicitly criticized that hegemony (as Cheryl Wall also notes in *Changing Our Own Worlds*). The work in that anthology was as varied as the writers' interests—both in genre and content. Verta Smart-Grosvenor's essay (on her kitchen) described black cultural nationalist criticism of the dominant racial group's domestic and social mores while it refigured our notions of "appropriate" oppositional sites.

What is the political work of an "imagined community," a "nation"? The idea of a "black nation" (with or without territorial sovereignty) is black America's popular consciousness of its own being. That consciousness makes imagining resistance coherent—both within the minds of individual black Americans and the strategizing of black American political groups. It provides a shorthand for constructing the heroic oppositional subject. That subject, as masculinist and heterosexist as it is, is a social construct generated by the work of the intellectual community of black nationalist cultural commentators, and provides an alternative to the U.S. state's attempt to create its own version of a black subject. Literary criticism as a site for the black nationalist subject's articulation is the "elsewhere" (in Raymond Williams's sense)—the site of political possibility with all of the tensions and marginalizations of any fought-over terrain. Black feminist resistance to the present terms of that "elsewhere" is part of the fighting.

WORKS CITED

Cade, Toni, ed. 1970. *The Black Woman: An Anthology.* New York: New American Library.

Cox, Oliver. 1959. *Caste, Class, and Race.* New York: Monthly Review Press.

Decker, Jeffrey. 1993. "The State of Rap: Time and Place in Hip Hop Nationalism." *Social Text* 34, 11.1: 53–84.

Mayfield, Julian. 1971. "You Touch My Black Aesthetic and I'll Touch Yours," in *The Black Aesthetic,* ed. Addison Gayle, Jr. Garden City: Doubleday-Anchor.

Mitchell, Timothy. 1991. "The Limits of the State: Beyond Statist Approaches and Their Critics." *American Political Science Review* 85.1 (March): 77–96.

Moses, Jeremiah Wilson. 1978. *The Golden Age of Black Nationalism, 1850–1925.* New York: Oxford University Press.

Neal, Larry. 1987. "The Social Background of the Black Arts Movement." *The Black Scholar* (January/February): 11–23.

Smart-Grosvenor, Verta. 1970. "The Kitchen Crisis," in *The Black Woman: An Anthology,* ed. Toni Cade. New York: New American Library.

Smith, David Lionel. 1991. "The Black Arts Movement and Its Critics." *American Literary History* 3.1: 93–110.

Spillers, Hortense. 1987. "Mama's Baby, Papa's Maybe: An American Grammar Book." *diacritics* 17.2: 65–81.

Wall, Cheryl, ed. 1989. *Changing Our Own Words: Essays on Criticism, Theory, and Writing by Black Women.* New Brunswick: Rutgers University Press.

8

Nationalism and Social Division in Black Arts Poetry of the 1960s

Phillip Brian Harper

1

This essay begins with an epigraph, not its own, but one from a key publication in the history of black American poetry. Dudley Randall's anthology *The Black Poets,* published in 1971, is significant not so much for the texts it provides of folk verse and literary poetry from the mid-eighteenth through the early twentieth centuries; rather, its import derives from its participation in a contemporary process of canonization performed on poetry from the Black Arts movement. The concluding section of Randall's anthology is titled "The Nineteen Sixties," and it is introduced by the short poem "SOS" by Imamu Amiri Baraka (LeRoi Jones), which is printed not in the main text but on the title page for the section:

> Calling black people
> Calling all black people, man woman child
> Wherever you are, calling you, urgent, come in
> Black People, come in, wherever you are, urgent, calling
> you, calling all black people
> calling all black people, come in, black people, come
> on in.[1]

It seems reasonable to infer that, as it occupies an epigraphic position in Randall's compilation, Baraka's "SOS" can be identified as emblematic of the poetic project of many young black writers of the late 1960s. And it is not particularly difficult to identify exactly in what this emblematic nature might consist. We know, after all, that radical black intellectual activism of the late 1960s was characterized by the drive for a nationalistic unity among people of African descent. As Larry Neal put it in 1968 in his defining essay "The Black Arts Movement,"

> Black Art is the aesthetic and spiritual sister of the Black Power concept. . . . The Black Arts and the Black Power concept both relate broadly to the Afro-American's desire for self-determination and nationhood. Both concepts are nationalistic. One is concerned with the relationship between art and politics; the other with the art of politics.[2]

Addison Gayle also embraces the nationalist impulse in his conception of the movement, outlined in his 1971 introduction to *The Black Aesthetic.* According to Gayle, "The Black Aesthetic . . . is a corrective—a means of helping black people out of the polluted mainstream of Americanism."[3] And in 1972 Stephen Henderson elaborated the development of this impulse through the late 1960s: "The poetry of the sixties is informed and unified by the new consciousness of Blackness. . . . a consciousness [that has] shifted from Civil Rights to Black Power to Black Nationalism to Revolutionary Pan-Africanism."[4] Thus do three of the Black Aesthetic's most prominent theorists conceive the importance of nationalist unity to the Black Arts movement.[5] For the moment, we can leave aside the various directions in which the nationalist impulse might develop as we attempt to identify its presence, in however rudimentary a form, in Baraka's poem.

In the introduction to their authoritative anthology, *Black Nationalism in America,* John Bracey Jr., August Meier, and Elliott Rudwick assert that

> the simplest expression of racial feeling that can be called a form of black nationalism is *racial solidarity.* It generally has no ideological or programmatic implications beyond the desire that black people organize themselves on the basis of their common color and oppressed condition to move in some way to alleviate their situation. The concept of racial solidarity is essential to all forms of black nationalism.[6]

It is precisely this essential impulse to racial solidarity that is manifested in Baraka's "SOS." Considered with respect to nationalism, the political import of the poem inheres not so much in the stridency and exigency of its appeal but rather in its breadth, in the fact that Baraka's call apparently includes all members of the African diaspora, as it is directed explicitly and repeatedly to "*all* black people," thereby invoking a political Pan-Africanism posited as characteristic of the Black Arts project. Moreover, the enjambment of the last two lines and their modification of the injunction definitively transform the SOS from a mere distress signal into a general summons for assembly. What is striking about Baraka's poem, however, is not that it "calls" black people in this nationalistic way but that this is *all* it does; the objective for which it assembles the black populace is not specified in the piece itself, a fact I take to indicate fundamental difficulties in the nationalist agenda of the Black Arts poets, as we will soon see.

In the meantime, I think it is useful to consider Baraka's "SOS" as a synecdoche for all of his poetic output of the 1960s, which constituted a challenge to other black poets to take up the nationalist ethic he espoused. Insofar as a significant number of black poets did heed his call, Baraka can certainly be seen as the founder of the Black Aesthetic of the 1960s and "SOS" as representative of the standard to which his fellow poets rallied. "SOS" is part of Baraka's collection *Black Art,* comprising poems written in 1965 and 1966 and published, along with two other collections, in the volume *Black Magic: Poetry, 1961–1967.*[7] Its message was subsequently engaged by other black writers from different generations and disparate backgrounds. In her 1972 autobiography, *Report from Part One,* Gwendolyn Brooks, who built her reputation on her expertly crafted lyrics of the 1940s and 1950s, makes Baraka's enterprise her own as she describes her new poetic mission in the early 1970s: "My aim, in my next future, is to write poems that will somehow successfully 'call' (see Imamu Baraka's 'SOS') all black people: black people in taverns, black people in alleys, black people in gutters, schools, offices, factories, prisons, the consulate; I wish to reach black people in pulpits, black people in mines, on farms, on thrones."[8] Sonia Sanchez, on the other hand, in her 1969 poem "blk / rhetoric" invoked Baraka's language to question what might happen after the calling had been done:

> who's gonna make all
> that beautiful blk / rhetoric
> mean something.
>   like
> i mean
>   who's gonna take

the words
        blk / is / beautiful
and make more of it
than blk / capitalism.
                                u dig?
        i mean
                like who's gonna
take all the young / long / haired
natural / brothers and sisters
and let them
                grow till
                                all that is
impt is them
                selves
                        moving in straight / ʾ
revolutionary / lines
                        toward the enemy
(and we know who that is)
                                like. man.
who's gonna give our young
blk / people new heroes
        (instead of catch / phrases)
        (instead of cad / ill / acs)
        (instead of pimps)
        (instead of wite / whores)
        (instead of drugs)
        (instead of new dances)
        (instead of chit / ter / lings)
        (instead of a 35¢ bottle of ripple)
        (instead of quick / fucks in the hall / way
          of wite / america's mind)
like. this. is an S O S
me. calling. . . . .
                        calling. . . . .
                                some / one
        pleasereplysoon.[9]

Sanchez's call—prefaced as it is by her urgent question and attended by the
entreaty to her listeners in the final line—is more pleading than Baraka's,
which is unabashedly imperative. I would suggest that the uncertainty that

characterizes Sanchez's poem is the inevitable affective result of writing beyond the ending of Baraka's "SOS," which it seems to me is what "blk / rhetoric" does. By calling into question what will ensue amongst the black collectivity after it has heeded the general call—succumbed to the rhetoric, as it were—Sanchez points to the problematic nature of the black nationalist project that characterizes Black Arts poetry.

What remains certain, in Sanchez's rendering—so certain that she need not state it explicitly—is the identity of the "enemy" against whom the assembled black troops must struggle. While Sanchez's elliptical reference might appear somewhat ambiguous at this point, especially after the emergence in the early and midseventies of a strong black feminist movement that arrayed itself against patriarchal forces, it seems clear enough that in the context of the 1969 Black Arts movement the enemy was most certainly the white "establishment." But this is the *only* thing that is "known" in Sanchez's poem, and while the identification of a generalized white foe is a central strategy in the Black Arts movement's effort to galvanize the black populace, here it provides a hedge against the overall uncertainty that characterizes the rest of the poem—a definitive core on which the crucial questions about the efficacy of nationalist rhetoric can center and thus themselves still be recognizable as nationalist discourse.

With its counterbalancing of fundamental inquiries about the future of the black nationalist enterprise by recourse to the trope of the white enemy, Sanchez's "blk / rhetoric" verges on the problematic that I take to be constitutive of the Black Arts project. Insofar as that project is nationalistic in character, then its primary objective and continual challenge will be, not to identify the external entity against which the black masses are distinguished—this is easy enough to do—but rather to negotiate division within the black population itself. I specifically invoke *negotiation* here and not, for instance, *resolution* because I want to claim that the response of Black Arts nationalism to social division within the black populace is not to strive to overcome it but, rather, repeatedly to articulate it in the name of black consciousness.

2

It has been widely held that the fundamental characteristic of Black Arts poetry is its virulent antiwhite rhetoric. For instance, as Houston Baker has noted, the influential black critic J. Saunders Redding disparaged the Black Aesthetic as representative of a discourse of "hate," a "naive racism in reverse."[10] And it is true that Baraka himself became known for a generalized antiwhite sentiment, often manifested in highly particularized ethnic and religious slurs, especially anti-Semitic ones. His "Black Art" provides an exemplary litany, calling for

> poems that wrestle cops into alleys
> and take their weapons leaving them dead
> with tongues pulled out and sent to Ireland. Knockoff
> poems for dope selling wops or slick halfwhite
> politicians Airplane poems . . .
> . . . Setting fire and death to
> whities ass. Look at the Liberal
> Spokesman for the jews clutch his throat
> & puke himself into eternity . . .
> . . . Another bad poem cracking
> steel knuckles in a jewlady's mouth.[11]

"Black People!" calls for the "smashing [of] jellywhite faces. We must make our own / World, man, our own world, and we can not do this unless the white man / is dead. Let's get together and killhim."[12] Similarly, Nikki Giovanni, in a poem that we will soon consider more fully, inquires urgently of her black reader, "Can you kill . . . / . . . Can you poison . . . / . . . Can you piss on a blond head / Can you cut it off . . . / . . . Can you kill a white man."[13]

   While the affective power of such antiwhite sentiment in much of the poetry certainly cannot be denied, it seems to me that the drama of interracial strife that this rhetoric represents also serves to further another objective of Black Arts poetry—the establishment of *intra*racial distinctions that themselves serve to solidify the meaning of the Black Aesthetic. In order to clarify this point, I would like to examine a few poems by key practitioners of the Black Aesthetic: Baraka, Sanchez, Giovanni, Haki Madhubuti (Don L. Lee), and June Jordan. These five poems have been widely anthologized as exemplary of the Black Arts project, yet I would argue that they are exemplary, not because they are *representative* of the poetics deployed in most Black Arts productions, but rather because they expose the logic of the Black Arts ethic that governs work from the movement generally, but whose operation is carefully suppressed in most of that material. I think that the strength of my claim will be augmented through the presentation of the complete poems, so I give the full texts here. First, Baraka's "Poem for Half White College Students":

Who are you, listening to me, who are you
listening to yourself? Are you white or
black, or does that have anything to do
with it? Can you pop your fingers to no
music, except those wild monkies go on
in your head, can you jerk, to no melody,
except finger poppers get it together
when you turn from starchecking to checking
yourself. How do you sound, your words, are they
yours? The ghost you see in the mirror, is it really
you, can you swear you are not an imitation greyboy,
can you look right next to you in that chair, and swear,
that the sister you have your hand on is not really
so full of Elizabeth Taylor, Richard Burton is
coming out of her ears. You may even have to be Richard
with a white shirt and face, and four million negroes
think you cute, you may have to be Elizabeth Taylor, old lady,
if you want to sit up in your crazy spot dreaming about dresses,
and the sway of certain porters' hips. Check yourself, learn who it is
speaking, when you make some ultrasophisticated point, check
     yourself,
when you find yourself gesturing like Steve McQueen, check it out,
     ask
in your black heart who it is you are, and is that image black or white,

you might be surprised right out the window, whistling dixie on the
     way in[14]

Second, Giovanni's "The True Import of Present Dialogue: Black vs. Negro":

Nigger
Can you kill
Can you kill
Can a nigger kill
Can a nigger kill a honkie
Can a nigger kill the Man
Can you kill nigger
Huh? nigger can you
kill

Do you know how to draw blood
Can you poison
Can you stab-a-jew
Can you kill huh? nigger
Can you kill
Can you run a protestant down with your
'68 El Dorado
(that's all they're good for anyway)
Can you kill
Can you piss on a blond head
Can you cut it off
Can you kill
A nigger can die
We ain't got to prove we can die
We got to prove we can kill
They sent us to kill
Japan and Africa
We policed europe
Can you kill
Can you kill a white man
Can you kill the nigger
in you
Can you make your nigger mind
die
Can you kill your nigger mind
And free your black hands to
strangle
Can you kill
Can a nigger kill
Can you shoot straight and
Fire for good measure
Can you splatter their brains in the street
Can you kill them
Can you lure them to bed to kill them
We kill in Viet Nam
for them
We kill for UN & NATO & SEATO & US
And everywhere for all alphabet but
BLACK

Can we learn to kill WHITE for BLACK
Learn to kill niggers
Learn to be Black men[15]

Third, Lee's "Move Un-Noticed to Be Noticed: A Nationhood Poem":

move, into our own, not theirs
into our.
they own it (for the moment): the unclean world, the
                              polluted space, the un-censor-ed
                              air, yr/foot steps as they
                              run wildly in the wrong
                              direction.
move, into our own, not theirs
into our.
move, you can't buy own.
own is like yr/hair (if u let it live); a natural extension of ownself.
own is yr/reflection, yr/total-being; the way u walk, talk,
            dress and relate to each other is *own*.
own is you,
cannot be bought or sold
                      can u buy yr/writing hand
                      yr/dancing feet, yr/speech,
                      yr/woman (if she's real),
                      yr/manhood?
own is ours.
all we have to do is take it
take it the way u take from one another.
        the way u take artur rubinstein over thelonious monk
        the way u take eugene genovese over lerone bennett,
        the way u take robert bly over imamu baraka,
        the way u take picasso over charles white,
        the way u take marianne moore over gwendolyn brooks,
        the way u take *inaction* over *action*.
move. move to act   act.
act into thinking and think into action.
try to think. think. try to think think think.
try to think. think (like i said, into yr/own) think.
try to think. don't hurt yourself, i know it's new.

try to act,
act into thinking and think into action.
can u do it, hunh? i say hunh, can u stop moving like a drunk gorilla?
                    ha ha che che
                    ha ha che che
                    ha ha che che
                    ha ha che che
move
what is u anyhow: a professional car watcher, a billboard for nothingness,
        a sane madman, a reincarnated clark gable?
either you is or you ain't!

the deadliving
are the worldmakers,
the image breakers,
the rule takers: blackman can you stop a hurricane?

"I remember back in 1954 or '55, in Chicago, when we had
13 days without a murder, that was before them colored
people started calling themselves *black*."
move.
move,
move to be moved,
move into yr/ownself, Clean.
Clean, u is the first black hippy i've ever met.
why u bes dressen so funny, anyhow hunh?
i mean, is that u, Clean?
why u bes dressen like an airplane, can u fly,
i mean,
will yr/blue jim-shoes fly u,
& what about yr/tailor made bell bottoms, Clean?
can they lift u above madness,
turn u into the right direction.
& that red & pink scarf around yr/neck what's that for, Clean,
hunh?   will it help u fly, yeah, swing, swing ing swing
            swinging high above telephone wires with dreams
            of this & that and illusions of trying to take bar-b-q
            ice cream away from hon minded niggers who
            didn't event know that *polish* is more than a
            sausage.

"clean as a tack,
rusty as a nail,
haven't had a bath
sence columbus sail."

when u going be something real, Clean?
like yr/own, yeah, when u going be yr/ownself?

the deadliving
are the worldmakers,
the image breakers,
the rule takers: blackman can u stop a hurricane, mississippi couldn't.
blackman if u can't stop what mississippi couldn't, *be it, be it.*
black man be the wind, be the win, the win, the win, win win:

> wooooooooooowe boom boom   wooooooooooowe bah
> wooooooooooowe boom boom   wooooooooooowe bah
if u can't stop a hurricane, be one.
> wooooooooooowe boom boom   wooooooooooowe bah
> wooooooooooowe boom boom   wooooooooooowe bah
be the baddest hurricane that ever came. a black hurricane.
> wooooooooooowe boom boom   wooooooooooowe bah
> wooooooooooowe boom boom   wooooooooooowe bah
the baddest black hurricane that ever came, a black
                  hurricane named Beulah,
go head Beulah, do the hurricane.
> wooooooooooowe boom boom   wooooooooooowe bah
> wooooooooooowe boom boom   wooooooooooowe bah
move
move to be moved from the un-moveable,
into our own, yr/self is own, yrself is own, own yourself.
go where you/we go, hear the unheard and do,
do the undone, do it, do it, do it *now,* Clean
and tomorrow your sons will
be alive to praise
you.[16]

Next, Sanchez's "chant for young / brothas & sistuhs":

yall

out there.   looooken so coool,

in yo / highs.

              yeah yall

                   rat there

         listen to me

screeaamen this song.

                   did u know i've

seen yo / high

                   on every blk / st in

wite / amurica

                   i've seen yo/self/

imposed/quarantined/hipness

                             on every

slum/

         bar/   revolutionary / st

& there yall be sitten.

                   u brotha.

u sistuh.

         listen to this drummen.

this sad / chant.

listen to the tears

flowen down my blk / face

                    listen to a

death/song being sung on thick/lips

by a blk/woman
                    once i had a maaan
                    who loved me so he sed
                    we lived togetha, loved togetha
                    and i followed wherever he led

                    now this maaan of mine
                    got tired of this slooow pace
                    started gitten high a lot
                    to stay on top of the race.

                    saw him begin to die
                    screeaamed.   held him so tight
                    but he got so thin so very thin
                    slipped thru these fingers of might

                    last time i heard from him
                    he was bangen on a woman's door
                    callen for his daily high
                    didn't even care bout the score.

                    once i loooved a man
                    still do looove that man
                    want to looove that man again
                    wish he'd come on home again

                    need to be with that maaannn
                    need to love that maaaannnn
                    who went out one day & died
                    who went out one day & died.

yall

out there   looooken so cooool

in yo / highs.

yeah.   yall

rat there

c'mon down from yo / wite / highs

and live.[17]

And, finally, "Okay 'Negroes,'" by Jordan:

Okay "Negroes"
American Negroes
looking for milk
crying out loud
in the nursery of freedomland:
the rides are rough.
Tell me where you got that image
of a male white mammy.
God is vague and he don't take no sides.
You think clean fingernails crossed legs a smile
shined shoes
a crucifix around your neck
good manners
no more noise
you think who's gonna give you something?

Come a little closer.
Where you from?[18]

These pieces, disparate as they are, share certain features. There are, to
be sure, the disparaging references to white society—Jordan's "male white
mammy," Sanchez's rendering of the heroin high, Baraka's invocation of
film celebrities as representative of the shallowness of white culture—all of
which fit neatly into characterizations of Black Arts poetry as essentially
antiwhite. But while these works might engage conceptions of white America as a negative force, the rhetoric of the pieces is not addressed—not di-

rectly at any rate—to the white society that is the ostensible target of their wrath. Indeed, the thematic context of the poems and their employment of the second-person pronoun *you* are clearly meant to conjure a specifically black addressee and thus to give the impression that the poetic works themselves are meant for consumption by a specifically black audience. In other words, the rhetoric of Black Arts poetry, in conjunction with the sociopolitical context in which it is produced, works a twist on John Stuart Mill's proclamation that "poetry is overheard," as it seems to effect a split in the audience for the work. Because of the way the poetry uses direct address and thus invites us to conflate addressee and audience, it appears that the material is meant to be *heard* by blacks and *over*heard by whites. I think, however, that this is appearance only, and it will be the serendipitous consequence of my primary argument to show that, while Black Arts poetry very likely does depend for its effect on the division of its audience along racial lines, it also achieves its maximum impact in a context in which it is understood as being *heard* directly by whites and *over*heard by blacks.

Clarification of that point is forthcoming. In the meantime, it is necessary to acknowledge the substantial polemical effect that is achieved through the *presentation* of Black Arts poetry as meant for black ears only, for it is this presentation that commentators have seized on when they have characterized the Black Arts movement as representing a completely Afrocentric impulse. As Gayle, for instance, puts it in his introduction to *The Black Aesthetic,* the black artist of the 1960s "has given up the futile practice of speaking to whites, and has begun to speak to his brothers. . . . to point out to black people the true extent of the control exercised upon them by the American society."[19] Gayle's claim is, in itself, not earthshaking; it is typical of the contemporary conceptions of the Black Arts movement's significance in black cultural history. What *is* notable is that Gayle's statement, in positing the Black Arts strategy as historically unique, establishes itself as a historical repetition, insofar as, nearly fifty years before, a black theorist of the Harlem Renaissance made a very similar claim about the nature of that movement. In his 1925 article on the flowering of the Harlem Renaissance, "Negro Youth Speaks," Alain Locke insisted that, "Our poets have now stopped speaking for the Negro—they speak as Negroes. Where formerly they spoke to others and tried to interpret, they now speak to their own and try to express."[20] The full irony of this repetition lies in the fact that it is precisely on the basis of the perceived failure of the Harlem Renaissance to engage black interests that Black Arts theoreticians find fault with the earlier movement. Neal specifically charges that the Harlem Renaissance "failed" in that "it did not address itself to the mythology and the life-styles

of the Black community."[21] Clearly, there is an anxiety of influence operative here, manifested in the powerful need among the Black Aestheticians to
disassociate themselves from the Harlem Renaissance; and this disassocia-
tion will be based on the later movement's apparently uniquely effective
manner of addressing itself to the interests of black people. By examining
this strategy, we can see more clearly both how social division within the
black community is fundamentally constitutive of Black Arts nationalism
and, relatedly, why it *is* so difficult for the Black Arts movement to postulate
concrete action beyond "black rhetoric," to project beyond the "call" manifested in Baraka's "SOS."

3

What is most striking about the way the poems under consideration—
which I have suggested distill the logic of the Black Arts project—address
themselves to the black community is their insistent use of the second-
person pronoun. This aspect of the poetry is notable not only because it is
the verbal indicator of the Black Arts poets' keen awareness of issues of audience and of their desire to appear to engage directly with their audience
(both of which I have already alluded to), but because the *you* references
also—and paradoxically, given the Black Aesthetic's nation-building
agenda—represent the implication of intraracial division within its Black
Arts strategy. It is clear, of course, that the use of the second-person pronoun of indefinite number implies less inclusiveness than would, say, the
use of the first-person plural, *we.* What remains to be explored is exactly on
what this apparent exclusivity—this implicit social division—is founded,
both grammatically and historically, in order for us to grasp more fully the
significance of Black Arts poetics.

The import of the second-person pronoun—both generally and in
the specific context of Black Arts poetry—derives largely from its special
grammatical status. Because *you* is a deictic, or shifter, whose reference
varies among a multitude of different subjects, it is always necessary to an-
chor that reference before we can interpret any linguistic construction in
which *you* appears. This would seem to be a relatively easy thing to accomplish, given that *you* is functionally fixed in a lexemic dyad through which
its meaning is conditioned and focused. Émile Benveniste has elucidated
the peculiar relation that obtains between the second-person pronoun and
the first-person (singular) pronoun, emphasizing that "'you' is necessarily
designated by 'I' and cannot be thought of outside a situation set up by

starting with 'I.'"²² Indeed, Benveniste suggests that these pronominal forms alone—exclusive of what we conventionally call the third-person pronoun—can properly be called personal because only the first and second persons are present in the discourse in which they are referenced. Having thus dismissed the genericized *he* as lacking this "sign of person," Benveniste then proposes a definition of *you* based on its inevitable relation to *I,* which itself always designates the speaking subject: "It is necessary and sufficient," he says, "that one envisage a *person* other than 'I' for the sign of 'you' to be assigned to that person. Thus every *person* that one imagines is of the 'you' form, especially, but not necessarily, the person being addressed 'you' can thus be [most accurately] defined as 'the non-*I* person.'"²³

Once we specify the referential field for *you,* however, it becomes clear that the more problematic task is identifying the referent for any *I* with which we are confronted. For, while it may be true that *I* and *you* are defined against one another—with *I* representing the speaker of an utterance and *you* representing the "non-*I* person"—this mode of anchoring deictic reference is useful only for specifying the subject represented in discourse; it provides us with no information about the subject articulating that discourse, which is always only imperfectly identified with the former. As Antony Easthope puts it, deriving his formulation from Lacan, "the 'I' as represented in discourse . . . is always sliding away from the 'I' doing the speaking," which makes for a profound crisis of identity for the speaking subject, who constantly oscillates between identification with the *I* represented in discourse (the realm of the *imaginary* in Lacanian terms) and recognition of the faultiness of such identification (the realm of the *symbolic*).²⁴

Numerous commentators have discussed the ramifications of such poststructuralist theories of the subject for socially marginalized groups, whose political agendas have often been considered as based on a primary need to forge stable identities in the first place and not on the deconstruction of the possibility of such identity.²⁵ Certainly, the Black Arts movement can very readily be seen as representing the impulse to establish a positive black subjectivity—based on nationalist ideals—in the face of major sociopolitical impediments to its construction. But poststructuralism's positing of the always imperfect discursive constitution of the subjective *I* does not, I think, *prohibit* the Black Aesthetic's construction of a powerful black nationalist subject; it merely stipulates that such construction is possible only from a position externally and obliquely situated with respect to the discursive *I.* I *will* argue, however, that the disjuncture between this as yet unidentified position and the discursive *I* itself precludes the constitution of an effective black nationalist *collectivity.* This is because the strategy

necessarily deployed by Black Arts poetry to establish a strong black nationalist subject—and through which it derives its meaning and power—is
founded on the oppositional logic that governs the pronominal language
characteristic of the work. That opposition is thematized in the poetry, not
in terms of the us versus them dichotomy that we might expect, however,
with *us* representing blacks and *them* whites; rather, it is played out along
the inherent opposition between *I* and *you,* both these terms deriving their
referents from within the collectivity of black subjects. Thus, the project of
Black Arts poetry can be understood as the establishment of black nationalist subjectivity—the forcible fixing of the identity of the speaking *I*—by
delineating it against the "non-*I* person," the *you* whose identity is clearly
predicated in the poems we are considering. So the *you* in Baraka's "Poem
for Half White College Students" is the African American who identifies
with the Euro-American celebrity, against which the speaking *I* of the poem
is implicitly contrasted. In Giovanni's and Lee's poems, *you* represents the
Negro subject whose sense of self-worth and racial pride has yet to be
proven. In Sanchez's "chant," *you* is the black junkie who finds solace in the
"wite" high of heroin, clearly meant to be associated with Euro-American
corruption. And in Jordan's "Okay, 'Negroes,'" *you* is the African American
who has not yet developed an understanding of the raciopolitical forces that
impinge on black subjectivity. Clearly, I oversimplify to the extent that the
referent of any given *you* might well vary even within a single poem. But my
point is that because, in spite of these shifts, the second person is much
more readily identified than the speaking *I* for any utterance, any *you* that
these Black Arts poets invoke can function as a negative foil against which
the implicit *I* who speaks the poem can be distinguished as a politically
aware, racially conscious, black nationalist subject. It seems to me that it is
this intraracial division on which the Black Arts project is founded and not
on any sense of inclusiveness with respect to the black community that we
might discern in Baraka's "SOS."

Indeed, once we have clarified the *I-you* division that underlies the
Black Arts concept of the black community, we can better understand the
intraracial division that is implicit in movement references to the "black"
subject itself. If it appears to us that Baraka's "SOS" embraces all members
of the black diaspora, this is only because we are forgetting that the designation *black,* from the middle 1960s through the early 1970s, represented
an emergent identification among nationalist activists and intellectuals and
not a generic nomenclature by which any person of African descent might
be referenced. Consequently, if Baraka is calling "all black people," he is already calling only those African Americans whose political consciousness is

sufficiently developed for them to subscribe to the designation *black* in the first place. All others—designated by *you* in the poems that utilize the pronominal rhetoric—will be considered as *negroes,* as in the titles of Giovanni's and Jordan's poems, a term that is intermittently transmuted into *niggers* in Giovanni's text.

4

Given these poems' authorization of their own black nationalist rhetoric, how then do we account for the historical and political factors in the movement's differentiation of the black body politic into disparate elements? Doesn't this division run counter to the solidarity we have taken to found black nationalism? Undoubtedly, a number of specific, local contingencies contributed to the development of the Black Arts movement's agenda and strategy. At the same time, it is possible, within the cultural-analytical context set up here, to identify a potential general motivation for the intraracial division so insistently deployed by Black Arts practitioners. That motivation is strongly related to the degree—noted above—to which Black Aestheticians of the 1960s sought to disassociate their movement from the Harlem Renaissance of the 1920s.

The Harlem Renaissance, apart from its evident cultural import, can be considered in sociopolitical terms as representing the culmination of a wave of black nationalist sentiment that lasted, according to Bracey, Meier, and Rudwick, from the 1880s until the onset of the Depression. During this period, they argue, "appeals to race pride and race unity became commonplace, and separate educational, religious, and economic institutions were more and more widely advocated" ("I," p. xl). On the other hand, they indicate the fundamentally ambiguous nature of this nationalist impulse by noting that these separatist appeals were mounted on behalf of a general accommodationist policy and not with a view toward ultimate black autonomy. They assert that while these separatist ideas "pervaded the spectrum of black social thought in the nineties and after the turn of the century . . . in general, they characterized the thinking of accommodators like Booker T. Washington more than that of protest leaders" ("I," p. xl). And they clarify further: "The ambiguous way in which nationalism has functioned in Negro thought was never more apparent than during this period. Almost always, except in the case of out-and-out colonization movements, separatism was advocated as a means of paving the way for full acceptance in American society" ("I," p. xli). To the degree that it conceived of this full ac-

ceptance as predicated on a Washingtonian *social* separatism (as opposed to
the ostensibly empowering *political* and *economic* separatism espoused by
the Black Power movement), and thus approximated alarmingly the agenda
of segregationist whites, the racial solidarity impulse of the turn of the century would be entirely out of sync with the black nationalism of the 1960s,
which was keenly sensitive to the possible co-optation of its agenda by
white interests. Consequently, just as we can identify in the Black Arts
movement the strong impulse to reject the cultural strategies of the Harlem
Renaissance, so too was it characterized by a profound need to disassociate
itself from the political objectives of the early black separatist movement. It
intensely repudiated the influence of the elders.

Black Aestheticians also—as is already widely recognized—rejected
the more immediate predecessor of the Black Power project, the civil rights
movement of the 1950s and early 1960s. While the actual temporal relation between these two movements is more complex than that of mere con-
secutiveness—as is roughly emblematized in the overlap of the careers of
Martin Luther King Jr. and Malcolm X—Black Power has nonetheless consistently been represented as a radical *progression* from the less urgent strategies of civil protest. Thus the notion of historical advance strongly influenced the Black Power movement's sense of itself in relation to both
turn-of-the-century and midcentury black political movements, and its
need to present itself as historically distinct from these other movements
can be discerned in the rhetoric of its poetic productions, the logic of which
transmutes that historical differentiation into the highly self-defensive division of the contemporary black population into disparate segments.[26]

It is also true, to develop the point further and in a slightly different direction, that the identification and consequent strong rejection of a puta-
tively ineffectual bourgeois accommodationism in whatever era of black
social and political history must have been a necessary undertaking for a
Black Arts movement characterized by an intense and potentially crippling
middle-class *ressentiment*. The Black Aestheticians' strong consciousness of
the need to appear rooted in the traditions of the folk was certainly not a
new phenomenon among mass political movements, nor is it the case that
movement intellectuals and the black masses were strictly dichotomized.
Nevertheless, for a movement that emerged in opposition to nonviolent
strategies that it represented as removed from the exigencies of everyday
black existence, the threat of being perceived as similarly alienated loomed
particularly large. It accounts, for instance, for the Black Aestheticians'
characterization of the emergent black studies movement of the late 1960s
and early 1970s as unacceptably "bourgie";[27] and the anxiety built up around

this possibility is evident in Stokely Carmichael's injunction of 1966: "We have to say, 'Don't play jive and start writing poems after Malcolm is shot.' We have to move from the point where the man left off and stop writing poems."[28] Thus is made clear the dominant sense of the suspect nature and relative ineffectuality of artistic and intellectual endeavors in the Black Power movement. It is a sense that is reiterated often in the poetry itself; for instance, Giovanni considers her inability to produce a "tree poem" or a "sky poem" in "For Saundra":

> so i thought again
> and it occurred to me
> maybe i shouldn't write
> at all
> but clean my gun
> and check my kerosene supply
>
> perhaps these are not poetic
> times
> at all[29]

And, much less typically, Sanchez worries explicitly that Black Power rhetoric will lead only to "blk / capitalism." It seems to me that it is the threatening unpredictability of exactly what will issue from nationalist organizing that accounts for Baraka's decision not to project beyond the call manifested in "SOS." The power of the work thus derives from the energy of the essential nationalist impulse itself and is not undermined by ambivalence regarding the different directions in which that impulse might develop.

Finally, I think that it is in order to quell such ambivalence that so much of the work employs a violent rhetoric, in which the mere repetition of references to killing the white enemy seems to be considered as the actual performance of the act. The positing of this violent rhetoric as performative language predicates the status of Black Arts poetry as being *heard* by whites and *over*heard by blacks. For if, in the performative logic of the Black Arts work, to be heard is to annihilate those persons who effect one's oppression, to be *over*heard is to impress upon one's peers just how righteous, how fearsome, how potently nationalistic one is, in contradistinction to those very peers who are figured as the direct addressee of the Black Arts works.

Which brings us back to where we began—with a consideration of conventional assessments of Black Arts poetry as primarily defined by its call for violence against whites. Clearly this rhetoric of violence, while certainly provoking various affective responses amongst white readers and auditors—responses that I don't pretend to address here—also represents the Black Arts movement's need to establish division *among blacks,* and, indeed, itself actually serves to produce such division. If we recognize the fundamental significance of this intraracial division to such black nationalism as is represented in the Black Arts project, then it seems to me that we are much closer to understanding the full social import of the nationalist imperative. Black Arts poetry can help us to do that because, as the most recent vital example of the nationalist impulse, it reflects the contradictions of the ideology in a particularly striking way. It behooves us to study those contradictions at this historical juncture as we begin to see in this country a new florescence of black nationalist consciousness whose cultural manifestations have yet to be fully realized and whose political ramifications have yet to be effectively theorized.

NOTES

This essay has benefited from the attention given to earlier versions of it by audiences at three different venues. For their helpful comments, criticisms, and suggestions, I would like to thank my colleagues at Brandeis and Harvard Universities and, especially, students and faculty in the English department at Johns Hopkins University. A revised and expanded version appears in my book, *Are We Not Men? Masculine Anxiety and the Problem of African-American Identity* (New York, 1996). I am also grateful for the opportunity to reprint the following poems: "SOS" and "Poem for Half White College Students," by Imamu Amiri Baraka (LeRoi Jones). © 1969 by Amiri Baraka (LeRoi Jones), reprinted by permission of Sterling Lord Literistic, Inc.; "The True Import of Present Dialogue: Black vs. Negro," by Nikki Giovanni. From *Black Feeling, Black Talk/Black Judgment.* © 1968, 1970 by Nikki Giovanni, reprinted by permission of William Morrow and Company, Inc.; "Okay, 'Negroes,'" by June Jordan. © 1970 by June Jordan, reprinted by permission of the author; "Move Un-Noticed to Be Noticed: A Nationhood Poem," by Don L. Lee (Haki Madhubuti). From *We Walk the Way of the New World.* © 1970 by Don L. Lee (Haki Madhubuti), reprinted by permission of Broadside Press; "blk/ rhetoric," by Sonia Sanchez. © 1969, 1978 by Sonia Sanchez, reprinted by permission of the author; "chant for young / brothas & sistuhs," by Sonia Sanchez. © 1970 by Sonia Sanchez, reprinted by permission of the author.

1. Imamu Amiri Baraka, "SOS," in *The Black Poets,* ed. Dudley Randall (New York, 1971), p. 181.

2. Larry Neal, "The Black Arts Movement," in *The Black Aesthetic,* ed. Addison Gayle Jr. (New York, 1971), p. 257.

3. Gayle, introduction, *The Black Aesthetic,* p. xxii.

4. Stephen Henderson, introduction to sec. 3, in *Understanding the New Black Poetry: Black Speech and Black Music as Poetic References,* ed. Henderson (New York, 1973), p. 183.

5. For an overview of the development of black nationalism in the Black Arts movement, see Houston A. Baker Jr., *The Journey Back: Issues in Black Literature and Criticism* (Chicago, 1980), esp. chap. 4, "In Our Own Time: The Florescence of Nationalism in the Sixties and Seventies," pp. 77–131.

6. John H. Bracey Jr., August Meier, and Elliott Rudwick, introduction, in *Black Nationalism in America,* ed. Bracey, Meier, and Rudwick (Indianapolis, 1970), p. xxvi; hereafter abbreviated "I."

7. See LeRoi Jones, *Black Magic: Poetry, 1961–1967* (Indianapolis, 1969).

8. Gwendolyn Brooks, *Report from Part One* (Detroit, 1972), p. 183.

9. Sonia Sanchez, "blk / rhetoric," *We a BaddDDD People* (Detroit, 1970), pp. 15–16.

10. Baker, *Afro-American Poetics: Revisions of Harlem and the Black Aesthetic* (Madison, Wis., 1988), p. 161.

11. Baraka, "Black Art," in *The Black Poets,* p. 224.

12. Baraka, "Black People!" in *The Black Poets,* pp. 226–27.

13. Nikki Giovanni, "The True Import of Present Dialogue: Black vs. Negro," in *The Black Poets,* pp. 318–19.

14. Baraka, "Poem for Half White College Students," in *The Black Poets,* p. 225.

15. Giovanni, "The True Import of Present Dialogue: Black vs. Negro," pp. 318–19.

16. Don L. Lee, "Move Un-Noticed to Be Noticed: A Nationhood Poem," in *Understanding the New Black Poetry,* pp. 340–43.

17. Sanchez, "chant for young / brothas & sistuhs," in *The Black Poets,* pp. 240–42.

18. June Jordan, "Okay 'Negroes,'" in *The Black Poets,* p. 243.

19. Gayle, introduction, *The Black Aesthetic,* p. xxi.

20. Alain Locke, "Negro Youth Speaks," in *The Black Aesthetic,* p. 17.

21. Neal, "The Black Arts Movement," p. 273.

22. Émile Benveniste, *Problems in General Linguistics,* trans. Mary Elizabeth Meek (Coral Gables, Fla., 1971), p. 197.

23. Ibid., p. 201.

24. Antony Easthope, *Poetry as Discourse* (London, 1983), p. 44.

25. For example, Joyce A. Joyce objects to the use of poststructuralist theory in black literary criticism; see Joyce A. Joyce, "The Black Canon: Reconstructing Black American Literary Criticism," *New Literary History* 18 (Winter 1987): 335–44.

26. It is also possible that the intraracial division effected in Black Arts poetry is a function of the black community's status as a sort of mutated colonial entity. During the late 1960s, analyses of the colonialized nature of black communities in the United States were forthcoming from both social scientists and black activists. Indeed, in their introduction to *Black Nationalism in America,* the editors posit just such a conception of black America, citing as their justification some contemporary studies in sociology and political

science. (See "I," p. lvi; among the material they cite, one article in particular clearly outlines the issues at stake in conceptualizing black communities as colonial entities. See also
Robert Blauner, "Internal Colonialism and Ghetto Revolt," *Social Problems* 16 [Spring
1969]: 393–408.) Given this, it is interesting to note that Abdul R. JanMohamed has
identified as one of the cultural manifestations of colonialism a mapping of the social entity along a Manichean duality that defines a morally "good" constituency—the colonizers,
more often than not—against one that is seen as inherently "evil"—the colonized. See
Abdul R. JanMohamed, *Manichean Aesthetics: The Politics of Literature in Colonial Africa*
(Amherst, Mass., 1983), and "The Economy of Manichean Allegory: The Function of
Racial Difference in Colonialist Literature," *Critical Inquiry* 12 (Autumn 1985): 59–87.
While I do not believe that the situation of black Americans can be posited unproblemati-
cally as a colonial one, its historical sine qua non—the slave trade—can certainly be considered as a manifestation of the colonizing impulse. Consequently, it seems possible that,
just as the economics of slavery developed in a particular manner after the initial appropriation of the "resources" from the African continent, there occurred concomitant mutations
in the cultural realm in which we can still trace the remnants of an essential colonial logic.
Thus, the *I-you* dichotomy that characterizes Black Arts poetry might represent the internalization within the black American community of the Manichean ethic that JanMohamed identifies with the colonial situation proper. It falls outside the scope of this essay to
trace the various mechanisms through which this internalization might have been effected,
but its possibility suggests a direction for further work on this topic.

27. A. B. Spellman, cited in James A. Emanuel, "Blackness Can: A Quest for Aesthetics," in *The Black Aesthetic,* p. 208.

28. Stokely Carmichael, "We Are Going to Use the Term 'Black Power' and We Are
Going to Define It Because Black Power Speaks to Us" (1966), in *Black Nationalism in
America,* p. 472.

29. Giovanni, "For Saundra," in *The Black Poets,* p. 322.

9

"Black Is Back, and It's Bound to Sell!" Nationalist Desire and the Production of Black Popular Culture

S. Craig Watkins

In 1970 poet-musician Gil Scott-Heron released his now legendary political treatise performed to music, "The Revolution Will Not Be Televised." The song revealed the extent to which the "black awakening" of the late 1960s and 1970s had imbued black cultural discourse with a strong dose of nationalistic fervor and revolutionary spirit.[1] Scott-Heron's song asserts that, for all of its seductive power and allure, television was irrelevant to the politics of black empowerment and social change. Scott-Heron's song championed the notion that any discourse worth tuning into would have to take place off the media culture stage. And while black performers during this period may have never heard of Antonio Gramsci, Theodor Adorno, or Stuart Hall, their view of the media as an instrument of social control revealed how critiques circulating in the academic world, unbeknownst to most, were also percolating in black cultural discourse.

Scott-Heron's claim that the "revolution will not be televised" remains poignant because it animates how black cultural politics during this period were undergoing a serious makeover in terms of both style and content. Even as "The Revolution Will Not Be Televised" contends that the popular media are irrelevant to black political intervention, it also, ironically, reveals the degree to which black Americans were already using the media as a site to imagine and construct a black nation worldview.

This essay focuses on a field not immediately associated with black nationality formation: popular media culture. Any serious consideration of black nationalism must recognize how notions of black peoplehood, community, and collective struggle penetrate the sphere of black popular culture. Likewise, such an analysis must recognize how black forms of expressive culture invigorate black nation discourse. Popular media culture has long been recognized by various advocates of black racial uplift as a necessary site of political struggle.[2] The terrain of popular media culture, for better or worse, is a vital aspect of black American life and a prominent factor in the modernization of black nationalist desire.

This essay probes some of the distinct ways black nation discourse is commodified in black popular culture. First, I outline how the transformation of black popular music in the late 1960s and 1970s foregrounds many of the tensions and contradictions that mark the commodification of black nationalism. Indeed, as the temperature of black American politics reached a boil in the late 1960s, the ways in which black Americans expressed themselves underwent dramatic change too.

Next, the essay considers the hyperpoliticization of rap music in the late 1980s. This particular moment in the fusion of black nationalism and black popular culture was facilitated by important social, economic, and technological shifts that enabled black youth to assert their vision of black nationalism in imaginative ways. More specifically, the essay examines rap music's most prolific black nationalist outfit, Public Enemy. In addition, I briefly consider the bourgeois nationalism of filmmaker Spike Lee. Lee's strategic posturing as a black cineaste is predicated, in part, on the notion that black capitalism represents a form of racial progress, uplift, and empowerment.

A main goal of this essay is to consider what black nationalism means to the post–civil rights generation of black youth. That is, how do they translate the legacy and currency of black nationalism into particular regimes of cultural politics? Ultimately, the essay considers how young African Americans appropriate nation discourse to enliven their own distinct modes of agency and intervention in the world of popular media culture.

"Say It Loud, I'm Black and I'm Proud!"

Throughout the twentieth century the political intonations of black popular music have been expressed in various genre forms and performance traditions—blues, jazz, rock 'n' roll, soul, and pop.[3] Still, the tumultuous decade of the 1960s is as good a period as any to situate an analysis of the popular diffusion and appeal of black nationalism. During this period black popular music performers incorporated elements of the social movements that were radically redefining U.S. race relations and notions of black racial identity. Moreover, as the tone of black politics became more strident and openly defiant, the demeanor of black expressive culture developed more explicitly political features.

Before the middle to late 1960s, the political inclinations of black popular music were usually coded, that is, clandestinely expressed in order to avoid white retaliation, censure, and commercial failure. The absence of explicitly political themes in black music can be attributed, in part, to the industrial milieus in which it was produced. That is, prior to the 1960s blacks were less likely to control the spaces where popular music was produced; thus the degree to which they could express an explicitly political message was seriously limited during studio recording sessions.

But if the political intonations of black popular music were once typically constrained, the social movements of the 1960s changed that, forever altering the manner in which the worlds of black popular culture and politics intersected. As black protest politics became more fragmented, the rise of a vibrant, though never coherent, nationalist movement dramatically reconfigured the terms and conditions under which black racial and cultural politics were practiced. Brian Ward argues that the politicization of the black popular music scene in the 1960s was made possible when three important barriers were removed.[4]

First, record industry executives who once eschewed any association of their product with black political commentary began to recognize the financial benefits such associations might produce in a period of great political activism. Second, the sheer intensity of black protest politics demanded at least some recognition if not support on the part of black performers. In other words, the movement made it suitable, indeed fashionable, to express more politically charged messages, images, and styles.[5] Finally, as the civil rights movement began to lose white financial support, its leaders aggressively enlisted the support of black performers in order to raise the money necessary to sustain the movement.

As the currents of black protest and political culture began to shift in the late 1960s, black nationalism emerged as a prominent expression of political intervention. Still, even as black nation discourse was penetrating the black public sphere, no consensus formed regarding how black artists and performers should employ it. Broadly speaking, then, certain forms of black cultural production cleaved around two forms of nationalism in the late 1960s and early 1970s: cultural and economic. Whereas the former was based on the creation of cultural expressions that rejected virtually anything associated with white America (i.e., food, film, clothes, language), the latter pivoted around the notion that blacks needed to become more economically independent. Moreover, economic nationalists did not necessarily reject association with white America but looked instead to develop ways in which blacks could accumulate capital and exercise greater economic control over their communities.

The production of even the most commercial forms of black popular music in the 1960s took shape within a vibrant debate about the role of culture in the social and political struggles waged by black Americans. The field of culture—theater, poetry, literature, music, cinema—had been largely ignored during the early years of the black social movement. However, by the middle to late 1960s, a very spirited and often contentious debate about the relevance of the arts to the liberation of blacks had formed. Cultural nationalists like Nikki Giovanni, Haki Madhubuti, Maulana Karenga, Harold Cruse, and perhaps most notably Amiri Baraka emerged as important cultural producers, commentators, and theorists primarily because they understood the role cultural arts could perform in mobilizing a black citizenry.

Nevertheless, black cultural nationalism was driven by different ideas and motivated by competing interests. On one end of this particular continuum was a politics that envisaged cultural production as a means to radicalize black racial consciousness and mobilize the masses. The nationalist-minded Black Arts movement, for example, used poetry, literature, and theater to cultivate a sense of peoplehood and community activism in its struggle for social justice. The Last Poets articulated both a message and style of black cultural resistance that anticipated the burgeoning hip hop movement. In addition, advocates of cultural nationalism also created a number of publishing presses—Broadside Press (Detroit), Free Black Press of California, Third World Press (Chicago)—in order to disseminate the ideological worldviews that drove the movement.[6] During the early to middle 1970s, even the first generation of formally trained black filmmakers—Charles Barnet, Haile Gerima, Julie Dash—were influenced by the rising currency of black nationalism as they sought to use independent cinema to articulate new notions of black racial identity and political activism.[7] And while the political orientation of the Black Panthers was more internationalist than nationalist, they too embraced the notion that black cultural production was a fertile source of social and political commentary. The Panthers established a soul music act—The Lumpen—in order to disseminate the ideology of the organization and, in their words, "stimulate action and make revolution."[8]

At the opposite end of this continuum stood performers who were part of a growing black star system. Although these performers were concerned, first and foremost, with commercial success and often fell short of singing outright about black liberation or revolution, many did nonetheless align themselves in more oblique ways with black nation rhetoric and style. What is most significant about the gravitation of black celebrities toward a black nationalist disposition is the extent to which it signaled a decisive shift in the sensibilities of a new generation of black audiences. In other words, as black Americans invested in new notions of blackness, popular music performers expressed more open solidarity with black political struggle in a number of different ways.

One common example was signaled by changes in hair or sartorial style. Indeed, the manner in which blacks politicized their hair and choice of clothing was crucial to cultural nationalism because it involved something that blacks could control: their bodies. This particular dimension of struggle understood that, in a racialized world-system, black bodies have always been important sites of social and political struggle. And though style politics have been a long-standing feature of black urban life, in the hyperpoliticized world of the 1960s and 1970s black performers were compelled to assess if their own sense of style complied with changing notions of black self-respect, empowerment, and glamour. Moreover, the emphasis on black style politics was as much a critique of whiteness as it was a celebration of blackness. In many ways, black cultural nationalists were rejecting the aesthetic values and codes that debase tightly curled hair, dark skin, and broad facial features. And while slogans like "black is beautiful" disclosed elements of racial chauvinism, they also demonstrated how blacks maneuvered to recode the sign of blackness.[9]

Black nationality formation also affected black music producers, who sought to manufacture a form of music that exuded a "blacker" mood or sensibility. Music critics and historians note that the texture of black popular music changed during this period of rising black consciousness. Ward, for example, argues that black producers began experimenting with tomtoms and elaborate Africanesque cross-rhythms. And while this attempt to create a more Afrocentric idiom in black popular music seldom involved deep and diligent study, it nevertheless resonated with a black public that made African language, culture, and history vogue.

Finally, several performers identified with the movement in song lyrics that expressed greater solidarity with black political struggle. For example, even as he was achieving undisputed status as the "Godfather of Soul," James Brown's blackness was openly challenged by some cultural nationalists. His occasional tendency to, shall we say, indecipherable lyrics, processed hair, and affiliation with the Republican Party struck some black nationalists as contradictory if not outright treasonous. However, by the late 1960s and early 1970s, Brown's lyrics, performances, and sense of style began to strike a more resonant cord with nationalist rhetoric and style. Indeed, songs like "Say It Loud, I'm Black and I'm Proud" and "Payback" expressed a more immediate and discernible connection to the generational mood shifts that were redefining black popular culture. In addition to lyric and stylistic changes, Brown also began working more closely with certain sectors of the movement, thus further shoring up his status in the black community by using his celebrity to support and raise money for black causes.[10]

Brown was not the period's only convert. The lyrics of many black performers began to develop a more direct association with the changing spirit of black political protest. Even Motown, widely known for its commitment to producing a brand of pop music that achieved unprecedented crossover success, broke occasionally from a hugely successful formula that required artists to eschew any explicit association with racial politics. Thus, when Marvin Gaye melodiously intoned "What's going on" and "What's happening brother," it was further confirmation that the black music scene was changing and signaled the degree to which even a pop-soul artist like Gaye could not resist the gravity of black protest.[11]

Perhaps the most impressive swing among Motown artists was the transformation of young Little Stevie into the mature Stevie Wonder. Much has been written about Barry Gordy's rigid contractual arrangements with Motown artists.[12] However, in 1971 Wonder secured a contract that gave him greater creative freedom and independence than any Motown artist had ever achieved. Wonder used his newfound freedom to explore the black musical continuum, producing numerous albums and songs that ingeniously incorporated elements of gospel, rhythm and blues, reggae, jazz, funk, soul, and pop. Equally important was the manner in which Wonder's music evoked the everyday landscapes of the black social world and changing notions of black social consciousness. It is also important to note that Wonder's genius was also possible because, like many black artists by the early 1970s, he produced and recorded his music in an industrial milieu that afforded him greater creative autonomy and control.

Even Gordy began to pay greater homage to the movement by producing recordings of important speeches and holding key fund-raising events, especially after the assassination of Martin Luther King Jr.[13] And though Brown, Gaye, Wonder, Gordy, and many other black celebrity performers never mistook themselves for black nationalists, their overtures to the provocative shifts in black politics revealed just how infectious the spirit of revolution was. In many ways, black popular music emerged as a key space to register the currents that were profoundly reconfiguring black racial consciousness.

If most black soul and rhythm-and-blues performers did not fashion a radical politic or revolutionary image, their commercial success did raise another important question: who would control the commodification of black popular music? This question was further buoyed by the rising tide of black nationalism and the call for blacks to struggle for greater economic independence and empowerment. Thus, as black performers began to identify more closely with the nationalist ethos of the time, black producers and entrepreneurs turned their attention to matters related to the managerial and administrative control of black music.

The degree to which black executives sought to exert greater control over the production of black music signaled an important shift in the political ethos of black Americans. More specifically, it demonstrated that blacks understood that genuine cultural and economic power in American society required some degree of control over or within the different spheres of industry. In the case of the music industry, that meant blacks would need to exert greater influence over the production and distribution of black music forms. Still, the rise of a small but highly successful cadre of black executives and entrepreneurs did not translate into a major overhaul of the dominant power relations in the music industry.

In fact, after observing the success of black-owned labels like Motown and other smaller, less widely known independent enterprises, the major record companies began creating their own black record labels and divisions with greater ferocity than ever before. In 1971, the Harvard Report produced a blueprint that outlined how the majors could devise highly calibrated strategies to sign and promote the crossover appeal of black music talent. Most important, the report signaled the degree to which black popular culture forms were becoming even more amenable to corporate merchandising. Ironically, at a time when blacks began to seriously contemplate greater control over black commodity culture, the major record companies sought to harness the potential crossover appeal of black music to their production strategies. In the face of expanding corporate power and influence, the ability of black executives to establish substantial control over black popular music became more difficult.

Besides, there was no consensus within the black movement regarding what constituted a viable expression of economic nationalism. Did it

mean promoting the development of a separate black economy, with its
own financial institutions and community-based organizations? Or did it
mean promoting a dynamic brand of black capitalism, powered by a bold
and spirited entrepreneurial imagination? Often the latter interpretation
reigned as a number of black entrepreneurs and executives positioned
themselves to benefit enormously from the racial, economic, and generational shifts that were creating a robust black consumer economy.[14] Although paramount to the livelihood of black working-class families and
their communities, the issue of economic empowerment also emerged as a
crucial theme in two spheres that, by the 1960s, had emerged as critical sites
of political struggle: the recording and broadcasting industries. Indeed, the
call for Black Power reverberated throughout the black music world and
reinvigorated dissatisfaction with a predominantly white-controlled music
industry's control over black artists and the music they created.

The ambiguity of Black Power politics, however, meant that it could
be variously translated. For instance, some used it to promote black capitalism. As a result, a select group of black Americans used the specter of Black
Power to accumulate greater political capital and influence during a period
of serious social unrest. Adolph Reed Jr. argues that the co-optation of
Black Power enabled an elite class of black politicos and business professionals to exercise greater leadership and control over the growing masses of
blacks who were becoming increasingly insurgent.[15] Thus the champi-
oning of black entrepreneurial capitalism often involved the abandonment
of some of the core principles of black nationalism, particularly ideas related to community uplift, group empowerment, and social change. So,
even though a small cadre of black entrepreneurs and executives accumu-
lated a degree of power and prestige in the music industry, it was generally
more individual- than community-based, celebrity-driven than politically motivated, and desirous of social mobility rather than social transformation.

If the notion of black capitalism impressed many as a viable means of
racial empowerment, the degree to which it could be successfully practiced
in the music industry was questionable given the unrelenting progression
toward corporate hegemony. In truth, the major record companies were already reestablishing command over the most important aspects—publishing, production, marketing, distribution—of the pop music industry.
Thus, a question particularly relevant in the twenty-first century began to
take shape, in earnest, in the late 1960s and 1970s: how could blacks assert
and maintain a modicum of control over black popular music even as it was
coming under greater corporate management? This particular question per-

colates even more intensely with the evolution and the transformation of hip hop culture.

Hip Hop Nationalism

If the black popular music scene of the late 1960s and early 1970s revealed a tempered association with black nationalist desire, a more robust alliance emerged by the late 1980s. Indeed, expressions of black insurgency reached an undeniable pitch in the kinetic rhymes and beats fashioned by hip hop artists. In many ways, the hyperpoliticization of black music in late twentieth-century America demonstrates just how complex race relations and the lived experiences of black youth had become.

In his analysis of black nationalist discourse in rap music, Jeffrey Louis Decker notes that two distinct forms emerged.[16] The first, "sixties-inspired hip hop nationalism," derives much of its creative energy from the Black Power movement of the 1960s, whereas the second, "Afrocentric hip hop nationalism," is inspired by the notion that ancient Egypt is the birthplace of civilization. Rap artists like Paris, Sister Souljah, and KRS-One represent sixties-styled nationalism while X-Clan, Lakim, and the Brand Nubian personify the Afrocentric strand.

Though many groups contributed to and complicated the expression of hip hop nationalism, no group was as commercially and critically successful as Public Enemy. In fact, Public Enemy is the prototype of the insurgent style. For example, the group pioneered a new sonic style in the production of rap music, fashioned an image that adroitly mined the racial signs in American culture, and achieved a popular following among a cross section of youth. Despite its revolutionary rhetoric and nationalist image, Public Enemy emerged as one of the first rap acts to cross over the racial, class, and national lines that shape the contours of global youth culture.

Of course any serious analysis of why black nation discourse reverberated so fiercely throughout the orbit of hip hop culture must consider the social and economic worlds young African Americans inhabit. The post–civil rights generation of African American youth inherited a world defined by sharp contradictions. It was typically assumed that this generation would be the chief beneficiary of the civil rights struggle for racial justice and equality. But for many black youth, a less optimistic experience became the reality instead. By the middle 1980s the college enrollment and rate of employment for black youth began an unexpected and precipitous decline. In addition, the rate of high school drop out, teen suicide, homicide, incarceration, and mortality showed steady and, in some cases, unprecedented increases.[17]

Furthermore, the hyperpoliticized themes that mark hip hop nationalism developed during a period in which patterns of economic bifurcation within the black American community became more pronounced. At one end of this bifurcated class structure were poor and working-class blacks isolated in ghetto communities that experienced serious social, economic, spatial, and demographic isolation. On the other end was a black middle and lower middle class buoyed by increased access to higher education and professional employment. Hip hop nationalism anticipated the racial mood shifts and growing discontent of a generation of young black Americans who were either disillusioned by the racial hostilities brought on by participation in the societal mainstream or dislocated from the center of social and economic life altogether.[18]

Equally important as the changing social and economic circumstances confronting black American youth was the demise of effective black political leadership. Following the watershed civil rights period, the black political establishment—both elected officials and civil rights organizations—experienced serious difficulty charting a new course of action in the face of increasing social conservatism and waning support for racial justice and equality. The crisis in black leadership also reflects the degree to which the social, economic, and political interests of blacks have become increasingly fragmented and varied, largely as a result of greater class differentiation.

The inability of the black political establishment to articulate a new vision of racial progress diminishes its appeal with young African Americans. Unable (or unwilling) to fashion a new political agenda, venerable organizations like the NAACP or the Urban League alienate many younger African Americans who consider the commitment to conventional forms of protest politics (i.e., boycotts, marches) antiquated and irrelevant to the crisis scenarios that are transforming black urban communities. And while Jesse Jackson's Rainbow Coalition promised to move black political activism in a more progressive direction, its movement into electoral politics seriously compromised its ability to produce substantive social or economic change. It was within the context, then, of ineffective black political leadership that young African Americans began seeking what they considered more compelling, assertive, and alternative forms of political expression.[19]

While some black youth tuned into (but not necessarily joined) more radical organizations like the Nation of Islam or the Five Percent Nation, others turned to the field of popular media culture as a location to articulate their specifically generational grievances and concerns. In the absence of a viable black political movement, rap philosophers like Chuck D, KRS-One, and Sista Souljah filled a very important void for many black youth. In fact, it was the ability and desire of message rappers to give voice to the concerns and lived experiences of a specifically black youth constituency that buoyed their popular status and cultural prestige. Message rappers resonate so strongly with youth because they assume the role of educator, entertainer, and spokesperson. For instance, KRS-One was one of the first public personalities to use the now commonly employed term "edutainment," signaling the degree to which he attempted to move the crowd in more ways than one.[20]

And yet, at the same moment the social, economic, and political circumstances of many black youth were worsening, the generation as a whole managed to accumulate both significant measures of symbolic capital and unprecedented access to popular media culture. Even as black youth are implicated in the nation's war on drugs, the largest prison industrial complex buildup in history, and a politically conservative backlash, they have achieved an equally prominent niche in a burgeoning global youth consumer economy.[21]

By the mid- to late 1980s, black youth were at the center of a virtual revolution in American popular culture as the musical expression of hip hop—rap—began to carve out a distinct and formidable niche in the pop music industry. To the extent that hip hop is preeminently a youth movement, it is also a historically specific formation that corresponds with the contours of late twentieth-century American life. The dominant practices in hip hop develop their creative shape in relation to a social world in which new forms and sites of political antagonisms proliferate. Even before a decisively black nationalist discourse began to penetrate, complicate, and broaden its scope, the hip hop movement had already developed into a fertile reservoir of youth culture and production.

Still, it is the subsequent role of technology and commercial culture, more than anything else, that continues to drive and animate provocative debates about the political tenor of hip hop culture. Does the intrusion of technology and commodification—most notably, the mass production, distribution, and merchandising of rap music—conspire to dull the oppositional edges of hip hop? Moreover, is the participation of black youth in the popular culture industry a legitimate expression of political dissent and empowerment? These questions, of course, rekindle debates about the capacity of capitalism to contain cultural practices that derive much of their energy along the social and economic margins of society. But rather than view technology and commercial culture as resources that stifle aggrieved populations, consider an alternative proposition instead: How do technology and commercial culture enable new repertoires of black youth agency, cultural production, and nation discourse?

While hip hop purists claim that commodification erodes the subversive demeanor and style of hip hop, the youth culture did not develop its most elaborate political expressions until after new technologies had been appropriated and the road to commercial success paved. In truth, the earliest rap recordings were mostly first-person narratives that boasted about the acquisition of status-conferring objects: jewelry, designer clothing, and women. And though narratives that portrayed women as sources of heterosexual male pleasure were certainly political, they did not embody the counterideological themes that would later be labeled "message rap."[22] The production of message rap developed as rap music, in general, was becoming commercial. Therefore, by enlarging the creative terrain of rap music production, technology and commodification forged open spaces that now include performance traditions that nourish rather than impoverish more socially provocative discourses. The formation of hip hop nationalism is a striking example.

While the fact that rap music crosses over into the wider (and more lucrative) sphere of white youth consumption is commonly noted, few, if any, address its appeal with a cross section of black youth. In addition to fashioning a repertoire of cultural politics that skillfully managed the racial fault lines of American life, Public Enemy astutely navigated the class differences *within* the black American community. Observing the group's bimodal appeal in black America, Kevin Powell writes that Public Enemy "rooted itself in the common experience of black people, especially young black people, and made us feel like we mattered, that our blackness was something beautiful, not a burden or something to run away from. And it didn't matter if you were from the ghetto or the burbs, a college student or flippin burgers at Micky D's. . . . Public Enemy, somewhere, somehow, spoke for all of us."[23]

For example, Public Enemy's strategic use of prison-based images and narratives resonated with a generation of dislocated black youth whose involvement with the criminal justice system increased sharply in the 1980s. Indeed, ever since the Nation of Islam sought them out as recruitment sites, American prisons have been a fertile source of black nationality formation. But if Public Enemy struck a chord with dislocated black youth, the group also hyped black nationalist–inflected themes that percolated through college campuses and black organic intellectual communities. The critiques of white racial hegemony or celebration of public intellectuals ranging from Malcolm X to Francis Scott-Welsing tapped additional sources from which black nationalist sensibilities could be nourished.

Ultimately, in the context of a relatively conservative media culture industry, Public Enemy's incendiary style was revelatory if not revolutionary. Public Enemy was, to paraphrase their sample of Malcolm X, "too black" and "too strong" for the pop music industry. For example, despite the group's popularity and worldwide prestige, few of their songs have been included in the program rotation of black appeal or pop radio formats. However, radio's refusal to play the heavy-hitting rhymes of Public Enemy served mainly to enlarge the group's revolutionary image and cultlike status. Moreover, because radio was virtually no option, Public Enemy adopted especially creative approaches to a medium that has become, in its own right, equally crucial in the promotion of popular music: video.

Public Enemy used the music video format not only to promote their products (i.e., music, caps, T-shirts) but also to animate their black nationalist politics. The rap group used especially inventive techniques to comment thoughtfully on the media's crusade in the making of the crack cocaine crisis ("Night of the Living Baseheads"), critique a burgeoning prison industrial complex ("In the Hour of Chaos"), and challenge a growing white political backlash ("I'm Going Back to Arizona"). So, if radio "shut down" Public Enemy, music video enlivened the group's construction of a revolutionary persona that both dramatized and popularized its nationalist message.

But if Public Enemy understood the politics of black youth disillusionment and alienation, the group also understood and grooved to the politics of pleasure. Even as Public Enemy's black nationalist project was enabled by important social, economic, and political changes, it was also affected by the savvy ways black American youth maneuver around a changing technological landscape. Public Enemy's production team, appropriately named the Bomb Squad, adopted a fresh, even radical approach to making rap music. This particular method relied heavily on the new technologies available in the world of pop music production—multitrack recording and sampling devices, digital technology, video, and later the Internet.[24] The manner in which they sampled sounds from the everyday lifeworld—conversational dialogue, police sirens, television news, gunshots, ambulances—was essential to their efforts to manufacture a sound and style of rap that vibed with the social milieu of young urban America. To be sure, the architects of the group's signature "bring the noise" style understood that the strategic use of the sounds and images that color the everyday life-world of black American youth could serve as a powerful source of social commentary and popular entertainment.

Interestingly, at the height of the group's success Public Enemy was as popular with black college students as with any other demographic. Even today, Chuck D is a regular figure on the college lecture circuit. The most arresting question of course is why young middle-class blacks, many of whom benefit from access to higher education and professional employment, would derive so much pleasure from identifying with the black nationalist–inflected beats and rhymes made popular by Public Enemy. At least three factors help to understand why Public Enemy's nationalist image strikes such a powerful chord with many middle- and lower-middle-class blacks. First, college-age blacks, at least since the 1960s, have been central to the formation of black nation discourse. Second, as the quality-of-life gap between middle- and working-class blacks widens, many young blacks struggle with varying degrees of race guilt and loyalty. Finally, the identification with black nationalism also illuminates the extent to which many black college students must wrestle with two conflicting identities: their status as both black and middle class.

The rise of hip hop nationalism animates the extent to which black nationality formation has been significantly influenced by college-age blacks. Carlton Ridenhour (Chuck D) and Hank Shocklee conceived of Public Enemy during their student days at Adelphi University.[25] It is quite notable that two figures central in a style of rap so evocative of black youth insurgency came of age in relatively middle-class environs. And while their middle-class status strikes some as contradictory, it reflects the degree to which black nationhood sensibilities are diffused throughout the class cleavages that structure black American life.

Members of Public Enemy not only anticipated but also lived the generational mood shifts that led many college-age blacks to begin sporting "Black by Popular Demand" T-shirts, X caps, and Afrocentric hairstyles. And yet the fascination of black youth with nationalism is more than a matter of style. In fact, it was largely the efforts of black students that led to the formation of black studies departments in colleges and universities around the United States in the late 1960s and early 1970s. Today, many black students enroll in black studies courses, read books by and about figures like Malcolm X, Angela Davis, Amiri Baraka, and Sonia Sanchez, and even go on to earn graduate degrees with a focus on African American studies.

Historian Clayborne Carson notes that though the rise of Black Power did not translate into greater political power for African Americans, it does continue to influence the arenas of intellectual and cultural life. The degree, then, to which many college-age blacks turn to nationalism as a source of identity politics, cultural expression, and self-empowerment reflects the rising tide of black nationalism on college campuses. In an essay examining this phenomenon, journalist Nicholas Lemann argues that "the power of nationalism is that it addresses all their major preoccupations, intellectual, psychological, and economic: it can be studied as an academic subject, it is a natural part of the adolescent identity crisis, and it provides a way of framing career decisions."[26] Though Lemann's charge that black youth's interests in black nationality represents an adolescent identity crisis is both reductive and wrongheaded, it does highlight that some college-age blacks must negotiate what, in reality, can be two seemingly incompatible experiences: their blackness and their middle-class mobility.[27]

As performers like Public Enemy employ message rap as a space to circulate counter narratives about American history, they establish a unique niche in the commodification of hip hop culture. Many message rappers cultivate a repertoire of narratives and performance traditions that call into question the absence of multicultural themes in school curricula. In addition, message rap artists consciously craft personas as public and organic intellectuals, that is, as producers of knowledge who are also connected to and engaged with the everyday circumstances and struggles of their communities.[28] Most important, message rappers and their audiences inventively use popular media culture to rewrite the historical memory of black figures typically omitted from official narratives of American history.

There is perhaps no greater evidence of this than the manner in which black youth built an entire culture industry based on Malcolm X as a symbol of race pride and black nationalism. Since his death in 1965, Malcolm X has been treated as a political outlaw and generally omitted from official narratives commemorating or even documenting American history. By the early 1990s, however, message rappers were as likely to sample an excerpt from Malcolm's "The Ballot or the Bullet" speech as they were a funky rhythm line from James Brown or George Clinton. The renewed interest in Malcolm X sparked a proliferation of rap songs, caps, T-shirts, books, and posters that saturated the American popular culture landscape. Indeed, mainstream cultural products like Spike Lee's Hollywood-financed biopic, *X*, or the new African American Heritage series stamp featuring Malcolm X can be attributed mainly to the way black youth iconized and literally inserted him back into the nation's historical memory.[29]

Other factors, too, explain the appeal of black nationalist desire among black college students. For instance, many middle-class blacks continue to experience varying degrees of race guilt. That is, they recognize that their economic status and life chances are, relatively speaking, far removed from those of African Americans who are unlikely to attend college or enter the salaried and professional classes. Public Enemy's iconization of black nationalism draws heavily from the intraracial politics expressed by Nation of Islam leader Louis Farrakhan. Since the middle 1980s, Farrakhan has become an intriguing figure for many black collegians. And although the Nation of Islam has never been successful at recruiting affluent blacks, Farrakhan has managed to tap into the psychological well of middle-class angst. Discussing Farrakhan's perplexing appeal in middle-class black America, Henry Louis Gates Jr. writes:

> The truth is that blacks—across the economic and ideological spectrum—often feel astonishingly vulnerable to charges of inauthenticity, of disloyalty to the race. . . . Farrakhan's sway over blacks—the answering chord his rhetoric finds—attests to the enduring strength of our own feelings of guilt, our own anxieties of having been false to our people, of having sinned against our innermost identity. He denounces the fallen in our midst, invokes the wrath of heaven against us: and his outlandish vitriol occasions terror and a curious exhilaration.[30]

And though few black college students join the Nation of Islam, they still find his political celebrity somewhat fascinating even if problematic. In a polemical yet perceptive analysis of Farrakhan's rise to national prominence, Adolph Reed Jr. writes that, for black college students, the Nation of Islam leader "forges identity with a power that counterattacks racism and isolation and soothes the anxiety around upward mobility or class maintenance."[31]

Moreover, many black collegians understand that their class status does not exempt them from either the personal indignities or institutionalized forms of racism, so black nation discourse strikes a resonant chord. Many middle-class blacks understand—and this is what makes their particular experience so profound—that despite their social, economic, and educational position, race is still likely to determine their place of residence, career mobility, and income. The desire to associate with black nationality formation, then, is not simply symbolic; it also perceptively acknowledges the degree to which the middle-class status of blacks can often be overshadowed by race. In fact, black middle-class life has never been commensurate to its white counterpart. Research suggests that middle-class whites still enjoy greater degrees of wealth as well as of professional and residential mobility than their black counterparts.[32]

In many ways, black nationalist desire among college-age blacks helps manage their paradoxical status in American society. The experiences of many young middle-class blacks on predominantly white college campuses generates some of the same hostilities and tensions typically associated with poor and working-class blacks—campus police harassment, preconceived notions about their intelligence, and even hate crimes and psychological abuse. The resonance, then, of hip hop nationalism with young middle-class blacks is yet another example of what Ellis Cose describes as the "rage of a privileged class," that is, a manifestation of how they struggle to reconcile their conflicting experiences of race and middle-class status.

Of course, sixties-inspired hip hop nationalism derives much of its symbolic efficacy from the period's black political insurgency. However, because hip hop nationalism draws so heavily from the image bank of the late 1960s, its fashioning of a black nation-world also reproduces many of the gender and sexual politics of the period. Consequently, Public Enemy's notion of black nationhood reflects a particularly gendered cultural imaginary.[33]

For example, the rap group is exclusively male, promotes a paramilitary image, and routinely uses icons from a pantheon of male leaders. What is most problematic about Public Enemy's cultural politics is the self-proclaimed view that the group represents the black nation when, in reality, it speaks most passionately to and about young black males. Consequently, its "Brothers Gonna Work It Out" ethos demonstrates, once again, how the issues and experiences of black women are marginalized and the state of black America is typically equated with the state of black men.[34]

Chuck D's often quoted comment that rap music is the black version of CNN reveals the degree to which a black-male worldview is often privileged in rap. Though not fully accurate, the assertion perceptively acknowledges that rap occasionally labors as an expression of counter journalism. On the one hand, the comment offers a discerning critique of how the reports produced by national news media organizations are often filtered through a white, middle-class lens. On the other hand, a close examination of the narratives that define message rap suggests that the issues most likely to be emphasized—prison life, urban violence, and the underground drug economy—are filtered through a male-centered lens. Thus, even as message rap makes black urban America the center of its gaze, it does so in a way that marginalizes the experiences of black women in this terrain.

Not surprisingly, despite the attempt to construct a revolutionary image, Public Enemy's articulation of black nationalism reveals many of the socially conservative tendencies that historically mark nationalist discourse. More generally, the tilt toward conservatism characterizes a tradition of black nationalism that seldom challenges hegemonic ideas about gender, patriarchal familial patterns, and sexuality. In other words, to the extent that young African Americans appropriate the conventions of sixties-style nationalism, they are also likely to enact the tendencies that turn this particular tradition of black nationalist desire in a backward- rather than forward-looking direction. So, as black youth embrace personalities like (pre-Mecca) Malcolm or Louis Farrakhan, they also reproduce what Adolph Reed Jr. characterizes as "the tension between militant posture and conservative program."[35]

"Black Is Back, and It's Bound to Sell!" The Commodification of Black Nationalist Desire

One of the most intriguing currents of black nationalism is the tendency of a black petite bourgeoisie to employ nation rhetoric as a means to accumulate capital. And though it is true that "black is back, and it's bound to sell" nationalism is unmistakably market driven, it is also indicative of the ever evolving relationship between black Americans and racial capitalism. The exuberant commodification of black nation discourse points, in numerous ways, to the inventive ways black cultural producers maneuver to exploit emergent fissures in a media-saturated economy, shifts in black racial consciousness, and the wider participation of blacks in consumer culture.

Surely, as black racial consciousness began to undergo serious revisions in the 1960s and 1970s, opportunities for new forms of commerce and cultural production developed. Consequently, as blacks began to actively construct new racial identities, entrepreneurs also began offering an array of commodities and services that promised to complement, popularize, and/or celebrate emergent expressions of blackness.[36] The relationship between black nationalism and commodity culture raises a question that, in truth, is difficult to answer: to what extent does commodification represent the erasure or the enlivening of black nationalist desire?

Perhaps no figure embodies the bourgeois tradition of black nationalism more than filmmaker Spike Lee. In fact, Lee's unprecedented success as an independent filmmaker has been bolstered by his strategic appropriation of black nationalism. In the process of carving out a formidable presence in American popular culture, Lee packaged himself as a guerrilla-style filmmaker determined not only to counter Hollywood depictions of black

American life but also to create a viable black independent film movement that was equal parts commerce and race uplift.

From the very beginning of his career, Lee understood how a strategic identification with the nationalist tendencies in black political culture could advance his desire to produce feature-length films. No matter how genuinely invested in black nationalism Lee is, he has utilized its appeal en route to becoming the most successful black film director in American history. Throughout his career Lee has often used media interviews to candidly express his disdain for the exclusivity typical of the Hollywood establishment. Lee's frontal assault on the industry was calculated insofar as he understood that he wanted to generate publicity while also building a strong base of black support. Lee carefully constructed himself as a black nationalist with a camera. Furthermore, the claim that his films "were about, for, and by black people" invoked the spirit and ferment that marked the Black Arts movement of the 1960s and 1970s.

To his credit Lee openly challenged the barriers that continue to limit the degree to which blacks participate in the film industry, particularly at the executive and creative levels. Even before he began to accumulate significant degrees of symbolic capital, he understood that real power in the media industry is oftentimes located away from public view—in boardrooms, executive offices, and in the skilled (screenwriting) and craft positions (director, cinematographer).

And Lee has engaged in an aggressive brand of cross-media promotion and entrepreneurship, producing—in addition to film—music, videos, books, apparel, and, most recent, a major advertising firm. Though many of his detractors criticize his varied business endeavors as a sign of crass commercialism, Lee's self-created style of media synergy is emblematic of the rules that currently govern a rapidly evolving and corporate-dominated media industry landscape.

But while Lee's merchandising efforts are not unique, what the filmmaker merchandises is distinctive: a peculiar mix of racial pride and cultural resistance. The way he maneuvers around the racial fault lines of American life works as both a political gesture and promotional tactic. In essence, his fight against film industry racism is both proper and problematic. The filmmaker's cultural politics, for example, invoke nationalist pride (stay black!) while commodifying it at the same time (buy black!). So, while Lee's representational politics have been the source of extensive commentary, his blend of race politics and commerce is equally arresting for the ways it evokes a tradition of black bourgeois nationalism that has a unique and dynamic history.

Of course, the commodification of black nationalist desire is marked by profound contradictions. For example, Public Enemy simultaneously enlivens the memory of black political struggle while packaging it for youth consumption. In fact, Public Enemy's black nationalist pose can be partially viewed as a strategic marketing device designed to carve out a potentially distinctive and lucrative niche in a vast popular culture marketplace. The architects of the group put a twist on a strategy that is commonly practiced in the age of music video—image management. One of the most significant influences of music video on popular music production is the ever increasing significance of a carefully packaged style and image. Public Enemy meticulously orchestrates a select range of symbols in order to create and, most important, sell a black nationalist image.

However, Angela Davis argues that the commodification of black protest politics typically emphasizes style and glamour over substance and social activism.[37] Images of young black men and women costumed in black leather jackets, Afros, and equipped with firearms are the dominant symbols of a period marked by serious social and political conflict. Davis notes that images from her past (most notably her Afro) are often used to recast her as fashion figure rather than political activist. Further, she contends that in many instances the legacy of black protest is used merely as a backdrop to market commodities. Ultimately, by associating black militancy with revolutionary style rather than revolutionary politics, images of the past are appropriated in a way that negates rather than enlivens social and political memory.

Conclusion

So, what does the state of black American popular culture indicate about the state of black American nationalism? How does the field of popular American culture enliven the memories, language, and style of black nationalism? It is, after all, the style and image of black nationalism and its relationship to commodity culture that is most pronounced. Still, is the emphasis on style and commodity production antithetical to the aspirations of black nationalism?

Ironically, the entrepreneurial spirit that characterizes so much of hip hop nationalism or the production of a "Spike Lee Joint" embodies key elements of black nationalist thought, particularly the notion of economic independence and empowerment. Black image makers use the legacy and appeal of black nation discourse to cultivate a creative community and movement that seeks to exploit emergent fissures in a vibrant media culture land-scape. The view that blacks should profit from the expressive cultures and commodities they create is a resonant theme in black popular culture. This particular theme has also been an element of black nation discourse throughout the twentieth century. In many ways, then, the cultural politics of black popular culture are spirited by the nationalist notion that blacks need to control the commodification of their culture. And while many black nationalists of the 1960s were principally concerned with the em-powerment of black communities rather than black celebrities, the notion of economic uplift has always created space for opportunistic and savvy en-trepreneurs to exploit surges in black nationality formation.

One of the most revealing indicators of how black youth revise the meaning and currency of black nationalism is best reflected in a phrase that is equally inventive and instructive, "keeping it real." While the slogan is most often viewed as a simplified discourse about racial authenticity, it is, in truth, far more discerning and evocative of a black nation ethos. The slogan is remarkably savvy and cognizant of the historical practices that have led to the theft, appropriation, and exploitation of black popular culture forms. As a result, it illuminates the degree to which black youth seek to assert a modicum of creative and economic control over the commodity cultures they help to create. The phrase recognizes, for example, that because black youth are central to the creation of hip hop culture they should also profit from and direct its commercial appeal. Indeed, as Greg Tate notes, rap music may be the first commodified form of black culture that blacks have ex-ploited as much as whites for financial gain.

To what extent, then, is black American participation in commercial culture imbued with black nationalist desire? Because it is a tremendously fertile source of racial pride, empowerment, and creative confidence, black popular culture strikes a resonant chord with black nation discourse. What is perhaps most interesting is that black youth do not see a contradiction be-tween their affinity for an imagined black world and the desire to get paid at the same time. So when critics charge that commodity culture has become a substitute for black political intervention, it is because they often fail to see how it has become, in effect, a site of intervention. In other words, the participation of black Americans in the production of commercial culture should not be read as a movement away from politics but rather as the movement of black political intervention into a very different terrain.

Much has been made of the fact that hip hop nationalism is no longer a commercially viable style and has, at least for now, lost its mass appeal. Still, it is important to recognize that many of the themes and interests that once distinguished hip hop nationalism—racial and generational pride, entrepreneurship, and control over black cultural production—are now permanent features of the hip hop landscape. So, even in an era when the rap music industry is dominated by studio gangstas, ca$h money thug$, ghetto fabulous chic, or the raucous tracks representing the "Dirty South," a subtly inflected black nationalist ethos continues to pulse throughout the ever broadening orbit of hip hop culture. In other words, in their struggle to "keep it real," what the hip hop generation is really saying is keep it black—black-inspired, black-controlled, with black appeal. In this sense, the legacy and the limitations of black nationalism continue to find expression in the popular cultures of young black Americans in ways that are pleasurable, promising, and problematic.

NOTES

1. Clayborne Carson, *In Struggle: SNCC and the Black Awakening of the 1960s* (Cambridge, Mass., 1981).

2. For examples of how various black political leaders have turned to the sphere of popular media culture, see, e.g., Louis R. Harlan, *Booker T. Washington: The Wizard of Tuskegee, 1901–1915* (New York, 1983). In the aftermath of the furor caused by the film *Birth of a Nation,* Washington and others invested in the film *Birth of a Race.* The making of the film is also discussed by Thomas Cripps, *Slow Fade to Black: The Negro in American Film, 1900–1942* (New York, 1993). Black political groups like the Nation of Islam have also turned to print media as a source of political advocacy and cultural production. See C. Eric Lincoln, *The Black Muslims in America* (Boston, 1973). Black Nationalist leader Marcus Garvey also maintained the importance of blacks participating in the production of media such as print and cinema.

3. As far back as the early twentieth century, blacks have creatively used music to express their ideas and critiques of American social relations. See, e.g., Angela Y. Davis, *Blues Legacies and Black Feminism: Gertrude "Ma" Rainey, Bessie Smith, and Billie Holiday* (New York, 1998) for a discussion of the social and political aspects of blues music. A broad body of literature also discusses the politics and social context of rock 'n' roll. Examples include George Lipsitz, *Time Passages: Collective Memory and American Popular Culture* (Minneapolis, 1990); Brian Ward, *Just My Soul Responding: Rhythm and Blues, Black Consciousness, and Race Relations* (Berkeley, Calif., 1998); and Louis Cantor, *Wheelin' on Beale: How WDIA-Memphis Became the Nation's First All-Black Radio Station and Created the Sound That Changed America* (New York, 1992). For a discussion of jazz, see also Scott Knowles DeVeaux, *The Birth of Bebop: A Social and Musical History* (Berkeley, Calif., 1997). The seminal analysis of the politics of black music is, of course, LeRoi Jones (Amiri Baraka), *Blues People* (New York, 1963).

4. Ward, *Just My Soul Responding,* pp. 388–92.

5. The politicization of American popular culture during the 1960s revealed the

extent to which the appetites and sensibilities of a new generation of youth compelled important thematic, genre, and stylistic shifts in various forms of popular culture. For a discussion of how the period's generational tensions collided with television censors, see Aniko Bodroghkozy, "'We're the Young Generation and We've Got Something to Say': A Gramscian Analysis of Entertainment Television and the Youth Rebellion of the 1960s," *Critical Studies in Mass Communication* 8, no. 2:217–30. Professional and amateur sports also experienced racial and generational tensions, most notably when boxer Muhammad Ali refused induction into the U.S. armed forces during the height of the Vietnam War. In 1968 Olympians Tommie Smith and John Carlos raised their black-gloved fists upright during a medal ceremony to protest American racism. For a historical account of black athletic protest, see Harry Edwards, *The Revolt of the Black Athlete* (New York, 1969).

6. See Jennifer Jordan, "Cultural Nationalism in the 1960s: Politics and Poetry," in *Race, Politics, and Culture: Critical Essays on the Radicalism of the 1960s,* ed. Adolph Reed Jr. (New York, 1986).

7. Clyde Taylor, "The LA Rebellion: New Spirit in American Film," *Black Film Review* 2, no. 2.

8. Ward, *Just My Soul Responding,* p. 414.

9. For a subtle analysis of blackness as a fluid and constantly evolving racial signifier, see Kobena Mercer, "'1968': Periodizing Politics and Identity," in *Cultural Studies,* ed. Lawrence Grossberg et al. (New York, 1991). For an intriguing historical account of the Black Power movement's influence on black cultural politics, see William L. Van Deburg, *New Day in Babylon: The Black Power Movement and American Culture, 1965–1975* (Chicago, 1992), and *Black Camelot: African American Culture Heroes in Their Times, 1960–1980* (Chicago, 1997).

10. Ward, *Just My Soul Responding,* pp. 388–92. Also see Nelson George's discussion of the economic and political factors that situate Brown's placement in a pantheon of black musical pioneers, *The Death of Rhythm and Blues* (New York, 1988).

11. For an excellent discussion of Marvin Gaye, see Mark Anthony Neal, *What the Music Said: Black Popular Music and Black Public Culture* (New York, 1999).

12. See Nelson George, *Where Did Our Love Go: The Rise and Fall of the Motown Sound* (1986).

13. See Barry Gordy, *To Be Loved: The Music, the Magic, the Memories of Motown: An Autobiography* (1994). Also see Ward, *Just My Soul Responding,* for an interesting analysis of Gordy's awkward tango with race politics, commerce, and black music.

14. See Janette Dates and William Barlow, *Split Image: African Americans in the Mass Media* (Washington, D.C., 1991) for a discussion of the advertising industry's discovery of black purchasing power.

15. Adolph L. Reed Jr., "Black Particularity Reconsidered," *Telos* 39 (Spring 1979): 71–93; reprinted as chap. 2 in this volume.

16. Jeffrey Louis Decker, "The State of Rap," in *Microphone Fiends,* ed. Andrew Ross and Tricia Rose (New York, 1994).

17. Indeed, the sociological literature on the dislocation of black American youths is vast. For analysis of the increased incarceration of black youth, see Janice Joseph, *Black Youths, Delinquency, and Juvenile Justice* (Westport, Conn., 1998). For an analysis of race and the criminal justice system, see David Cole, *No Equal Justice: Race and Class in the*

American Criminal Justice System (New York, 1999). See also Clarence Lusane's assessment of how the war on drugs has led to dramatic increases in black American incarceration, *Pipe Dream Blues: Racism and the War on Drugs* (Boston, 1991). See also Olga M. Welch and Carolyn R. Hodges, *Standing Outside on the Inside: Black Adolescents and the Construction of Academic Identity* (Albany, N.Y., 1997), for a study of black youth and the educational system. For an evaluation of homicidal violence and black youth, see Lisa D. Bastian, *Young Black Male Victims: National Crime Victimization Survey* (Washington, D.C., 1994).

18. For analysis of the isolated worlds many poor black American youth inhabit, see LeAlan Jones and Lloyd Newman (with David Isay), *Our America: Life and Death on the South Side of Chicago* (New York, 1997); Elijah Anderson, *Code of the Street: Decency, Violence, and the Moral Life of the Inner City* (New York, 1999); Douglas S. Massey and Nancy Denton, *American Apartheid: Segregation and the Making of the Underclass* (Cambridge, Mass., 1993); and William Julius Wilson, *When Work Disappears: The World of the New Urban Poor* (New York, 1996). For analysis of the world many middle-class black youth inhabit, see Joe Feagin and Melvin Sikes, *Living with Racism: The Black Middle Class Experience* (Boston, 1994); Mary Pattillo-McCoy, *Black Picket Fences: Privilege and Peril among the Black Middle Class* (Chicago, 1999); and Yanick St. Jean, "Black Habits of the Heart: The American Dream and the Black Middle Class," Ph.D. diss., University of Texas at Austin, 1992.

19. Of course the recent troubles of the NAACP can be partially attributed to the organization's inability to attract a substantial base of young African Americans. In fact, during his brief tenure as president of the organization Ben Chavis adopted a more strident tone that was designed to appeal to a younger generation of black political activists. However, because the NACCP has typically adopted a more moderate-to-liberal position, Chavis's overtures toward a more militant philosophy were considered too risky insofar as they might cut off traditional streams of financial support. For an interesting analysis of the state of black American politics near the close of the twentieth century, as well as the rise and fall of Jesse Jackson, see Manning Marable, *Black American Politics: From the Washington Marches to Jesse Jackson* (London, 1985), and *Beyond Black and White: Transforming African American Politics* (New York, 1995); Clarence Lusane, *African Americans at the Crossroads: The Restructuring of Black Political Leadership and the 1992 Elections* (Boston, 1994); Adolph Reed Jr., *The Jesse Jackson Phenomenon: The Crisis of Purpose in Afro-American Politics* (New Haven, Conn., 1986).

20. KRS-One, or Kris Parker, has become a visible proponent of the role hip hop culture can perform in mobilizing young African Americans. In addition to the many lectures he delivers around the world he is also working to create what he calls a Hip Hop Institute in Atlanta, Georgia.

21. See, e.g., S. Craig Watkins, *Representing: Hip Hop Culture and the Production of Black Cinema* (Chicago, 1998).

22. For a discussion of the formation of message rap, see Ernest Allen, "Making the Strong Survive: The Contours and Contradictions of Message Rap," in *Droppin' Science: Critical Essays on Rap Music and Hip Hop Culture,* ed. William Eric Perkins (Philadelphia, 1996).

23. Kevin Powell, "Enemy Territory," *Vibe* (September 1994).

24. In fact Public Enemy has the distinction of the first platinum-selling recording

act to turn to the Internet as a way to launch the release of a new album. As a result of conflict with both Def Jam Records and Polygram (the latter purchased Columbia's 50 percent stake in Def Jam), the group has elected to try the Internet as a way to get around major record label distributors and secure a larger share of record sales. For a discussion of this pioneering move that many believe will define the music industry in the Internet age, see Neil Strauss, "Rap Revolutionaries Plan an Internet Release," *New York Times,* April 16, 1999.

25. See Chuck D (with Yusuf Jah), *Fight the Power: Rap, Race, and Reality* (New York, 1997).

26. Nicholas Lemann, "Black Nationalism on Campus," *Atlantic,* January 1993, 31–36.

27. It is difficult to describe the rage and mistrust many black college students experience once they discover that so much of America's racial history is systematically excluded from the textbooks typically assigned during the primary and secondary years of education. Whereas college is usually a period of exploration, experimentation, and personal development, for many black youth it can also facilitate greater race consciousness and pride.

28. For a discussion of organic intellectuals, see Antonio Gramsci, *Selections from the Prison Notebooks* (London, 1971).

29. Largely as a result of hip hop culture the range of Malcolm X–related cultural products produced in recent years is nothing less than remarkable. Several dozen books have been published covering a broad spectrum of perspectives and publishing houses, including Molefi Asante, *Malcolm X as Cultural Hero: And Other Afrocentric Essays* (Trenton, N.J., 1993); Joe Wood, *Malcolm X: In Our Own Image* (New York, 1992); Michael E. Dyson, *Making Malcolm: The Myth and Meaning of Malcolm X* (New York, 1994). In addition, several pictorial volumes have been published as well as reissues of previously published works, including the collaboration between Malcolm X and Alex Haley, *The Autobiography of Malcolm X* (New York, 1992). The reissue of the autobiography made several best-seller lists, including that of the *New York Times.* In addition to Spike Lee's biopic, other films and television programs have been created. Independent filmmaker Orlando Bagwell produced and directed *Malcolm X: Make It Plain* (Blackside and ROJA Productions, 1994). Also, each of the major television networks has run special news programs that either featured the life and times of Malcolm X or the Spike Lee film.

30. Henry Louis Gates Jr., *Thirteen Ways of Looking at a Black Man* (New York, 1997).

31. Adolph Reed Jr., "The Rise of Louis Farrakhan," *Nation,* January 21, 1991.

32. See Feagin and Sikes, *Living with Racism,* for a discussion of the ways in which race shapes the everyday worlds of middle-class blacks. For an excellent empirical analysis of the economic differences between middle-class blacks and whites, see Melvin L. Oliver and Thomas M. Shapiro, *Black Wealth/White Wealth: A New Perspective on Racial Inequality* (New York, 1995). For a discussion of the factors that work against black mobility in the corporate sphere, see Sharon M. Collin, *Black Corporate Executives: The Making and Breaking of a Black Middle Class* (Philadelphia, 1997). For a discussion of the problems that confront the formation of black suburbs, see Massey and Denton, *American Apartheid.*

33. For a critique of the gender and sexual politics of sixties-style black national-

ism, see Elaine Brown, *A Taste of Power: A Black Woman's Story* (New York, 1992), and Angela Davis, "Black Nationalism: The Sixties and the Nineties," in *Black Popular Culture,* ed. Gina Dent (Seattle, 1992).

34. This trend is also typical in academic studies of black urban communities. In his analysis of how social scientists and anthropologists commonly study black urban communities, Robin D. G. Kelley notes that most ethnographers focus on the public spaces occupied by black men. As a result, many of their findings and conclusions about black communities are often based on studies that exclude women from any substantive consideration. See Robin D. G. Kelley, *Yo' Mama's Disfunktional!: Fighting the Culture Wars in Urban America* (Boston, 1997).

35. Reed, "The Rise of Louis Farrakhan."

36. See Van Deburg, *A New Day in Babylon,* for a discussion of the various products—clothes, hairpieces, music, magazines, food—that emerged to service a thriving black nationalist movement.

37. Angela Y. Davis, "Afro Images: Politics, Fashion, Nostalgia," in *Soul: Black Power, Politics, and Pleasure,* ed. Monique Guillory and Richard C. Green (New York, 1998).

10

After *The Fire Next Time:* James Baldwin's Postconsensus Double Bind

Will Walker

After January of 1964, literally as well as in the minds of his critics, James Baldwin went South. This essay explores Baldwin's representation of the impact of his southern tour and the rise of the Black Power movement on his long essay *No Name in the Street,* a memoir of the desegregation movement of the 1960s. It is, particularly, in this essay that Baldwin's critics claim that he moved away from an identification with American liberalism, construed as the most significant political manifestation of western humanism, to a strong embrace of the political philosophy of black nationalism(s), its supposed antithesis. My claim is that those who advance this argument have misread Baldwin and have misunderstood the complicated ideas and practices that have been considered "black nationalist" in one way or another. The argument proceeds in three phases. First, I situate Baldwin as a liminal cultural worker, betwixt and between the concrete aspirations and cultural practices of African American communities and a very specific form of left-leaning liberalism, associated in the early sixties with a Jewish literary establishment. Second, I adumbrate the rhetorical form of the revolutionary nationalism Baldwin's critics claim he adopted, a rejectionist version of the American Dream narrative, often referred to as the American Jeremiad.[1] I conclude that Baldwin's own complicated nationalism was in concordance with the revolutionary black nationalist narrative of political bondage to liberal norms and of emancipation through the creation of innovative forms of civil society. Where Baldwin differed stridently with the revolutionary nationalists was over the issue of cultural nationalism. Bald-

win rejected all forms of racial essentialism on the grounds of a deep historical sense of cultural and racial hybridity, which he often described in terms
of sibling rivalry. It is around this issue of a radical rhetorical posture shared
with the revolutionaries and a deep desire for hybrid forms of civil society
that Baldwin's critics have misunderstood him.

Baldwin as Liminal Intellectual

James Baldwin died an exile in Saint Paul de Vence on November 30, 1987.
He had not been a political exile in the sense of having been expelled from
the land of his citizenship, the United States. Rather, his exile was the result
of a sort of intellectual double bind, a double bind with which his life had
in many ways always been fraught. As a black intellectual, he was caught between two definable ideological formations of the black freedom movement of the 1950s and 1960s: the first phase of civil rights reform (1954–
65), which expressed its demands in the redemptive national language of
the liberal consensus narrative, and the second phase of black nationalist
politics (1965–72), which articulated its demands in terms of a racial particularism that foregrounded the experiences, memories, practices, and aspirations of black Americans as something distinct from the redemptive
politics of the United States. Hence, Baldwin's intellectual double bind—
that he was neither a consensus liberal who appealed to the American
promise of racially inclusive freedom and equality, nor a black nationalist
who appealed to the redemptive practice of closing ranks because America
was irredeemable and unable to regenerate itself, yet who was devoted to the
full emancipation of African Americans—makes him one of the most perplexing and troubling of African American cultural critics. Edward Said's
characterization of the intellectual as an outsider, existing between the ostensibly natural bonds of racial/national "filiation" and the apparently circumstantial "affiliations" elicited by the winds of social, political, and
economic change, fits Baldwin's predicament well.[2] The perplexing nature
of Baldwin's critical self-situating, his intellectual double bind, has led to
claims and counter claims concerning the significance of his legacy.

Among his claimants, Kendall Thomas has most recently attributed
Baldwin's social and political marginality from the Black Power movement
to his sexual identity, his homosexuality. Thomas excavates Baldwin to
show how a homophobic chauvinism, a "virulent masculinism," undergirds
the rhetoric of a contemporary black identity politics that still bears the essentialist marks of its nationalist origins. He shows little concern with Bald-

win's own development and intellectual positions; Baldwin is a foil for the
critique of racial essentialism within black nationalism, a critique that does
not take into account Baldwin's own contributions to the moral language of
black cultural nationalist politics. For Thomas, Baldwin's marginality from
the bonds of his natal community and filiative associations is ultimately an
"exemplary instance of someone who refused to make this false, and ultimately fatal, choice" between the racial and sexual sources of the African
American self.[3] While Henry Louis Gates Jr. also makes use of Baldwin in
his attack on contemporary nationalist antiracist politics, his most profound analysis of Baldwin is an attempt to make sense of Baldwin's supposed change in political rhetoric between 1963 and 1972, after the
publication of *The Fire Next Time*.

Gates is among those who have attempted to make some sense of the
impact of the Black Power movement on Baldwin's trajectory as a writer.
His argument is essentially that after *The Fire Next Time* Baldwin consciously abandoned the complexity that prevented his writings from serving
ideological and political ends. He lost his "cultural authority," according to
Gates, because, in the shift from civil rights reform to the cultural politics of
Black Power, Baldwin became a rhetorical ape of the new black nationalist
ideologues, "mouth[ing] a script that was not his own." Gates relies heavily
on Baldwin's long essay *No Name in the Street* to support his thesis that
Baldwin permitted himself to be "instructed by those who had inherited his
mantle of cultural authority, 'the new power generation,'" by merely serving up the "populist slogans of the day and return[ing] them with a Baldwinian finish."[4] What is lost in Gates's account of Baldwin's "narrative of
decline" between the publication of *Fire* and *No Name in the Street* (though
Gates's claim is that the "decline" model is too simple a model for Baldwin,
since his "late essays" demonstrate an "intellectual resurgence") are the ways
in which Baldwin's early writings anticipated the rhetorical strategies of the
Black Power movement, and in some respect went beyond them, without
being identified with them. Gates fails to analyze the way in which Baldwin's critical repertoire made him as marginal to the civil rights movement
as it did to the Black Power movement. Baldwin should be understood as a
cultural critic who drew from the jeremiadic tradition of American nationalism *and* the antiracist rhetoric of black nationalism(s) to construct a postmodern traditionalist rhetoric. His rhetoric was shaped then by the belief
that the United States was not only postmodern and postcolonial (shaped
by a deep suspicion of western humanistic metanarratives) but also traditional (shaped by a proclivity toward forms of group life). His cultural
criticism, a hybrid narrative of western liberal humanism and racial

particularism, was formed to meet the exigencies of this conjunction, a conjunction that mirrored his own in-betweenness. For this reason Baldwin was viewed suspiciously by both liberals and black nationalists after the publication of *The Fire Next Time.*

Baldwin and the Liberal Consensus

In situating Baldwin as a cultural critic, it is important to remember that he began his career writing for magazines controlled by a group of Jewish cultural workers known as the New York Intellectuals. Had it not been for the role that Jewish ethnicity played in constituting the group and the particular twist that it placed on the questions concerning American identity that its members sought to address, Baldwin's historic legacy could well be tied to that of the New York Intellectuals. The group clearly functioned for Baldwin as a "social marginality facilitator," in Jerry Watts's terminology; that is to say, an institution that protects, nurtures, and promotes the black artist who finds him- or herself stranded between intellectually resourceless black communities and indifferent or hostile mainstream white communities.[5] In the preface to his collected nonfiction, *The Price of the Ticket,* Baldwin himself asserts the role of Jewish magazines as social marginality facilitators by situating his writing career in its relationship to the New York Intellectuals, whom he claims "saved his life" by giving him his start as a writer. The list of names—Saul Levitas of the *New Leader,* Elliot Cohen and Robert Warshow of *Commentary,* and Philip Rahv of *Partisan Review*—reads as a who's who of the Jewish intellectuals who saw themselves at the center of American highbrow life in the postwar era. These editors functioned as a kind of midwife to James Baldwin, the cultural critic and public intellectual, their journals being the vehicle through which his writings were first disseminated.

The New York Intellectuals began as a group of second-generation Jewish radicals committed to anticommunism *and* radical democracy in the late 1930s. Alexander Bloom has characterized them as an extremely "individualist lot," located between the Old World traditions of their parents, from which they consciously distanced themselves, and the American mainstream, from which they were alienated due to their Jewish immigrant status. Their cosmopolitanism exhibited their movement away from what Irving Howe has called the "world of our fathers," and their socialism (internationalism) suggested their critique of the American consensus. This status as intellectual outsiders changed after World War II when they moved to a position of "uneasy liberalism" in the postwar era, a liberalism described by Elliot Cohen, writing for *Commentary* in 1952, as one in which "the American system offered the best chance for the future." Bloom sums up this transition as a move that made the New York Intellectuals "liberal intellectuals for the nation rather than radical intellectuals critical of it." Baldwin began writing for the magazines controlled by the New York Intellectuals in the postwar era, just at the time when many in the group had begun to believe that "maybe *here*, right on our own doorstep, is the long yearned-for political alternative, after all."[6]

My point is that Baldwin began his literary career affiliated with a group of Jewish intellectuals who were torn between two moments: a moment of ideological cosmopolitanism that downplayed Jewish ethnicity and highlighted the alienated status of the (Jewish) intellectual in the 1930s and 1940s, and a post–World War II moment, in which the New York Intellectuals emerged as "a distinctive hybrid: . . . intellectual[s] with a strong attachment to both [their] ethnic and national roots."[7] This tension between an aspiration for a nation-state that embodied a humanistic universalism and a strong desire for self-understanding within one's own ethnic and racial traditions also shoots through Baldwin's cultural criticism. I do not wish to argue for a causal relation between Baldwin's stance and that of the New York Intellectuals, but to point in the direction of an elective affinity that is surely one reason (other than his obvious literary talents) the New York Intellectuals facilitated Baldwin's writing career. Remembering the patronage that the New York Intellectuals paid to Baldwin, Nathan Glazer wrote: "I was on the editorial staff then; how he came to us I don't recall, but I do recall our pleasure that a remarkable young Black writer— how remarkable, we didn't yet know—had come to us. At that time, *Commentary* was a much more exclusively Jewish magazine than it would later become, and all we could think of suggesting to Baldwin was that he write about Blacks and Jews." Glazer's remark points toward the role that ethnicity played in the patronage that facilitated Baldwin's writing career. The liberalism that Baldwin and the New York Intellectuals of the postwar era articulated was a liberalism imbued with the cultural politics of identity.

Baldwin's intellectual negotiation of competing ideological allegiances placed him in what Said would call an exilic state. Said writes, "The exile exists therefore in a median state, . . . beset with half involvements and half detachments, nostalgic and sentimental on one level, an adept mimic or a secret outcast on another. Being skilled at survival becomes the main imperative, with the danger of getting too comfortable and secure constituting a threat that is constantly to be guarded against."[8] This description fits Baldwin's postconsensus essays well; they depict Baldwin as both "nostalgic and sentimental" for the type of political practice promoted by Martin Luther King Jr. and Malcolm X. But that they reveal Baldwin as nostalgic for *both* leaders demonstrates the complicated nature of Baldwin's own social criticism.

Black Nationalism and the Critique of Modernity

The Fire Next Time made James Baldwin famous. Yet, it is a mystery why. Yes, Baldwin did renounce black separatism, in the form of the Nation of Islam, favoring an integrationist politics based on a deep notion of common human suffering and a belief in the political utility of love. One can make the case that the profundity of this social vision of human brotherhood and sisterhood is certainly one reason for the success of *Fire*. But *Fire* also articulated a common black nationalist theme of the rejection of American ideals based on the belief that white supremacy was the limit of American democracy. It is this aspect of coupling the black nationalist negative critique of American democracy with an affirmative hope in the American future that made *Fire* so complex a document, which meant so many things to so many different people. After the publication of *Fire,* Baldwin emphasized the negative critique he shared with nationalists rather than the affirmative hope that had caused mainstream liberals to laud him; hence, his oeuvre has been read as a narrative of decline by his liberal critics.

The hybrid narrative of prophetic critique, which is the product of this strange coupling of negation and affirmation, of criticism and hope, also makes Baldwin one of the most complex social critics of the 1960s. Baldwin's critical repertoire was not ordered by the well-worn jeremiadic dialectic of a discrepancy between American liberal principles of the nation's founding and American practices, but was articulated in terms of a continued national captivity to racist practices and American achievement, the aspiration for an *other* America, another country. What is the case for Baldwin's black nationalist bona fides, which were often denied by revolutionary black nationalists? I begin with a characterization of the negative criticism articulated historically by black nationalism(s).

Cornel West has characterized the difference between the cultural criticism of black nationalists and the cultural criticism of black American exceptionalists as the difference between a deep-seated pessimism concerning the efficacy of American ideals and a disappointment concerning the ability of Americans to live up to those ideals. On West's view, disappointment with America on the part of African American critics assumes that the critic has had some reasonable expectation that America would fulfill its promise, realize its dream. Conversely, black nationalists expect nothing from America; their deep-seated pessimism deconstructs the narrative frame that structures the ideals of the American experiment. Given this reading of black nationalism, one would have to consider Baldwin a nationalist. He was not disappointed that Americans could not live up to American ideals. But West has offered a more sustained formulation of black nationalism. He writes:

> Black nationalists usually call upon black people to close ranks, to distrust most whites (since the reliable whites are few and relatively powerless in the face of white supremacy) and to promote forms of black self-love, self-defense, and self-determination. [Black nationalism] views white supremacy as the definitive systemic constraint on black cultural, political, and economic development. More pointedly, black nationalists claim that American democracy is a modern form of tyranny on the part of the white majority over the black minority. For them, black sanity and freedom requires that America not serve as the major framework in which to understand the future of black people. Instead, American civilization—like all civilizations—rises and falls, ebbs and flows. And owing to its deep-seated racism this society does not warrant black allegiance or loyalty. White supremacy dictates the limits of the operation of American democracy—with black folk the indispensable sacrificial lamb vital to its sustenance. Hence black subordination constitutes the necessary condition for the flourishing of American democracy, the tragic prerequisite for America itself.[9]

Taking West's characterization of black nationalism, I will, first, elaborate on what I have meant by the negative critique that Baldwin shares with black nationalism(s) and, second, square what West has characterized as black nationalism's "closing ranks" mentality with Baldwin's strong commitment to cultural and racial hybridity, his affirmative hope concerning what America could become.

In Baldwin's essay *No Name in the Street,* this critique is so uncompromising that it seems to overwhelm the affirmative hope that the liberal establishment so readily understood as the traditional form of the American Dream narrative. *No Name* is Baldwin's effort to reinterpret the history of the civil rights movement and his own part in it for a new generation of black nationalist activists. The essay is also Baldwin's bid to place himself within a line of black nationalist exemplars who have represented a certain kind of cultural criticism. In *No Name,* this kind of criticism is what I have designated negative critique. It is what separates Baldwin from King and links him to Malcolm X.

By 1963, Baldwin had begun to proclaim the end of the age of Europe, of the legitimate authority of western culture in general, and of American ideals in particular. In *No Name,* he takes this element of his critical repertoire to be his connection to the black nationalist tradition of cultural critique. Baldwin writes: "All of the western nations have been caught in a lie, the lie of their pretended humanism; this means that their history has no moral justification, and the West has no moral authority. Malcolm, yet more concretely than Frantz Fanon—since Malcolm operated in the Afro-American idiom, and referred to the Afro-American situation—made the nature of this lie, and its implications relevant and articulate to the people whom he served."[10] Baldwin's use of Malcolm X as an exemplar of critical practice is a crucial gesture toward the tradition of black nationalist critique but not the black nationalist program of closing ranks and the development of a black economic and political infrastructure, a concept he considers with a deep skepticism (*No Name,* p. 475).[11] Baldwin's emphasis that this is an indigenous form of social criticism, linked to the exemplarism of Malcolm X, not Fanon, is also a significant factor in understanding Baldwin's linkages to black nationalism(s). By 1971, Fanon's *The Wretched of the Earth* had sold some 750,000 copies. Nationalist leaders had proclaimed Fanon the patron saint of cultural nationalism, and it had been said that "every brother on a rooftop can quote Fanon."[12] What these brothers on the rooftop had taken from Fanon was the idea that African American cultural forms and practices were a uniting force for Africans of the diaspora and should stand at the center of revolutionary political practice. Baldwin departed from the black nationalists on this cultural aspect of the freedom struggle. He saw African American cultural forms as uniquely American, a product of the conditions of natal alienation and cultural resistance to white supremacist practices. Thus Baldwin strives to maintain his black nationalist bona fides, even while evading a chauvinistic cultural nationalism, by finessing Malcolm X's Islamic affiliations and by making negative critique the most important thing about Malcolm's exemplarism.

Negative critique is criticism aimed at what Said has called the sensitive "nodal point of a culture." In this case it links core western humanistic values to the domination of "other" peoples. The French philosopher Antoine-Nicolas de Condorcet, in a work that may be regarded as the Enlightenment's culminating attempt at self-interpretation, made this link between western humanistic values and domination clear. Condorcet described the civilizing project of modernity as consisting of the "true perfection of mankind": the "abolition of inequality between nations and the progress of equality within nations." Condorcet went on to suggest that the progress of the human race would have to pass a stage wherein the eradication or civilizing of African and Asian savages would have been carried out by either the law of force or the enculturating force of reason.[13]

The tradition of black nationalist critique, which West has delineated above and which Baldwin links to Malcolm X, is characterized by making racial domination the precondition for the flourishing of western modernity. Baldwin, as is often the case, bases his critique of modernity on a racial theodicy, which may be described usefully here as a representation of the intended and unintended consequences of the modern project, of the effects of disciplined reason on black persons. Baldwin continues by quoting Dostoyevsky, a primary demythologizer of the notion of European progress from the standpoint of the unjustified suffering of the weak. Baldwin cites Dostoyevsky's *The Idiot* concerning the antinomies of modernity: "I don't believe in the wagons that bring bread to humanity, for the wagons that bring bread to humanity, without any moral basis for conduct, may coldly exclude a considerable part of humanity from enjoying what is brought; so it has been already" (*No Name*, pp. 492–93). The argument that Baldwin lifts from Dostoyevsky's demythologizing of European modernity is that the progress which modernity promised was predicated on arbitrary exclusionary practices. Baldwin's racialized theodicy maintains that victims are those blacks who "paid the price for the prosperity of white Americans" (*No Name*, pp. 494). In this regard Baldwin believes the western nations have been caught in a lie, "the lie of their pretended humanism."

In order to maintain the mask of civilization, of "pretended humanism," Baldwin, in Arnoldian terms, maintains that whites understand the oppositional political practice of black nationalists as the activity of barbarians at the gate: a cultural threat against the perceived orderliness that preceded the civil rights movement. He thus displaces the *ressentiment* that usually attaches to the victim status onto whites.

> Now, not even the people who are the most spectacular recipients of the benefits of this prosperity are able to endure these benefits: they can neither understand them nor do without them, nor can they go beyond them. Above all, they cannot, or dare not, assess or imagine the price paid by their victims, or subjects, for this way of life, and so

they cannot afford to know why the victims are revolting. They are
forced, then, to the conclusion that the victims—barbarians—are
revolting against established values—which is both true and not
true—and, in order to preserve these values, however stifling and
joyless these values have caused their lives to be, the bulk of people
desperately seek out representatives who are prepared to make up in
cruelty what both they and the people lack in conviction. (*No Name*,
p. 496)[14]

Baldwin goes further in his displacement of the victim status onto whites by
appealing directly to what West has called the role of blacks as the "sacrificial lamb vital to the sustenance" of white supremacy.

Baldwin's frequent use of the figures of the Christ and the scapegoat
to represent the suffering of African Americans has led some critics to claim
that Baldwin's criticism was driven by a victim-status ideology that depicts
the suffering of African Americans as redemptive.[15] Stanley Crouch maintains that this notion is so pronounced in Baldwin that it has influenced a
generation of African American writers. Crouch writes that "much of Afro-
American fiction . . . derives from a vision set down by James Baldwin, who
described the downtrodden as saintly. According to Baldwin, those who
had suffered most knew life best; had more to tell the world. . . . Baldwin
insisted that somewhere in the soul of those black folk were truths that
might set everyone free."[16] Crouch also links Baldwin's version of blacks as
sacrificial victims to the negative critique of black nationalists Malcolm X
and Eldridge Cleaver.

Crouch is right in making this connection, for the victim status of
blacks in the rhetoric of nationalists is different from the representation of
blacks as victims in civil rights discourses, though he would like to characterize this difference as a contrast between the "complex vision of universal
humanism" that undergirds civil rights discourses and the "intellectual barbarism" and "condescending self-regard" of "ethnic nationalism."[17] The
contrast does not get us far in understanding a critic as subtle as Baldwin.
He shared the nationalist's view of black victimhood—it was a constitutive
factor in the construction of American national identity. And he structured
his negative critique to illuminate this process. He also shared the so-called
complex humanism of the civil rights movement. He simply had another conception of the human condition than did King, who, according to Crouch,
discovered the "intersection of mutual identification that allows those outside a minority or special interest group to fight for its principles." This intersection, of course, was the common liberal inheritances of freedom,

equality, and justice which King fashioned into a redemptive protest narrative. The important point here is that though the narrative focused on a common inheritance, it *did* figure blacks as victims, as redemptive figures. Baldwin's humanism highlighted the common condition of suffering, of which the experience of African Americans was an instance, a constitutive instance, in the construction of American identity.

Baldwin's negative critique highlights the experience of blacks as the scapegoat, the sacrificial victim. But he sets himself apart from the most exemplary practitioner of sacrificial politics, Martin Luther King Jr., who used the victim status of blacks to compel white Americans to redeem a fallen past of American ideals, by deploying the metaphor of the sacrificial victim instead as a nonredemptive figure, as one who does not redeem the community but confirms its guilt:

> The failure of the private life has always had the most devastating effect on American public conduct, and on black-white relations. If Americans were not so terrified of their private selves, they would never have needed to invent and could never have become dependent on what they still call the "the Negro problem." This problem, which they invented in order to safeguard their purity, has made of them criminals and monsters, and it is destroying them; and this not from anything blacks may or may not be doing but because of the role a guilty and constricted white imagination has assigned to blacks. That the scapegoat pays for the sins of others is well known, but this is only legend, and a revealing one at that. In fact, however the scapegoat may be made to suffer, his suffering cannot purify the sinner; it merely incriminates him the more, and it seals his damnation. The scapegoat, eventually, is released, to death: his murderer continues to live. The suffering of the scapegoat has resulted in seas of blood, and yet not one sinner has been saved, or changed, by this despairing ritual. Sin has merely been added to sin, and guilt piled upon guilt. In the private chambers of the soul, the guilty party is identified, and the accusing finger, there, is not legend, but consequence, not fantasy, but truth. People pay for what they do, and, still more, for what they have allowed themselves to become. And they pay for it simply: by the lives they lead. (*No Name*, pp. 477)

Here, Baldwin is at his nationalistic *and* humanistic best; he connects the privations of private lives to the social dis-ease and the cultural dis-order of racial hierarchy, which white America seeks to preserve through the archaic ritual of scapegoating. According to Baldwin, the ritual is an act of cultural projection, which identifies African Americans with such un-American vices as slothfulness and cross-racial sexual aggression.[18] This attribution of criminal and monstrous qualities to blacks is described as "the Negro problem," and, according to Baldwin, its purpose is to "safeguard the purity" and innocence of America's social order. The importance of Baldwin's association of this act of projection with ritual scapegoating and its connection to the negative critique of black nationalism(s) can be illuminated by René Girard's analysis of the "monstrous double," the surrogate victim.

Girard argues that primitive societies maintained social order by imputing the violent and socially divisive principles and practices of a community to a substitute victim, a scapegoat. The scapegoat is considered a "monstrous double," a marginal figure who exists both inside and outside the community, possessing all the "possible differences within the community," and constituting "both a link and a barrier between the community and the sacred."[19] The unacknowledged similarity of the sacrificial victim to the members of the community allows for the transfer of the violent social forces from the community to the scapegoat. Girard lists slaves, children, and prisoners of war as fitting into this category of surrogate victim. In addition, Girard notes that scapegoating requires a misunderstanding of the function of the act on the part of those who perform it.[20] According to Baldwin, the "Negro problem" is a case of just such misunderstanding. The crisis in American culture described as the "Negro problem" permits the "guilty imagination" of whites, who created a social order in which blacks would be socially and culturally denigrated, to remain in a state of innocence.[21] For Baldwin, the Negro is America's "monstrous double," the bastard son, the racial hybrid, who embodies the crisis of blood union and cultural miscegenation that threatens the racial distinctions on which American society had been built. It is, according to Baldwin's best lights, the threat of the blood contamination of whites that sets in motion racial violence toward blacks that has produced a "despairing ritual," which has "resulted in seas of blood." As Girard has noted, "blood contagion" begets ritual sacrifices that "confirm an affinity between sexuality and those diverse forms of violence that invariably lead to bloodshed."[22]

It is here that Baldwin's negative critique parts company with that of revolutionary black nationalism(s). Baldwin's articulation of blacks as the sacrificial victims of American culture is predicated on his view that blacks are culturally American, not African. Cultural nationalism understands African American practices to be continuous with the practices of peoples of the African diaspora throughout the world. Baldwin maintains that blacks in North America are natally alienated, they have been entirely cut off from an African cultural heritage. The ritual scapegoating in which whites engage is, therefore, part of a sibling rivalry among American brothers. As Girard has stated, the "double and the monster are one and the same being." This legacy of the Americanization process is either suppressed or derided by black nationalism(s), but its affirmation as an explanatory category is the linchpin of Baldwin's cultural criticism. In *No Name*, Baldwin uses the "bloodstained land" of the South as a metaphor for his view that, in America, the intimacy of blood between blacks and whites has been repressed through acts of racial violence. Baldwin's 1964 journey to the South permitted him to see the shared cultural intimacy between blacks and whites, which is the legacy of centuries of enslavement and Jim Crow law. This turn to the South allows Baldwin to make much more vivid the notion of cultural and sexual miscegenation that is the most important element in distinguishing his cultural criticism from that of revolutionary black nationalist criticism. Concerning the repressed acknowledgment of blood union in the South, Baldwin writes:

> Because the South is, or certainly was then, so closed a community, their colors struck the light—the eye—far more vividly than these same colors strike one in the North: the prohibition, precisely, of the social mingling revealed the extent of the sexual amalgamation. Girls the color of honey, men nearly the color of chalk, hair like silk, hair like cotton, hair like wire, eyes blue, gray, green, hazel, black, like the gypsy's, brown like the Arab's, nostrils, thin, wide lips, thin lips, every conceivable variation struck along incredible gamuts—it was not in the Southland that one could hope to keep a secret! And the niggers of course didn't try, though they knew their white brothers and sisters and papas, and watched them daily, strutting around in their white skins. . . . And the white men couldn't bear it—knowing that they knew; it is not only in the Orient that white is the color of death. (*No Name*, p. 491)

Baldwin's claim is that blacks and whites are not separate peoples; they are both Americans. The fact that blacks share a common land, culture, and blood with whites is the repressed "secret" behind American nationalism.[23] The knowledge of this blood intimacy breeds the need for the sacrificial death to maintain the racially chauvinistic virility of the American Dream. Nowhere has Baldwin clearly dramatized this connection between race, sex, and violence more than in his 1965 short story "Going to Meet the Man."

In "Going to Meet the Man," Baldwin tells the story of a sexually impotent, small-town southern policeman engaged in the violent repression of civil rights demonstrators. The sheriff is unable to engage in sexual intercourse with his wife until he remembers the ritual violence meted out against the demonstrators and the lynching of a black man.

> He thought of the boy in the cell; he thought of the man in the fire;
> he thought of the knife and grabbed himself and stroked himself and
> a terrible sound, something between a laugh and a howl, came out of
> him and dragged his sleeping wife up on one elbow. . . . He thought
> of the morning and grabbed her, laughing and crying, crying and
> laughing, and he whispered as he stroked her, as he took her, "Come
> on sugar, I'm going to do you like a nigger, just like a nigger, come
> on, sugar, and love me just like you'd love a nigger." He thought of
> the morning as he labored and she moaned, thought of the morning
> as he labored harder than he ever had before, and before his labors
> had ended, he heard the first cock crow.[24]

The content of the story, to which this passage is the conclusion, consists of all the elements of what Richard Slotkin has described as a regeneration through violence, the "structuring metaphor of the American experience."[25] According to Slotkin, the Puritan captivity narratives were the first literary articulations of the American myth. The narratives consisted of the capture of a white woman, who represented the New England political body, by Indians. Her capture represents the possible defilement of the entire Puritan community; conversely, her emancipation signifies the collective body's promised redemption.[26] "Going to Meet the Man" is the African American version of the captivity narrative. Baldwin uses it to elaborate the American ritual of scapegoating. The cited passage is preceded by a passionate hunt for an African American victim, who is presumed to have raped a white woman. The entire community, men, women, and children, converge on the victim, and by fire, rope, and blade they lynch "the most beautiful and terrible object." It is this image, along with the image of a bloodied civil-rights worker, that the sheriff remembers in Baldwin's portrayal of the miscegenistic violence that takes place in the bed of white America. Baldwin represents the memory of this violence, which included the castration of the lynching victim, as regenerating the sheriff, restoring his virility. This regenerative act of violence permits the sheriff to "labor harder than he ever had before" to the dawn of a new day when he hears the "first cock crow."

Baldwin's most significant metaphor for American society is the prophetic, familial trope of the divided house. He uses the trope to continue his demythologization of the American myth, which is inextricably linked to his discussion of African Americans as the intimate other that orders American society. Hence, Baldwin's critique of the constitution of American political culture is always an explication of the blood that blacks and whites share. Baldwin's critique is therefore genealogical, as he maintains that an understanding of this truth would heal the nation. This demythologization of the American Dream, Baldwin writes, is analogous to the "dirty joke that is at the heart of the Virgin Birth" (Christ is not a bastard, he has human paternity) and which sustains orthodox Christianity in the same way that rigid categories of black and white sustain the American Dream.

Baldwin uses the figure of the house to explain the student revolts and rise of Black Power as both continuous with and subverting American redemptive history. He accomplishes this by placing what Hannah Arendt has characterized as the political contestation of the highly moral claims of white student rebels and the degenerate practices of violence by the Black Power movement within the interpretive frame of the American myth.[27] He depicts the moment as a rupture in the sibling rivalry which undergirds American culture: "When the heir of a great house repudiates the house, the house cannot continue, unless it looks to alien blood to save it; and here were the heirs and heiresses of all the ages, in the street along with that blood always considered to be most alien, never lawfully to be mixed with that of the sons and daughters of the great house" (*No Name*, p. 548). What we see here is a rhetorical extension into the twentieth century of what George Forgie has described as one of the primary metaphors deployed in political argumentation in the antebellum period.

Forgie describes the American cultural criticism of the antebellum period as crisis-centered, structured by the metaphor of the divided house, and produced by both a generational conflict between heroic Founding Fathers and post-Revolutionary sons, and a sibling rivalry between sons of the fathers over the meaning of their legacy in a "post-heroic age."[28] Baldwin uses this trope to contend that the national crisis over integration is a crisis of blood, a struggle over whether democratic blessings are so scarce that a racial genetics of national redemption will continue to obfuscate the blood union of blacks and whites. In Baldwin's depiction of the social uprisings of the late sixties, good white sons (student radicals) join the bad sons (Black Power advocates) to turn against the Fathers who had bequeathed them an inheritance of white supremacy. The violence that ensued, contra Arendt,[29] was not simply the violence of the nation-state maintaining its place as the only institution that controls the instruments of violence but was part of the reciprocal violence from which white America has been unable to extricate itself since enslavement and the founding of the American white supremacist nation-state.[30] Baldwin's metaphor of the house at once invokes and debunks the normative drama of American redemptive history by making race central to that story.

Conclusion

James Baldwin's uncompromising negative critique of American political culture extends beyond black nationalist critiques in terms of the complexity of its psychological depth and discussion of how both white and black identities have been constructed in the Americanization process. The attacks on his critical practice by people such as Amiri Baraka and Eldridge Cleaver go to Baldwin's construction of black cultural nationalism, not his negative critique of the American consensus narrative and the forms of life built around it. Whereas Baldwin maintained that an embrace of black identity as existentially empowering would be a first step toward social emancipation, he believed it could be nothing more than that, a first step. Though revolutionary black nationalists such as Stokely Carmichael referred to black cultural nationalism as only an interim strategy on the road toward political modernization and a new cultural pluralist society, it is clear that most nationalists saw cultural nationalism as a permanent institution of the political society they were striving toward.[31] Baldwin saw it as a necessary step toward a world in which black and white would no longer be socially salient identities.[32]

NOTES

1. See Sacvan Bercovitch, *The American Jeremiad* (Madison, 1978).

2. Edward Said, *The World, the Text, and the Critic* (Cambridge, Mass., 1983).

3. Kendall Thomas, "'Ain't Nothin' Like the Real Thing': Black Masculinity, Gay Sexuality, and the Jargon of Authenticity," in *The House That Race Built: Black Americans, U.S. Terrain,* ed. Wahneema Lubiano (New York, 1997), p. 122. Though Thomas is concerned with Baldwin's sexual alienation, he recognizes Baldwin's double marginality as well when he writes that "while Baldwin may have left America because he was black, he left Harlem, the place he called 'home,' because he was gay."

4. Henry Louis Gates Jr., "The Welcome Table," in *Lure and Loathing: Essays on Race, Identity, and the Ambivalence of Assimilation,* ed. Gerald Early (New York, 1994), pp. 160, 155.

5. Jerry Gafio Watts, *Heroism and the Black Intellectual: Ralph Ellison, Politics, and Afro-American Intellectual Life* (Chapel Hill, N.C., 1994), pp. 15–16.

6. Alexander Bloom, *The New York Intellectuals and Their World* (New York, 1986), pp. 6–7, 184. Italics are original.

7. Robert S. Boynton, "The New Intellectuals," *Atlantic Monthly* (March 1995): 62.

8. Edward Said, *Representations of the Intellectual* (New York, 1994), p. 49.

9. Cornel West and Henry Louis Gates Jr., *The Future of the Race* (New York, 1986), p. 73.

10. James Baldwin, *No Name in the Street,* in *The Price of the Ticket: Collected Non-Fiction, 1948–1985* (New York, 1985), p. 492. Subsequent references to this collection will be noted parenthetically in the body of this essay.

11. Baldwin writes that "black capitalism" is a "concept demanding yet more faith and infinitely more schizophrenia than the concept of the virgin birth."

12. William L. Van Deburg, *New Day in Babylon: The Black Power Movement and American Culture, 1965–1975* (Chicago, 1992), pp. 58–59.

13. Marquis de Condorcet, *Sketch for a Historical Picture of the Progress of the Human Mind* (London, 1955), pp. 173–79.

14. Baldwin is, of course, making reference to the rise of the New Conservatism, which invoked an appeal to traditional values as a strategy for dealing with the changing social order created by integration policies such as busing and affirmative action.

15. See Albert Murray, *The Omni-Americans: Some Alternatives to the Folklore of White Supremacy* (New York, 1970); Jerry Watts, *Heroism and the Black Intellectual: Ralph Ellison, Politics, and Afro-American Intellectual Life* (Chapel Hill, N.C., 1994); Stanley Crouch, *Notes of a Hanging Judge: Essays and Reviews, 1979–1989* (New York, 1990).

16. Crouch, *Notes of a Hanging Judge,* p. 202.

17. Ibid., pp. x, xii, xv.

18. In an early essay, "Many Things Gone," Baldwin uses scapegoating as he does here, as an explanation for black cultural degeneracy. He writes: "But there is a complementary faith among the damned which involves their gathering of the stones with which those who walk in the light shall stone them; or there exists among the intolerably degraded the perverse and powerful desire to force into the arena of the actual those fantastic crimes of which they have been accused, achieving their vengeance and their own destruction through making the nightmare real. The American image of the Negro lives also in the Negro's heart; and when he has surrendered to this image life has no other possible reality" ("Many Things Gone," in *The Price of the Ticket,* p. 74).

19. René Girard, *Violence and the Sacred,* trans. Patrick Gregory (Baltimore, 1977), pp. 8, 271.

20. Ibid., p. 7.

21. W. E. B. Du Bois, the critic who first announced that the "problem of the twentieth century is the problem of the color-line," makes a similar point concerning the rhetoric of racial scapegoating and the maintenance of American cultural order. He writes:

"But, alas! while sociologists gleefully count his bastards and his prostitutes, the very soul of the toiling, sweating black man is darkened by the shadow of a vast despair. Men call the shadow prejudice, and learnedly explain it as the natural defense of culture against barbarism, learning against ignorance, purity against crime, the 'higher' against the 'lower' races." W. E. B. Du Bois, *The Souls of Black Folk* (New York, 1995), p. 50.

22. Girard, *Violence and the Sacred,* p. 35.

23. Baldwin's description of Americans as a biracial people is all the more relevant given the recent disclosure that Thomas Jefferson did indeed father at least one child of his slave Sally Hemmings. Jefferson evidently did keep his personal desires "secret" while espousing a plan of colonization or of racial apartheid that would protect the pure aesthetics of American civil society. Concerning the physical and moral reasons for rejecting the incorporation of blacks into the American nation-state, Jefferson describes racial differences as absolute. His description of blacks, unlike Baldwin's, takes no note of common characteristics that would suggest racial amalgamation. This is all the more surprising given the fact that Jefferson's plantation included slaves who were the products of interracial sexual liaisons. Concerning a racial aesthetics of American culture, Jefferson writes: "And is this difference of no importance? Is it not the foundation of a greater or less share of beauty in the two races? Are not the fine mixtures of red and white, the expressions of every passion by greater or less suffusions of colour in the one, preferable to that eternal monotony, which reigns in the countenances, that immovable veil of black which covers all the emotions of the other race? Add to these, flowing hair, a more elegant symmetry of form, their own judgment in favor of the whites, declared by their preference of them, as uniformly as is the preference of the Oranootan for the black woman over those of his own species. The circumstances of superior beauty, is thought worthy attention in the propagation of our horses, dogs, and other domestic animals; why not in that of man?" Thomas Jefferson, "Notes on the State of Virginia," in *Thomas Jefferson: Writings,* ed. Merrill D. Peterson (New York, 1984), pp. 264–65. It must also be noted that Jefferson's thoughts on race were not just part of a general consensus; his position was on the cutting edge of racial thought.

24. James Baldwin, *Going to Meet the Man* (New York, 1965), p. 217.

25. Richard Slotkin, *Regeneration through Violence: The Mythology of the American Frontier, 1600–1860* (Middletown, Conn., 1973), p. 5.

26. Ibid., pp. 94–95.

27. See Hannah Arendt, *On Violence* (New York, 1970).

28. George B. Forgie, *Patricide in the House Divided: A Psychological Interpretation of Lincoln and His Age* (New York, 1979), pp. 3–53.

29. Arendt is unaware of how close she is to this Baldwinian insight when she states that "violence has remained mostly a matter of theory and rhetoric where the clash between *generations* did not coincide with a clash of tangible interest groups. . . . Negro students . . . regarded and organized themselves as an interest group." Arendt continues the errors of social scientists in viewing blacks as an interest group while whites ("generations") are not in political struggles over democratic goods. Of course, the language itself is part of a liberal rhetorical consensus that blurs the role of race in political contestation, legitimating the activity of the white students and deligitimating that of the blacks. See Arendt, *On Violence,* p. 18.

30. Concerning the "vicious circle" of violence that necessitates the creation of a scapegoat to stop its expansion, René Girard has written that "when a community succeeds

in convincing itself that one alone of a number is responsible for the violent mimesis besetting it; when it is able to view this member as the single 'polluted' enemy who is contaminating the rest; and when the citizens are truly unanimous in this conviction—then the belief becomes reality, for there will no longer exist elsewhere in the community a form of violence to be followed or opposed, which is to say, imitated and propagated." Girard, *Violence and the Sacred*, pp. 81–82.

31. See Stokely Carmichael and Charles Hamilton, *Black Power: The Politics of Liberation in America* (New York, 1967).

32. This lends some credence to Eldridge Cleaver's charge that Baldwin had a "racial death wish." Cleaver misses the point in attributing Baldwin's position to a self-loathing of blacks and not viewing the abolition of racial identities as part of Baldwin's iconoclastic humanism. See Eldridge Cleaver, *Soul on Ice* (New York, 1968).

11

Theses on Black Nationalism

Jeffrey Stout

Introduction

The following theses characterize and extend an account of black nationalism inspired by the work of James Baldwin and Ralph Ellison. I refer to my remarks as "theses" in order to acknowledge the high proportion of assertion to argumentation in them. To make a satisfying argument out of these theses I would need to adduce a good deal of evidence in support of my claims about black nationalism, to defend my assumptions about how Baldwin and Ellison should be read, and to explain how they differ from each other.[1] But given that the account might possess some interest in its own right even if I am wrong in associating some part of it with Baldwin or Ellison, I will concentrate here on making its main features clear. If my references to Baldwin and Ellison inspire some readers to look at them with fresh eyes, so much the better.

In speaking of these writers as critics of black nationalism, I do not mean to imply that they differed in all respects from their nationalist opponents. Similarities as well as differences will come into focus as the discussion unfolds. I am aware of the arguments that have been made for claiming both authors *as* nationalists, but for two reasons I choose not to classify them in that way: first, because they did not think of themselves as nationalists; and, second, because the question of whether they *really were* nationalists tends to generate a verbal dispute that is better sidestepped pragmatically than responded to directly. My principal concerns in extending their critique include accounting for the vagaries of the concept of black nationalism, the decreasing importance of its ideological component, and the continuing attractiveness of black nationalist style to many African Americans who have come of age since the 1960s. The point is not, however, to define black nationalism, to "theorize" it in the usual sense, or to bury it, but rather to identify and clarify the most important issues that have arisen in connection with it.

At the most general level, these issues turn out to be the questions of how the racial and national communities in which we all find ourselves ought to be conceived and what role those communities ought to play in our lives. In short, how much, and in what way, should we care about such communities? At a more specific level of analysis, it becomes clear that concern for such communities is often a matter of piety, aspiration, and anger. These are powerful sentiments, to say the least. They are sometimes elevating, often dangerous. What, then, shall we make of them?

Thirty-Five Theses

1. Black nationalism concerns itself with the African American people, considered as a community. Communities are groups constituted by something their members take themselves to share. A group whose members shared, say, a common biological origin, but did not recognize one another as "one of us," would not qualify in this sense as a community. On the other hand, a group whose members shared nothing but the disposition to recognize one another as fellow members would qualify. The African American people do plainly qualify as a community in this sense, regardless of what one thinks of the various dubious claims that have been made by black nationalists concerning what they have in common.

2. When Baldwin expressed the wish "that the Muslim movement [i.e., the Nation of Islam] had been able to inculcate in the demoralized Negro population a . . . *more individual* sense of its own worth,"[2] he implied that the thing shared by the African American people need not and should not be a sense of fusion, in which individuals experience a loss of separate identity as they merge collectively into an undifferentiated mass. The members of a community do not necessarily experience their bond intensely or agree with one another on matters of high importance. Neither need they imagine themselves to be the vehicles of a common will.[3] The African

American people, like other peoples, have only rarely and fleetingly, if ever, been bound together so tightly as that. This should be considered a good thing, not something to be overcome by corrective measures.

3. Imagined communities are groups in which members are linked, each to each, not merely by face-to-face interaction and the forms of mutual recognition and personal attachment it generates but by collectively imagining what they share in some way.[4] For example, an imagined community might take shape as a result of shared stories, true or false, about the original kinship of its members at the dawn of creation. Some black nationalists tell stories of this kind about an ancient African past, but the stories are not believed by enough African Americans to constitute an imagined community larger than a sectarian group. The primary factor responsible for forging black Americans into an imagined community was rather the crucible of oppression. The melding of various kinship stems into one people began in slave ships crossing the Atlantic, where the experience of oppression started to generate images of a shared fate and belief in a shared destiny.

4. Ethical discourse is the activity in which we hold ourselves and one another answerable for the commitments we undertake when evaluating individuals, groups, their actions, their emotions, their traits of character, and their ways of life. The communities individuals form are, for obvious reasons, among the most important topics of ethical discourse—not least of all when they are imagined in racial or national terms. Less obvious perhaps is the fact that the very activity of holding one another answerable for the commitments we undertake when discoursing on ethical topics is something that tends to create discursive communities across the boundaries of ethnicity and race. The shared activity of holding one another answerable need only be brought to attention *as* something shared to constitute a community in its own right. If an oppressed group, identifying with the discursive activities of its prophets, holds its oppressors answerable for unjust acts, and the oppressors respond by trying to justify their behavior, the resulting exchange tends to bring into existence the prerequisites for a discursive community, embracing both oppressed and oppressors.[5] It is this kind of community that Baldwin was trying to foster consciousness of and identification with when he stressed that "the oppressed and the oppressor are bound together in the same society; they share the same criteria," and when he called on "relatively conscious whites and the relatively conscious blacks . . . [to] achieve our country, and change the history of the world."[6] Black nationalism, like many other forms of nationalism, tends to ignore or to undermine discursive communities of this kind.

5. To identify a group of people as *blacks* is to substitute one of their features—the color of their skin—for their whole persons. There is nothing intrinsically wrong with the trope being employed, which rhetoricians call a synecdoche. We do not object to the captain who calls out "Twenty sail!" when specifying the number of ships on the horizon or to the presiding officer who counts noses when trying to determine whether our assembly has a quorum. The trouble comes when substituting a visible feature for a person is linked with a second substitution—a metonymical reduction— intended to specify something else all members of the group in question essentially share, something that supposedly makes them what they are, qua group members. To make a double substitution of this kind is to issue an inferential license. The license authorizes an inference from the visible presence of one thing, a feature that members of a group can be seen to share, to the existence of something else that constitutes their shared social identity. The visible feature comes to stand for both the person to whom it belongs and the underlying characteristic that is taken to confer social identity. Where the underlying characteristic is taken to explain or justify superior social status, the visible feature functions as an emblem of that status. Where the underlying characteristic is linked inferentially to inferior social status, the visible feature functions as a social stigma.

6. Racism is like sexism in its reliance on inference tickets that transform a person's visible features into stigmata of his or her group's inferior social status by implying explanations and rationalizations of the social identity he or she shares with others. Nationalism, because it cannot always denote social identity by convenient reference to visible features of the human body, such as skin color and genitalia, must often employ cultural artifacts to play the roles of emblems and stigmata. Uniforms and flags, for example, function as emblems of nationality on the battlefield. The Star of David functioned as a stigma during the reign of National Socialism. Once supplied with a suitable set of visible markers, nationalism can, and typically does, disseminate stigmatizing inference tickets of its own. That it often takes over, and thereby reinforces, the markers of race and gender should not be surprising.[7]

7. A social system in which racism, sexism, and nationalism operate simultaneously is therefore one in which multiple visible markers function in tandem with inference tickets to establish and maintain social identities. Alienation from one's imputed identities tends to be experienced in such a system as invisibility, as Ellison demonstrated eloquently in *Invisible Man*.[8]

8. Black nationalism responds to denigration of blackness and glorification of whiteness not by eschewing the visible markers essential to white

racism but by changing their valences. The more extravagant forms of black nationalism simply reverse the valences. That is to say, they authorize inferences concerning whiteness and blackness that invert those authorized in the social system of white superiority. As Baldwin put it, referring to the outlook of Elijah Muhammad, "the sentiment is old; only the color is new":

> We were offered, as Nation of Islam doctrine, historical and divine proof that all white people are cursed, and are devils, and are about to be brought down. . . . But very little time was spent on theology, for one did not need to prove to a Harlem audience that all white men were devils. They were merely glad to have, at last, divine corroboration of their experience, to hear—and it was a tremendous thing to hear—that they had been lied to all these years and generations, and that their captivity was ending, for God was black.[9]

A more moderate form of black nationalism might refrain from mere reversal of the valences of whiteness and blackness in white racism, but it would still have to change them. Black nationalism need not denigrate whiteness per se, but it does seem always to involve treating blackness as emblematic of something worthy of respect or admiration. That this is one source of its appeal to black people who have been stigmatized by white racism should go without saying, but it is worth keeping in mind as part of the explanation for black nationalism's survival.

9. Of course, while all forms of black nationalism valorize blackness, they are hardly alone in doing so. Martin Luther King Jr. is never classified as a black nationalist, yet he did use the concept of "negritude" to valorize blackness. He, like Elijah Muhammad, envisioned black Americans as a people. He, too, figured blackness as emblematic of something that black Americans share and in which they should take pride. But it seems likely that King was echoing the rhetoric of black nationalists when he made this move. The same can be said for other prominent critics of black nationalism, like Baldwin and Ellison, who also owed more than they always cared to admit to the movement they criticized.

10. Larry Neal was probably inflating such unacknowledged debts when, in an essay originally published in 1970, he termed Ellison a black nationalist. While distancing himself from Ellison's famous remark that "style is more important than political ideologies," Neal emphasized "the obvious theme of identity" in *Invisible Man,* the narrator's relentless search for a "usable" African American past, and Ellison's deep engagement with

"the murky world of [African American] mythology and folklore, both of which are essential elements in the making of a people's history." Speaking more sweepingly, Neal went on to claim that "some form of nationalism is operative throughout all sections of the black community. The dominant political orientations shaping the sensibilities of many contemporary black writers fall roughly into the categories of cultural nationalism and revolutionary nationalism."[10] It is hard to know what to make of such remarks.

11. Since 1970 or so, debates over black nationalism, though often as heated as ever, have seldom been clear. Emotions run strong, but it is hard to say exactly what is at stake. It is common to find a pair of interlocutors locked in fierce disagreement over whether black nationalism is a good or a bad thing but unable to agree even on what it is that the one champions and the other abhors. But if the committed black nationalist favors one thing while the equally committed antinationalist opposes something else, on what do they really disagree? To what have they committed themselves apart from conflicting attitudes toward a label? Definitions and theories of black nationalism abound, yet their very abundance is apt to make one wonder whether there is anything specifiable for all the sound and fury to signify, something that could retain the interest of disputants even when made clear.

12. The most instructive way of interpreting Neal's remarks is to suppose that they tell us more about what was happening to black nationalism as the sixties came to a close than they tell us about Ellison. If Ellison could now be counted as a black nationalist, then black nationalism itself had changed. In the process of becoming more inclusive, black nationalism had begun trying to absorb into its own canon figures formerly counted as paradigmatic opponents of the movement. Something was happening to the notion of black nationalism itself. The rules governing application of the label were changing.

13. Neal clearly intended his inclusive use of the term "nationalism" as a conciliatory gesture. While moderating his own nationalism, Neal had come to see less of himself in the figure of Ras (*Invisible Man*'s unforgettable caricature of a black nationalist at the point of complete frustration). Meanwhile, he may have come to see deeper concern in Ellison's writing for the peoplehood of black people than he had previously suspected. Classifying Ellison as a cultural nationalist implied that, to count as a nationalist, one need not share the revolutionary nationalist's aspiration to achieve some form of political sovereignty for African Americans. But what would a cultural nationalist favor? Neal did not say. Because the ideological com-

ponent of black nationalism was becoming fuzzy, the movement was increasingly concerned with promoting attitudes of a certain kind toward black culture.

14. As black nationalism has become less a matter of ideological commitment, it has also become more a matter of preferring some means over others for purposes of self-expression. It has increasingly become, in other words, a matter of style. Ellison saw this development coming in this stunning passage from his marvelous essay from the late 1970s, "The Little Man at Chehaw Station":

> The proponents of ethnicity—ill concealing an underlying anxiety, and given a bizarre bebopish stridency by the obviously American vernacular inspiration of the costumes and rituals ragged out to dramatize their claims to ethnic (and genetic) insularity—have helped give our streets and campuses a rowdy, All Fool's Day, carnival atmosphere. In many ways, then, the call for a new social order based upon the glorification of ancestral blood and ethnic background acts as a call to cultural and aesthetic chaos. Yet while this latest farcical phase in the drama of American social hierarchy unfolds, the irrepressible movement of American culture toward integration of its most diverse elements continues, confounding the circumlocutions of its staunchest opponents.[11]

The only comment I would add to this, two decades later, is that "the irrepressible movement of American culture toward integration of its most diverse elements" has become a far more worrisome thing, played out on a global scale in terms dictated by multinational corporations anxious to cash in on the diasporic identifications of consumers. The culture into which black nationalist style is now being absorbed is one in which successful rap artists, novelists, and professors become blips on the screen of an unending infomercial and one in which commodities of all sorts are packaged as emblems of ethnic identities and marketed scientifically to the appropriately susceptible demographic enclaves. The "All Fool's Day, carnival atmosphere" is still here, and growing more chaotic, but now you can purchase its emblematic accoutrements from the local mall and subscribe to instant access to representations of diversity from your local cable provider.

15. Black nationalism was already in the process of becoming a style, and ceasing to be an ideology, in the late 1960s. Today many young people and merchandisers see it as a lifestyle that one literally buys into through the purchase of clothing reminiscent of Africa, sneakers endorsed by basketball

stars, and tickets to the movies of Spike Lee.[12] What teenagers and the business elite agree on tends these days to become social fact in America. For the professional class there will soon be interior decorators who for a fee will order first editions of Du Bois for the mahogany bookcase in the living room. The alternatives to cultural-nationalism-as-lifestyle are not ideologies, like democratic socialism and libertarian republicanism, but other lifestyles made available on the same terms, like the one in which pretend colonialists drive Land Rovers while wearing clothing from Banana Republic. The former enclave is no more likely to provide resistance to the most important oppressive forces at work in this setting than the latter. If the Ellisonian dictum that "style is more important than political ideologies" now applies with a double irony to black nationalism itself, this hardly means that the movement has gradually come around to accepting an Ellisonian notion of what makes style important. Ellison's dictum expressed his commitment to the ethical-aesthetic ideal of living one's life as if one were creating a work of art, an ideal he seems to have associated with both Ralph Waldo Emerson and Duke Ellington. The political significance of recalling this commitment today is that it projects the image of a human being too marked by individuality to be content with the lifestyle options the merchandisers are selling. The social practices Ellison valued were all ones in which individuality, and thus resistance to the commodification of identity, is cultivated. Resistance to the commodification of identity, today, is the essential starting point for a politics of resistance. Some nationalists may want to canonize Ellison retrospectively, but neither *Invisible Man* nor Ellison's essay collections fit easily within their canon. His style offers a means for resisting the most important features of contemporary culture that is wholly lacking in the repertoire of black nationalism.

16. The two groups most insistent on defining *black nationalism* narrowly appear to be, on the one hand, radical nationalists intent on retaining the most extreme claims that have entered the movement's rhetorical repertoire during its most militant moments; on the other hand, black conservatives intent on holding everyone to their left equally responsible for those claims. The former are content to treat black nationalism as the badge of their rhetorical extremism. The latter are really trying to make liberals pay for the breadth of their toleration. Hyperbolic black nationalism is just sublime enough, by virtue of the strong intimation of danger it offers, to mesmerize both parties. Their attitudes toward it, pro and con, are both forms of fixation on the sublime. Small wonder, then, that the resulting debate is fruitless, or that it qualifies as entertainment on "Crossfire" and the college lecture circuit.

17. The question that really divides Neal from Ellison is how much and in what way African Americans (and other peoples in the geographical vicinity) should care about their own peoplehood, given that there are other things (and peoples) worth caring about. Answering this question well is infinitely more important than deciding which answers to count as nationalist. Beyond a certain point, the term just gets in the way. If nationalists want to redefine their "ism" for the purpose of converting their old opponents into so-called nationalists, and we find this confusing, we can always respond by using the new definition as a standing license to substitute *definiens* for *definiendum*. By thus eliminating the term "nationalism" itself when it seems a distraction, we can easily turn our attention back to the question of how much and in what way one should care about the peoplehood of one's people under circumstances like ours.[13]

18. David Theo Goldberg claims that the concepts of "race and nation are largely empty receptacles through and in the names of which population groups may be invented, interpreted, and imagined as communities or societies."[14] Yet if Goldberg is right about this, there may be no point in trying to say, once and for all, what black nationalism is, nor in stipulating how, generally speaking, the expression "black nationalism" should be used. If some friend, foe, or theorist of something called black nationalism tells us what black nationalism is or what the term means, we can always set aside the question of whether the *definiendum* has been correctly defined and ask instead whether the *definiens* identifies a topic worth debating and investigating. If it does, then the *definiendum* has served a useful function by leading us somewhere, after which we are free to eliminate it (temporarily) from the discussion and use the *definiens* in its place. The only criterion of success in such matters is the practical one of knowing how to find one's way around the discursive terrain we occupy, which is partly a matter of knowing how to cope with the ambiguities one is likely to encounter there.

19. Black nationalism puts the discourse of race and the discourse of nation together. It does so by projecting an imagined national community—a people—for whom blackness serves as an emblem. What is it, then, that black Americans share, as black nationalists imagine them? There have been many answers to this question, but here are some of them:

(a)   a common biological or ontological essence;
(b)   a common origin in a particular place, namely, Africa;
(c)   a common history of suffering and humiliation, based on ascriptions of racial identity linked to denigrated social status;

(d)   a common culture, including music, food, folkways, stories, and rites;

(e)   a common destiny, given the likelihood that the entire people will endure the same fate from here on out;

(f)   a common interest in the achievement of certain ends, such as return to the place of origin, political sovereignty in some newly assigned territory, or economic and cultural self-determination; and

(g)   a common interest in employing the means thought necessary to achieve their legitimate ends, such as mass emigration, revolutionary violence, or economic and cultural separatism.

Items (a)–(d) are essentially retrospective and refer to the putative sources of African American peoplehood. These items may be grouped thematically under the heading of piety—given that they have all been treated in black nationalism as sources on which African Americans depend for their existence and progress through life and to which African Americans therefore ought to respond with appropriate expressions of gratitude and loyalty. Item (c) is also a focal point for the expression of anger. Items (e)–(g) are essentially prospective and refer to the people's future. They may be grouped thematically under the heading of aspiration. The ends and means of black nationalists can themselves of course be broken down into political, economic, and cultural elements, which have received varying interpretations and varying degrees of emphasis at different times.

20. It should be obvious from the structure of this scheme that it provides for the possibility of countless permutations of the basic themes of black nationalism and no criterion for drawing the line, once and for all, between black nationalism and its siblings. This is as it should be, for it is unhelpfully ahistorical to say that black nationalism has an essence. It would be possible to specify a type of black nationalism in relation to this scheme by assigning an appropriate interpretation to each item on the list. The spectrum of interpretations for each item ranges from weak to strong. With respect to most items, the more an interpretation emphasizes separation or difference of African Americans from other groups, the stronger that interpretation would be. A thinker who assigned weak interpretations to each item would not count as a nationalist at all. A thinker who assigned strong interpretations to each item would count as an extreme nationalist. But it is also possible to assign strong interpretations to some items while assigning moderate or weak interpretations to others. The type Neal refers to as cul-

tural nationalism, for example, would assign a strong reading to (d) and a strong reading to the cultural component of (f) while assigning weaker readings to some other variables.[15] One interesting implication of the scheme is that only types of black nationalism which assigned relatively strong interpretations to the political component of (f) would qualify as types of nationalism, according to Benedict Anderson's influential definition of the latter notion. Anderson, the most important recent theorist of nationalism as a global phenomenon, takes a nation to be an imagined political community that is "both inherently limited and sovereign."[16] By emphasizing political sovereignty in this way, Anderson's definition of nationalism entails that most varieties of black nationalism that have flourished in the United States would not qualify as species of the basic genus. This is important to keep in mind for two reasons: first, because it displays a major source of terminological confusion in discussions of black nationalism as a global phenomenon; second, because it helps explain why black nationalism in the United States has been underestimated as an influence on nationalisms (*simpliciter*) in geographical areas other than the United States.

21. Ellison and Baldwin both embraced a conception of African American peoplehood emphasizing (c) the community's common history of suffering, (d) the value of its cultural heritage, and (e) its common destiny. They rejected (a) the notion of a shared biological or ontological essence. They acknowledged but played down the significance of (b) the notion of a common place of origin, by distinguishing it from (a) and assimilating it to (c) and (d). Africa, for them, was simply a mapmaker's arbitrary name for an expansive, culturally diverse, geographical region in which many distinct peoples have lived. Having ancestors from part of what we now call Gambia would not connect anyone to an African essence equally instantiated in what we now call Egypt or Algeria. Ellison and Baldwin envisioned no such essence.[17] Nor did they imagine that there was once an African golden age. The historical fantasies of today's Afrocentrists would be grist for Ellisonian parody. Baldwin rejected the similar fantasies of an earlier generation by saying that "in order to change a situation one has first to see it for what it is: in the present case, to accept the fact, whatever one does with it thereafter, that the Negro has been formed by this nation [i.e., America], for better or worse, and does not belong to any other—not to Africa, and certainly not to Islam."[18]

22. Black nationalism is an affair of piety if there ever was one. In this, it has much in common with nationalism of other kinds.[19] At their worst, nationalists everywhere have invented and then venerated wholly fabricated pasts, the phoniness of which is palpable to anyone not caught up in collec-

tive wishful thinking. Black nationalists have concocted more than a few of their own. When Baldwin introduced his discussion of the Nation of Islam in "Down at the Cross" by reflecting at length on his early experiences in the Christian church, he effectively established ironic distance from both his own former piety and Elijah Muhammad's Muslim variety, allowing his doubts about the former to undercut the appeal of the latter as well. "Being in the pulpit was like being in the theatre," wrote Baldwin of his days as a youth preacher; "I was behind the scenes and knew how the illusion was worked."[20] The stage has been set for us to see through the illusions at work in Elijah Muhammad's preaching as well:

> This truth is that at the very beginning of time there was not one
> white face to be found in all the universe. Black men ruled the earth
> and the black man was perfect. This is the truth concerning the era
> that white men now refer to as prehistoric. They want black men to
> believe that they, like white men, once lived in caves and swung from
> trees and ate their meat raw and did not have the power of speech.
> But this is not true. Black men were never in such a condition.[21]

The cure for such illusions, as Baldwin put in "Everybody's Protest Novel," consisted of frank acknowledgment that black and white Americans, oppressed and oppressors, "both alike depend on the same reality."[22] The piety of the Nation of Islam simply could not, from Baldwin's point of view, do justice to the realities of mutual dependence among peoples in America.

23. Ellison's *Invisible Man* can be read, on one level, as a rigorous rethinking of what black Americans owe, culturally speaking, to the traditions of black American life. It is this pious dimension of the novel that makes Neal want to canonize it, but the kind of piety Ellison expresses toward the traditions of his people, especially toward the tradition of the blues, is a more nuanced and subtle thing than any form of black nationalism thus far developed in the United States appears able to accommodate. One reason for this is Ellison's way of connecting it to the more general question of what all Americans owe, culturally speaking, to the multiple traditions of American life, black and white. Ellison's detailed acknowledgment of dependence on the various cultural sources of American life is, to my mind, one of the supreme accomplishments of our literature. It is at odds with any form of piety grounded in identification with only one people.[23]

24. Black nationalism is not only a vehicle for expressing piety, directed toward the past, but also a vehicle for expressing aspirations, directed

toward the future. Ellison and Baldwin charged it with unrealism on the second count as much as on the first. Even relatively curtailed forms of black nationalist aspiration seemed to them a tissue of fantasies. Where black nationalism in the United States amounts to anything more than vague and noncontroversial calls for self-help, self-respect, and recognition—when, for example, it strives for some fairly definite form of separation from American culture, the broader economic system, or the civic nation—it comes up against some hard realities. Among these are that the more ambitious objectives entertained by black nationalists, such as political sovereignty for black America, cannot be achieved by any known means; that few black Americans would be willing to emigrate to a homeland, either in Africa or somewhere in the United States, even if it somehow became available; and that milder forms of separatism, be they economic or cultural, would themselves entail costs that few black Americans would be willing to endure.

25. The declining significance of political ideology within black nationalism now manifests itself in a nostalgia for the sixties. Many people initially attracted to black nationalism have been prepared to admit that the political, economic, and cultural aspirations with which the movement started are unrealistic, but they have been reluctant nonetheless to abandon identification with the movement. Perhaps the reason they do not see themselves as having left the nationalist fold is that they retain the old aspirations of black nationalism in the modified form of velleities. Full-fledged aspiration involves intending an end, willing the means necessary for the achievement of that end, and believing that the end can be achieved. A velleity, in contrast, involves what might be called subjunctive or counterfactual willing: if the situation *were* different from the actual one in certain relevant respects, I *would* . . . The velleities of contemporary black nationalism lend it a somewhat wistful tone. This tone expresses a longing for a previous state of affairs in which the original aspirations of the movement at least *seemed* credible.

26. If black nationalism has been weakened in the United States by the apparent unrealism of its aspirations, one reason for the movement's success in attracting interest and respect in this context has surely been its capacity to express anger. Some blacks who would admit to finding the pieties of the movement puerile and the political program of the movement unpalatable still turn to black nationalist oratory for cathartic release of their outrage against injustice and hatred. They are attracted by its rhetoric of excess—the obviousness of the villains, the clarity of the passions invoked, the fantasy of imagined vengeance. They are looking for "excessive

gestures, exploited to the limit of their meaning."[24] The nastiest product of this rhetoric, which has of course received much attention, is the scapegoating of Jews.[25] Some black intellectuals who distance themselves from anti-Semitism are nonetheless arguing these days that only a rhetoric of excess can do expressive justice to the realities of black anger and descriptive justice to the excessive brutalities that have provoked it. Their hope, apparently, is that the scapegoating function of the rhetoric, in which white devils and Jews are made to personify the evils that flow from racial oppression, can be separated from the rhetoric's other devices for expressing the full depth and extent of those evils. They read the early speeches of Malcolm X for the same reason they read Richard Wright's novels, as indispensable witnesses to an excessively bad situation. They suspect that Baldwin and Ellison, who criticized both black nationalist rhetoric and Wright's "protest novels" for their excesses, simply failed to respond adequately to the experience of suffering and injustice blacks have endured in this country.

27. It would be foolish to think that we face a choice between Malcolm X's speeches and Wright's novels, on the one hand, and the writings of Baldwin and Ellison, on the other. There are good reasons for keeping all of them on our shelves and syllabi. They do different things for us that need doing. But we should never underestimate the resources that Baldwin and Ellison offer for coming to terms with outrage and with outrageous circumstances.

28. The point of departure for Ellison's fiction was the realization "that it was not enough"[26] for him simply to be angry, or simply to present horrendous events or ironic events. He transmuted his anger into the literary analogue of a blues sensibility, which hovers at the borderline between tragedy and comedy, borrowing tonalities from each. Anyone who thinks that the anger isn't there or isn't deep isn't reading very carefully. The comic elements are called upon in accordance with the maxim that the "greater the stress within society the stronger the comic antidote required,"[27] but they are called upon in such a way that they are never allowed to cancel out the force of the tragic elements to which they respond. The comic elements in Ellison's prose are deliberately compensatory, which is to say that they keep close company with grief and despair but ultimately modify and transcend them.

29. Ellison's doubts about Wright's success as a novelist aspiring to social realism centered on the incongruity between Wright's depiction of black American circumstances and Wright's own existence as a writer. There seemed to be nothing in the depiction that could account for the possibility of someone "as intelligent, as creative or as dedicated as [Wright] him-

self."[28] Ellison concluded that Wright had not adequately accounted for the cultural sources of his own existence and progress through life. Ellison therefore set himself the literary task of reimagining his social circumstances as a black American so that an articulate protagonist—one capable of a blues sensibility, like his own—could be rendered intelligible in them. The narrator-protagonist of *Invisible Man* would be "a blues-toned laugher-at-wounds who included himself in his indictment of the human condition."[29] The prime difficulty Ellison had to face in rendering such a character intelligible was that of describing evils of the kind he had experienced and the life of an articulate, spiritually resilient protagonist as products of the same situation. The ethical and political interest of the task lay in its requirement that he attend simultaneously to the reasons for anger, the temptations to despair, and the grounds for hope in his situation. It is no accident that Ellison's preface refers to the novel as "a raft of hope," or that the novel ends by referring explicitly to "the lower frequencies" as the register in which he "speaks for" his reader.[30]

30. It is precisely those who ground their hope religiously in sources that transcend our social situation who are most likely to dismiss Ellison's effort as unnecessary and self-deceptive. Prophets of a supernatural God, whether nationalist or universalist, Muslim or Christian, are not singing the blues when they lament this-worldly pain, excoriate this-worldly evil, and proclaim hope in a transcendent redeemer. In their eyes, the intimations of goodness in our current social situation, including the prophet's own voice, always have transcendent sources, so the situation itself can be described as essentially rotten without causing a problem of self-referential consistency for the describer. Meanwhile, anger and despair can be given full play in a rhetoric of excess, because the hoped-for compensatory factors are believed to be both wholly other and backed by omnipotent force. The rhetorical exercise of the prophet is to bring oneself (and the audience) as close to despair as possible, in the name of a realistic view of evil, and then, after pausing for breath, to veer heavenward at the last moment, thanking Allah or Jesus for the gift of hope against hope. Baldwin and Ellison were both aware of this kind of prophetic style, and self-consciously avoided it in their own prose. They had good reasons, I believe, for doing so—reasons rooted in their preference for a blues sensibility according to which good and evil, powers divine and satanic, are all mixed up both in our social situation and in ourselves and are to be dealt with by means of whatever this-worldly social magic and lyrical coping we can muster.[31] Once they made this move, they had no choice, on pain of despair, but to locate grounds for hope in the social situation itself. Their hopefulness, which Ellison sometimes mislead-

ingly called "optimism," does not derive from gilding the lily. They took evil and anger as seriously as any American writer has. Coping lyrically with evil is not a way of ignoring it or minimizing it but a way of mitigating it, of surviving it, of enduring.

31. Harry Frankfurt writes that "A person who cares about something is, as it were, invested in it. He *identifies* himself with what he cares about in the sense that he makes himself vulnerable to losses and susceptible to benefits depending upon whether what he cares about is diminished or enhanced. Thus he concerns himself with what concerns it, giving particular attention to such things and directing his behavior accordingly."[32] Both Baldwin and Ellison cared in this sense about the peoplehood of their people. They suspected that black nationalists were preoccupied with it.[33] To be preoccupied with something is to care about it in such a way that other things tend, over time and not merely for a moment or two, to be excluded from one's concern.

32. Baldwin made a point of highlighting Elijah Muhammad's "single-mindedness," and implied that the exclusivity of his preoccupation was the source of his power over others.[34] Ellison's portrait of Ras in *Invisible Man* displays the comic (and potentially tragic) consequences of allowing one's life—or the life of one's people—to be dominated by exclusivistic concerns. Both authors wanted to make room for the identifications, cares, and concerns of democratic participation in American national life, as well as for membership in the international communities of literary artists. They did not suppose, however, that making room for these other concerns diminished the intensity of their own concern for the peoplehood of African Americans. When, late in his life, Malcolm X came into close contact with Muslims outside the Nation of Islam, he found himself identifying with an imagined community broader in scope than the people with which he had previously been preoccupied as a black nationalist. This did not mean that he cared less about the peoplehood of American blacks but only that his concern no longer possessed the exclusivity of a preoccupation. The moral of his last conversion is that nationalism, far from having a monopoly on concern for one's people, tends often to disfigure that concern and to shrink the heart that harbors it.

33. In the works of Baldwin and Ellison, the exclusivity of nationalism appears as a narrowing of the human soul, as contributing to the formation of selves less capable, on the whole, of caring about all the things worth caring about. Because the concerns of democratic participation and artistic creation expand one's capacity for caring, they thought, such concerns tend to complement and enrich whatever other concerns one might

have that are worth having. Democratic and artistic practices also have the virtue of putting the relative importance of all concerns in perspective and of providing the discursive and imaginative means for testing their actual worth. There are too many goods to pursue and celebrate, too many evils to confront and resist, to let any one object of concern crowd the others out of our hearts, however prominent it may seem for a time.

34. Black nationalism is one part piety, one part aspiration, and one part anger. At its best it has expressed all three of these attitudes with clarity and power. Yet, like other nationalisms (not least of all, the form of nationalism most white Americans embrace), it has been known to degenerate into something ludicrous or hideous. Its piety has had trouble escaping fantasy, patriarchy, and power-worship. Its aspirations have sometimes been marred by delusions of grandeur and dreams of vengeance. Its anger, which begins as a just response to suffering and injustice, has at times passed over into hatred and scapegoating. We know from examples of black nationalism in contexts outside the United States that these dangers can all be avoided when leaders and writers set their minds to it and the path to national sovereignty is not permanently blocked.[35] But here in the United States, where no one since Marcus Garvey has been able to make the goal of national sovereignty for African Americans seem plausible to many of the people meant to benefit from it, the movement has had trouble maintaining its balance.[36] In the end its staying power is the thing that really needs explaining. No small part of the explanation, sadly, is the paucity of attractive political alternatives.[37]

35. "Today blood magic and blood thinking, never really dormant in American society, are rampant among us. . . . And while this goes on," Ellison remarked some time ago, "the challenge of arriving at an adequate definition of American cultural identity goes unanswered."[38] We have all in the meantime become complicit in the new social contract that condemns the wretched of all races and nations to consume, if anything at all, a stream of images, insignia, and other substances that dull their sensibilities. This is the bleak tide against which Ellison launched his "raft of hope." Have I made it seem too bleak? Not if the scene includes the raft and its maker, and the place he stood upon when crafting it, and the materials he built it from; and the traditions, African and American and European, from which he drew those materials; and all the people and practices and institutions, fragile and fallible as they might be, that inspired and sustained him in the making. The hope that Ellison holds out to us consists partly in the pious acknowledgment, within his writing, of everything that made his writing possible. It also consists in his style. Kenneth Burke once referred to style as

something we will greatly need if "a dismal political season is in store for us." Style, that is, "as a campaign base for personal integrity . . . as the *beneath-which-not,* as the *admonitory and hortatory act,* as the *example* that would prod continually for its completion in all aspects of life, and so, in Eliot's phrase, 'keep something alive.'"[39] This, I believe, is what Ellison wanted his style to be.

NOTES

1. I have learned much about both authors and about black nationalism itself in conversation with Al Raboteau and Cornel West, and from the students the three of us have taught and advised at Princeton. I want especially to acknowledge my indebtedness to the following books and dissertations written by those students: Victor Anderson, *Beyond Ontological Blackness: An Essay on African American Religious and Cultural Criticism* (New York, 1995); Lawrie Balfour, *The Evidence of Things Not Said: James Baldwin and the Promise of American Democracy* (Ithaca, N.Y., 2001); Bethel Eddy, "The Rites of Identity: The Religious Naturalism and Cultural Criticism of Kenneth Burke and Ralph Ellison," Ph.D. diss., Princeton University, June 1998; Eddie S. Glaude Jr., *Exodus! Race, Religion, and Nation in Early Nineteenth-Century Black America* (Chicago, 2000); William D. Hart, *Edward Said and the Religious Effects of Culture* (Cambridge, 2000), esp. chap. 2; and Willie Earl Walker III, "Prophetic Articulations: James Baldwin and the Racial Formation of the United States," Ph.D. diss., Princeton University, June 1999.

2. James Baldwin, *Collected Essays* (New York, 1998), p. 333.

3. Bernard Yack, *The Problems of a Political Animal: Community, Justice, and Conflict in Aristotelian Political Thought* (Berkeley, Calif., 1993), chaps. 1 and 2.

4. I borrow the term "imagined communities" from Benedict Anderson, *Imagined Communities,* rev. ed. (London and New York, 1991), p. 6.

5. See Nicholas Wolterstorff, *Until Justice and Peace Embrace* (Grand Rapids, Mich., 1983), pp. 100, 104.

6. Baldwin, *Collected Essays,* pp. 17, 346f.

7. As feminists and womanists have often pointed out, black nationalism tends on the whole simply to mirror, and not to invert, the sexism of its principal opponents. See, e.g., Patricia Hill Collins, "Learning to Think for Ourselves: Malcolm X's Black Nationalism Reconsidered," in *Malcolm X in Our Own Image,* ed. Joe Wood (New York, 1992), pp. 59–85. See also Wahneema Lubiano, "Black Nationalism and Black Common Sense: Policing Ourselves and Others," in *The House That Race Built,* ed. Wahneema Lubiano (New York, 1998), pp. 232–52. Anti-Semitism and gay-bashing are other forms of stigmatization that black nationalism sometimes takes over uncritically from the surrounding culture. Cornel West considers the impact of black nationalism on black-Jewish relations in *Prophetic Fragments* (Trenton, N.J., and Grand Rapids, Mich., 1988), pp. 171 ff. He claims that "early forms of black nationalism—though never dominant in the black community—were, in part, xenophobic, especially antiwhite and, at times, anti-Semitic"

(p. 172). In *Race Matters* (Boston, 1993), West criticizes "black nationalist spokesmen like Farrakhan and Jeffries" for suggesting that "Jewish power" is an appropriate name for the forces "subordinating black and brown peoples" (p. 74). He also refers to the murder of Yankel Rosenbaum in 1991 as "chilling testimony to growing black anti-Semitism in this country. Although this particular form of xenophobia from below does not have the same institutional power of those racisms that afflict their victims from above, it certainly de- serves the same moral condemnation" (p. 75). West argues, in effect, that black anti- Semitism and such related attitudes as "patriarchal and homophobic prejudices" all tend to undermine the "black freedom struggle" by making it complicit in practices of stig- matization (p. 79). Compare "Negroes Are Anti-Semitic Because They're Anti-White," in Baldwin, *Collected Essays,* pp. 739–48.

   8.   Ralph Ellison, *Invisible Man* (1952; New York, 1990).

   9.   Baldwin, *Collected Essays,* pp. 319, 315.

   10.   Ellison's remark on style and ideologies appears in "A Very Stern Discipline," in Ralph Ellison, *Going to the Territory* (New York, 1986), p. 294. Larry Neal discusses Ellison in his essay "Ellison's Zoot Suit," reprinted in *Speaking for You: The Vision of Ralph Ellison,* ed. Kimberly W. Benston (Washington, D.C., 1990), pp. 105–24. The quotations given here all appear on p. 115, the reference to Ellison's remark on p. 114.

   11.   Ellison, *Going to the Territory,* p. 21f.

   12.   Black nationalism, as an evolving set of attitudes toward the peoplehood of African Americans, needs now to be situated in relation to what David Hollinger calls "three formidable constituencies" that are pulling the American nation-state "in different directions": "One is a business elite that, in an age of international corporations, finds more and more of its employees and factories abroad. This elite has some need for the American state, but it can get along without attending very carefully to the needs of the nation, the people who constitute the community of American citizens. The second constituency identifies with one or more diasporas and sees the United States more as a site for transna- tional affiliations than as an affiliation of its own. The proponents of diasporic conscious- ness sometimes look to the state for entitlements, but, like the business elite, they have little incentive to devote themselves to the welfare of the [civic] national community. In the meantime, a third constituency has claimed America with a vengeance. This third con- stituency is made up of a great variety of Middle Americans, evangelical Christians, advo- cates of family values, and supporters of Newt Gingrich and of Rush Limbaugh. Many of these Americans are suspicious of the state except as an enforcer of personal morality, but they claim the nation as, in effect, their own ethnic group." *Postethnic America* (New York, 1995), pp. 15f. It is in the interest of the business elite to transform all forms of diasporic consciousness, functionally speaking, into obsession with lifestyle enclaves by commodify- ing the symbolic means of identification. This process of commodification may now be re- placing the racism implicit in the third constituency's use of ethnic symbolism as the most important challenge facing those of us who oppose injustice. People obsessed with buying their way into prestige within an ethnically defined lifestyle enclave are giving the business elite want they want in two ways: first, through the transfer of cash; second, by remaining oblivious to the widening gap between the managerial-professional class and the underclass in all three constituencies.

   13.   For discussion of the kind of pragmatic approach I am taking here, see William James, "What Pragmatism Means," in his *Pragmatism* (Buffalo, N.Y., 1991), pp. 22–38.

For a more technical treatment of the same sort of approach, see W. V. Quine's classic discussion of explication as elimination in *Word and Object* (Cambridge, Mass., 1960). For analogous explications of epistemological terms, see Jeffrey Stout, *The Flight from Authority* (Notre Dame, Ind., 1981), chaps. 1 and 4. For a similar approach to hermeneutics, see Jeffrey Stout, "What Is the Meaning of a Text?" *New Literary History* 14, no. 1 (1982): 2–12.

14. David Theo Goldberg, *Racist Culture: Philosophy and the Politics of Meaning* (Oxford and Cambridge, Mass., 1993), p. 79.

15. The scheme shows why Neal's distinction between revolutionary and cultural types of black nationalism tends to confuse the issue. The notion of revolutionary nationalism focuses on a type of means for achieving nationalist aspirations, whereas the contrasting notion of cultural nationalism appears to focus on either a type of nationalist end which may or may not exhaust a particular nationalist's aspirations, or an object of nationalist piety. Neal increases the confusion by referring to both of his basic types as "political orientations." He says neither whether they are exhaustive nor whether it is possible, without contradicting oneself, to hold both orientations at once. He does not say what qualifies cultural nationalism as cultural and what qualifies it as political. If the mark of cultural nationalism is that it aspires to achieve cultural objectives (or cultural objectives alone) by political means, whereas revolutionary nationalism aspires to achieve political objectives (as well as cultural ones?) by political means, what about the attempt to achieve political objectives by nonrevolutionary means? Neal's typology and others like it had better be left aside.

16. Anderson, *Imagined Communities*, p. 6.

17. For a critique of black essentialism, see Anderson, *Beyond Ontological Blackness*.

18. Baldwin, *Collected Essays*, p. 333.

19. Benedict Anderson says that part of the difficulty in clarifying the notion of nationalism "is that one tends unconsciously to hypostasize the existence of Nationalism-with-a-big-N (rather as one might Age-with-a-capital-A) and then to classify 'it' as *an* ideology. . . . It would, I think, make things easier if one treated it as if it belonged with 'kinship' and 'religion,' rather than with 'liberalism' or 'fascism.'" *Imagined Communities*, p. 5. My own emphasis on the pious and aspirational aspects is intended in part to explain why nationalism should be grouped with religion. The notion of religion I am assuming here is indebted to George Santayana, *The Life of Reason*, 5 vols. (New York, 1905–6), esp. vol. 3, *Reason in Religion*. For an excellent interpretation of the relevant themes in Santayana, see Henry Samuel Levinson, *Santayana, Pragmatism, and the Spiritual Life* (Chapel Hill, N.C., 1992). My approach does not imply, however, that nationalism should not be grouped with fascism. For a brilliant analysis of fascism as "a bastardization of fundamentally religious patterns of thought," see Kenneth Burke, "The Rhetoric of Hitler's 'Battle,'" in *The Philosophy of Literary Form*, 3d ed. (Berkeley, Calif., 1973), pp. 191–220, esp. p. 219. My thoughts on the relation between nationalism and religion respond in part to Hart, *Edward Said and the Religious Effects of Culture*. See also Hart's discussion of Santayana and Levinson in his "Cornel West: Between Rorty's Rock and Hauerwas's Hard Place," *American Journal of Theology and Philosophy* 19, no. 2 (1998): 151–72.

20. Baldwin, *Collected Essays*, p. 308.

21. Ibid., p. 325.

22. Ibid., p. 17.

23. See Eddy, "Rites of Identity," chap. 5, for a superb discussion of Ellison's treatment of "the vernacular pieties of an American identity." Chapter 2 of the same work offers an interpretation of Kenneth Burke's conception of piety, which forms part of the background against which Ellison's treatment of piety can be understood. Eddy shows that Ellison needs to be seen, in part, as belonging to a tradition of cultural criticism that descends from Emerson and includes Santayana and Burke. I am here only skimming the surface of an aspect of Ellison's work that Eddy has considered in depth.

24. Roland Barthes, *Mythologies,* trans. Annette Layers (New York, 1972), p. 16. Barthes is referring here to wrestling, not to the speeches of Louis Farrakhan, but much of what he says would apply to the latter as well. For blacks who take delight in Farrakhan's rhetoric of excess without ever thinking of converting to his sect, the oratory conjures up a spectacle that functions expressively more or less as a professional wrestling match does. As Barthes argues in reference to wrestling, "What is . . . displayed for the public is the great spectacle of Suffering, Defeat, and Justice. Wrestling presents man's suffering with all the amplification of tragic masks. . . . Suffering which appeared without intelligible cause would not be understood. . . . On the contrary suffering appears as inflicted with emphasis and conviction, for everyone must not only see that the man suffers, but also and above all understand why he suffers" (p. 19 f.). "But what wrestling is above all meant to portray," Barthes continues, "is a purely moral concept: that of justice. The idea of 'paying' is essential to wrestling, and the crowd's 'Give it to him' means above all else 'Make him pay' " (p. 21).

25. Cornel West argues as follows in *Prophetic Thought in Postmodern Times* (Monroe, Me., 1993): "In fact, the media will project Farrakhan as attracting black folk because he is anti-Semitic and [imply that] black folk want to hear anti-Semitic rhetoric. There is no doubt in my mind that Farrakhan has deep xenophobic elements in his rhetoric, but that is not why the majority of black people come to listen to him, you see. They come to listen to him because he symbolizes boldness. And they don't join his organization because they don't see the kind of moral integrity they want" (p. 72). As I see it, Farrakhan's boldness consists in having the courage of his pieties (which include the assertion of black pride), his aspirations (which include the "Make them pay" element of vengeance against the forces of evil as he imagines them), and his anger (which includes his anger at the perpetrators of injustice as he imagines them). By increasing the audience's sense of danger, an effect he achieves through mythic amplification and personification of the forces of evil, Farrakhan is able to make himself more believable in the audience's eyes as a personification of boldness. But this means that the "mythic amplification and personification of the forces of evil" are essential to the performance, even if we take the personification of hyperbolic boldness to be the main attraction for an audience too long made to feel meek and powerless. If I am right about this, two points deserve emphasis: first, that scapegoating appears indispensable to the process through which Farrakhan "symbolizes boldness" in his own person; and, second, that the prospect of being emboldened, of having one's self-image vicariously enlarged and empowered, can be part of what makes scapegoating so attractive psychologically to those who resort to it. For most members of the audience, the scapegoating of Jews may be an affair of the imagination that stops short of licensing actual violence, but this hardly suffices to make the sentiments being expressed (or the selves being shaped) ethically acceptable. Scapegoating and various other forms of sacrifice are major themes in Ellison. See, e.g., Ralph Ellison, *Shadow and Act* (New York,

1972), p. 124, and the treatment of lynching in *Going to the Territory,* pp. 177 ff. For a discussion of Ellison on sacrifice, see Eddy, "Rites of Identity," chap. 6.

26. Ellison, *Going to the Territory,* p. 53.

27. Ibid., p. 185. Ellison understands that comparable motives were at work in both Ralph Waldo Emerson and Walt Whitman, two authors who have often been dismissed, as Ellison often is today, for being either too optimistic or too insensitive to evil. See, e.g., ibid., p. 311.

28. Ellison, *Shadow and Act,* p. 120. See p. 252 for a similar argument against Amiri Baraka (then called LeRoi Jones).

29. Ellison, *Invisible Man,* p. xviii.

30. Ibid., pp. xx, 581. What Ellison meant by a raft of hope would seem to be what Kenneth Burke, his friend and interlocutor, meant by a "structure of encouragement" in the following passage: "Suppose that, gnarled as I am, I did not consider it enough simply to seek payment for my gnarledness, the establishment of communion [between writer and reader] through evils held in common? Suppose I would also erect a structure of encouragement, for all of us? How should I go about it, in the sequence of imagery, not merely to bring us most poignantly *into* hell, but also *out* again?" Burke, *The Philosophy of Literary Form,* p. 160; Burke's emphasis. My emphasis on the reference to "the lower frequencies" in the novel's last line is influenced by conversations with Al Raboteau.

31. See Baldwin's discussion of the blues in "Down at the Cross": "In all jazz, and especially the blues, there is something tart and ironic, authoritative and double-edged. White Americans seem to feel that happy songs are *happy* and sad songs are *sad,* and that, God help us, is exactly the way most white Americans sing them. . . . Only people who have been 'down the line,' as the song puts it, know what this music is about" (*Collected Essays,* p. 311, Baldwin's emphasis). I am saying that readers of Baldwin and Ellison who complain about these authors' ability to come to terms with black rage and the systemic evils of racism are making the mistake of wanting their sad songs to be sad. Both of these writers had been "down the line." Ellison, who thought Emerson and Whitman had developed a lyrical sensibility analogous to the blues, discerned the sadness in their happy songs. He credited them, too, with having been "down the line." For a discussion of the blues and the theme of comic transcendence in Ellison, see Eddy, "Rites of Identity," chap. 7: "I believe Ellison chooses the blues, in part for piety's sake because he knows where he comes from and the sources of his being, but also because he believes that the blues, with its comic component, has more resources for coping with the absurdities [of life] . . . than does tragedy" (p. 266). Again, I am only touching on an issue that Eddy considers rigorously.

32. Harry G. Frankfurt, *The Importance of What We Care About* (Cambridge, 1988), p. 83, italics in original.

33. Nicholas Wolterstorff defines nationalism as "a nation's preoccupation with its own nationhood" in his book, *Until Justice and Peace Embrace,* p. 104.

34. Baldwin, *Collected Essays,* p. 324.

35. The best example of a fully realized, ethically acceptable form of black nationalism, to my mind, is that of C. L. R. James, the most prominent intellectual involved in the struggle for West Indian independence. His greatest work, *Beyond a Boundary*

(Durham, N.C., 1993), would bear comparison with *Invisible Man* as a set of artistic variations on the themes of piety, aspiration, and anger.

36. It is important to keep in mind that Malcolm X is only one of many members of the movement to reorient themselves, ethically speaking, by increasing identification with Islam as an international community. Indeed, there are whole groups that seem to have done so. When they do so, however, the preoccupations of nationalism are at least somewhat modified, if not transformed into something qualitatively different. The imprecision of the term "nationalism" once again makes it hard to say whether such groups are any longer committed to nationalism. If we adopt Wolterstorff's definition (see n. 33 above), and gloss the notion of preoccupation as I have glossed it, they would not be. But we can count them as "nationalist," while also putting "nationalism" in a more favorable light, either by rejecting Wolterstoff's definition or by glossing the notion of preoccupation in a way that doesn't imply exclusivity of concern. Once again, the terminological question is less important than the question of whether one's caring for the peoplehood of one's people should ever be exclusivistic. Islam, Christianity, and Judaism often deal with the latter question under the heading of "idolatry," which in this context means giving to creatures (or even to creatures of one's own imagination) what belongs only to God. All three of these traditions have generated forms of religiously legitimated preoccupation with nationhood *and* religiously motivated critiques of such preoccupation as idolatrous. For a discussion of relevant themes in Christian theology, see Robert Merrihew Adams, "The Problem of Total Devotion," in *Rationality, Religious Belief, and Moral Commitment,* ed. Robert Audi and William J. Wainwright (Ithaca, N.Y., 1986), pp. 169–94.

37. When accounting for which leftist political movements from the fifties and sixties are surviving in the early years of the new millennium, it is important to keep in mind the nature of the new environment. Communism has dropped out of the picture altogether, for obvious reasons relating to global political change. Black nationalism seems to have adapted in part by allowing its political aspirations to be transformed into a pattern of velleities and lifestyle ambitions. In radical democracy, the velleity aspect is somewhat present (for lack of concrete ideas about how to make things better), but because the lifestyle aspect is largely missing, the movement has had difficulty adapting to the new setting. It remains visible only because a few eloquent spokespersons have managed fifteen minutes of fame on television—only to see their message reduced to sound bites. But adapting to the new setting is not necessarily a good thing. (As Ellison taught, there are virtues in being invisible.) The deeper reason for the marginality of radical democracy is that it does not fit in very well with the perceived interests of any of the three basic constituencies identified by Hollinger. It will succeed only if it builds a fourth constituency capable of challenging the others and if it refuses to get sucked in by the system of information-exchange being controlled by the business elite.

38. Ellison, *Going to the Territory,* p. 21.

39. Burke, *The Philosophy of Literary Form,* p. 160 f.; Burke's emphasis.

Eddie S. Glaude Jr. is associate professor of religion and Africana studies at Bowdoin College. He is the author of *Exodus! Religion, Race, and Nation in Early Nineteenth-Century Black America* (2000).

Farah Jasmine Griffin is professor of English at Columbia University. She is the author of *Who Set You Flowin'? The African-American Migration Narrative* (1995) and *If You Can't Be Free, Be a Mystery: In Search of Billie Holiday* (2001), editor of *Beloved Sisters and Loving Friends: Letters from Rebecca Primus of Royal Oak, Maryland, and Addie Brown of Hartford, Connecticut, 1854–1868* (1999), and coeditor of *A Stranger in the Village: Two Centuries of African-American Travel Writing* (1998, with Cheryl J. Fish).

Phillip Brian Harper is associate professor of English at New York University. He is the author of *Framing the Margins: The Social Logic of Postmodern Culture* (1994) and *Are We Not Men? Masculine Anxiety and the Problem of African-American Identity* (1996).

Gerald Horne is professor of history and communication studies at the University of North Carolina, Chapel Hill. He is the author of *Black Liberation/Red Scare: Ben Davis and the Communist Party* (1994), *Fire This Time: The Watts Uprising and the 1960s* (1995), and *Race Woman: The Lives of Shirley Graham Du Bois* (2000).

Robin D. G. Kelley is professor of history and Africana studies at New York University. He is the author of *Hammer and Hoe: Alabama Communists during the Great Depression* (1990), *Race Rebels: Culture, Politics, and the Black Working Class* (1994), *Into the Fire: African Americans since 1970* (1996), and *Yo' Mama's Disfunktional!: Fighting the Culture Wars in Urban America* (1997). He has also coedited *Imagining Home: Class, Culture, and Nationalism in the African Diaspora* (1995, with Sidney J. Lemelle).

Wahneema Lubiano is associate professor in the Program in Literature and the Program in

African and African American Studies at Duke University. She is the editor of *The House That Race Built: Black Americans, U.S. Terrain* (1997).

Adolph L. Reed Jr. is professor of political science at the New School for Social Research. He is the author of *W. E. B. Du Bois and American Political Thought: Fabianism and the Color Line* (1997) and *The Jesse Jackson Phenomenon* (1986). He has also edited two volumes, *Without Justice for All: The New Liberalism and Our Retreat from Racial Equality* (1999) and *Race, Politics, and Culture: Critical Essays on the Radicalism of the 1960s* (1986).

Jeffrey Stout is professor of religion at Princeton University. He is the author of *Flight from Authority: Religion, Morality, and the Quest for Autonomy* (1981) and *Ethics after Babel: The Languages of Morals and their Discontents* (1988).

Will Walker works with Public/Private ventures, an action-based social policy think tank. He is currently working on a book about faith-based initiatives, race, and public policy.

S. Craig Watkins is associate professor of radio, television, and film at the University of Texas at Austin. He is the author of *Representing: Hip Hop Culture and the Production of Black Cinema* (1998).

Cornel West is Alphonse Fletcher Jr. Professor at Harvard University. He is the author of numerous books, including *Race Matters* (1993), *The American Evasion of Philosophy: A Genealogy of Pragmatism* (1989), *Keeping Faith: Philosophy and Race in America* (1993), and *Prophesy Deliverance! An Afro-American Revolutionary Christianity* (1982). He has also coauthored numerous books.

E. Frances White is dean of the Gallatin School for Individualized Study at New York University. She is the author of *Sierra Leone's Settler Women Traders: Women on the Afro-European Frontier* (1987) and *Dark Continent of Our Bodies: Black Feminism and the Politics of Respectability* (2001) and coauthor of *Women in Sub-Saharan Africa: Restoring Women to History* (1999, with Iris Berger).